WORDS MARKED BY A PLACE

Words Marked by a Place

Local Histories in Central Oregon

JAROLD RAMSEY

Oregon State University Press   Corvallis

Portions and versions of some of the essays in this book have appeared in the following periodicals, under these titles:

> Excerpt from Maudy's Year," *Northwest Review* 45:3 (2007), 161–168; "Airacobra: In Memoriam 2nd Lt. Robert l. Cranston," *Northwest Review* 48:1 (2010): 58–76.

> *Sageland*: "The Birth of a County," part 1 (Winter 2014): 16–26; part 2 (Summer 2014): 42–55; "Echoes of the Railroad" (2011): 18–30.

> *The Agate*: "Homestead Orchards," "A Young Pilot's Last Letters," 3 (Spring 2015): 14–18; "The Mystery Homesteaders," 4 (Fall 2015): 3–11; "Henry Larcom Abbot in Central Oregon," 5 (Spring 2016).

The following publishers have given permission to use quoted materials from copyrighted works.

> Oregon Historical Society, for quoted and graphic materials from Robert Sawyer, ed., "Abbot Railroad Surveys," *Oregon Historical Quarterly* 33, nos. 1 and 2 (March 1932 and June 1932).

> Binford and Mort, for Howard Turner, "Madras," in *Jefferson County Reminiscences*, 1998 (1957).

> Pictorial Histories Publishing Co., for Rick Mitchell, *Airacobra Advantage: The Flying Cannon*, 1992.

Acknowledgment is made for use of excerpts from:

> H. L. Davis, *Team Bells Woke Me and Other Stories*, William Morrow and Co. (1953); copyright by H. L. Davis; copyright renewed 1981 by Elizabeth T. Hobson.

> H. L. Davis: *Collected Essays and Stories*. Moscow: University of Idaho Press, 1986.

> William Carlos Williams, "Kenneth Burke," in *Selected Essays of William Carlos Williams*. New York: New Directions, 1969.

Library of Congress Cataloging in Publication Control Number: 2018006147 (print)

♾This paper meets the requirements of ANSI/NISO Z39.48-1992 (Permanence of Paper).

Oregon State University Press
121 The Valley Library
Corvallis OR 97331-4501
541-737-3166 • fax 541-737-3170
www.osupress.oregonstate.edu

For George Aguilar, of Wolford Canyon and Warm Springs

"The local is the only thing that is universal. The classic is the local fully realized, words marked by a place."

—William Carlos Williams

Contents

List of Illustrations ix

Preface xi

Acknowledgments xvii

One   HENRY LARCOM ABBOT IN CENTRAL OREGON, 1855 1

Two   "A VISIT FROM SAM ANAXSHAT," FROM *MAUDY'S YEAR* 25

Three   OUR HOMESTEAD ORCHARDS 43

Four   THE RAILROAD ERA AND ITS LEGACY 59

Five   THE BIRTH OF JEFFERSON COUNTY: PART ONE 71

Six   THE BIRTH OF JEFFERSON COUNTY: PART TWO 81

Seven   LOCAL HISTORY ON STAGE: FIVE SKITS 95

Eight   THE MYSTERY HOMESTEADERS 117

Nine   "WORDS MARKED BY A PLACE"
           In Search of a Central Oregon Lingo 135

Ten   FARMERS AND OLD IRON 151

Eleven   ROWBOAT RESCUE ON THE DESCHUTES, 1940 159

Twelve   AIRACOBRA
           In Memoriam 2nd Lieutenant Robert L. Cranston, 1924–1944 167

Notes 191

Bibliography 195

Index 199

Illustrations

Henry Larcom Abbot at West Point 3
Modern map of Pacific Railroad Survey explorations in Oregon, 1855 9
Official 1855 Pacific Railroad Survey map 10
Cascade Range skyline, by John Young, 1855. 13
Abbot's party at Tygh Valley, by John Young, October 1855. 14
Boegli's Orchard at The Cove, 1920s 46
McCoin Orchard on Gray Butte, 2017 49
Homestead orchard tour at Cyrus Orchard, 2012. 50
Oregon Trunk and Des Chutes Railroad lines at North Junction, 1910 61
Railroad Day in Madras, 1911 62
Construction of Crooked River railroad bridge, 1910 63
1915 map of Crook County, after creation of Jefferson County 75
Oregon governor Oswald West, 1914 78
William Boegli, first judge of Jefferson County, 1914–1916 78
William U'Ren, adviser to "Madras for county seat" faction 83
First Jefferson County courthouse, Culver, 1914–1916 85
Madras *Pioneer* cartoon on the county seat conflict, 1916 87
"Courthouse raid" in Culver, January 1, 1917 91
"Singing Moonshiner" Centennial skit, Camp Sherman, June 2014 108
Wedding portrait of Gay and Ethel Larkin. 119
Ben Larkin's Madras harness shop, ca. 1913 120
Larkin homestead site east of Blizzard Ridge today 125
Fourth of July celebration at Elkins place, 1915. 128
Header and header box in harvest, Agency Plains, ca. 1912 152
Derelict header in a farm machinery boneyard. 153
Old grain separator, Agency Plains 155
Crooked River below The Cove, before the dams 160
Pioneer photo of Thad Dizney and Doc Akiyama in rowboat. 163
Old North Hangar at Madras Airport, 2017 171
Bell P-39Q Airacobra 176
Robert Cranston and Vivian Duganzich, California, 1943 185
Cranston's map of Madras, March 1944 187

Preface

Some years ago, my mother—she was born in 1906 and died in 2007, at 101—visited us when we were living in Rochester, New York, and one day I took her to the Margaret Woodbury Strong Museum (now known as the Strong National Museum of Play). The Strong Museum is one of the great museums of American material culture, and they had just opened a lavish exhibit of middle-class home furnishings from the 1840s to about 1910.

Understand that my mother was born in Opal City, a little Central Oregon railroad town that never quite got itself born. Her parents were homesteaders, and she grew up under those special east-of-the-mountains, frontier/ homestead conditions. She was never defensive about the limitations of her origins; indeed, she was proud of where she came from—but I think that as an adult she assumed that on some cultural levels she *was* cut off from the American mainstream. So I wondered what she would make of the Strong Museum's exhibit.

We started through it, and after a while I realized that my mom was lagging far behind. I went back, and found her in the 1870s "Gilded Age" section, in a state of great excitement. "Look at that!" she exclaimed, pointing to a big ornate coffee grinder. "We had one of those at home! And look at this kitchen range—it's almost identical to my mother's. See, it's a 'Home Comfort' like ours!" And so on around the reconstructed 1870s kitchen: she was identifying with nearly everything on display, and I realized that she was connecting her childhood memories of her mother's kitchen in Opal City, out on what was then at least the frontier, with the main patterns of American domestic culture (as formulated by the Strong Museum). She was surprised, and gratified—only thing was, of course, that the exhibit she was looking at portrayed popular material fixtures of American life in the 1870s, whereas the homestead kitchen in her mind dated from about 1915. But still, if not up-to-date or trendy in 1870 terms, it was all satisfyingly congruent with the national cultural mainstream, after all!

Such are the personal discoveries that good museums like the Strong, and many regional and local museums, can afford us, when they allow us to engage both the local foreground and the regional and national backgrounds of our history. It is not an easy interpretive balance. But surely it is one worth striving to find and maintain, in the pursuit of historical understanding.

This relationship between "local history" and "history-at-large" was a theme in my 2003 book *New Era*, and it is more prominent in this book. *Words Marked by a Place* is in some respects a follow-on to *New Era*. Both books have grown out of a lifelong fascination with the history and lore of the rugged country around Madras, where I grew up and now live. But since finishing the first book, I've gotten very involved with our Jefferson County Historical Society and its museum, and with the planning and mounting of official centennial celebrations for Madras and neighboring towns and for the coming of the railroads and, in 2014, for Jefferson County itself (which covers an area about the size of Delaware and now has the most racially and ethnically diverse population of any county in Oregon).

This hands-on experience has considerably stretched and broadened my understanding of the place of local history in the historical scheme of things; in particular it has impressed upon me the value of "doing" history in ways other than *writing* about it. What I've discovered is that for many people, their serious love of history best realizes itself in museum work; in genealogical research; in historical pageants, re-enactments, and skits; in the diverse activities of historical societies.

Academic historians, of course, generally ignore such grassroots endeavors, or view them condescendingly. In his interesting book on local history as a field, *Re-Thinking Home*, Joseph Amato has almost nothing to say about activities other than research and writing. It's undeniable that, despite good intentions, local history pageants can mangle their subjects, often by forcing them to conform to the popular myths of the West (or the South, or the Midwest, or wherever), a la Hollywood, and that museums of town or county history can become grandmothers' attics of donated artifacts, each telling a small story, perhaps, but not adding up to anything like a comprehensive story of one locale among others.

But the tacit disdain of many professional historians for the work of their "unpublished" counterparts strikes me as unfair, and intellectually shortsighted. "All History is Local!" is no doubt a bumper-sticker oversimplification—but it does convey a useful element of truth. It reminds us that, at bottom, the experiencing of history is inevitably localized and personal, as it was, poignantly, for my mother in the Strong Museum, as she saw her childhood memories of kitchenware in a national cultural context. My point is that we most fully experience our lives in relation to the past through two sets of mental "lenses" that are at once opposites and yet complementary to each other. One is "wide-angle," panoramic, visioning with a broad regional or even national scope; the other is "close-up," intent on viewing in detail what's near at hand and foregrounded. Operating a sort of mental "zoom button" between the one lens and the other in everyday affairs is so natural to most of us from childhood on that it must be part of our inherent mental circuitry. If so, then why does it seem to be inoperative in so much historiography?

The point may seem obvious, but let's push it a little further by considering a few examples of what can go wrong in "doing" and presenting history if we ignore the zoom button and employ either the close-up or the wide-angle lens exclusively. The second kind of problem first: One of the most influential propositions ever made by an American historian was Frederick Jackson Turner's "frontier thesis," arguing that the American frontier was a major determinant of our development as a nation, and that it came abruptly to an end in the late nineteenth century—"no more free land," an end to westering and all that. Turner's point about the closing of the frontier is based on US Census records—but what about the case of Central Oregon, where my grandparents on both sides and thousands of other families homesteaded on what they understood to be an inviting new frontier of "free land" that opened up in the early 1900s? Sweeping conclusions about the closing of the frontier drawn from Turner's thesis, it turns out, would have profited from some "close-up" reconsiderations, based on conspicuous local exceptions like this one.

The same kind of distortion can happen in the realm of local history. At one time our county historical society used as its identifying logo an image of a hand-carved wooden ox-yoke—a graphic icon of the Oregon Trail, for sure. But as a symbol of Central Oregon pioneering, which in fact involved farm wagons and harnessed horses and mules and, ultimately, the railroads, *not* oxen, it was a misrepresentation, a stereotype carelessly plucked from the grab bag of mythic images of "The West" and imposed on the true story of how the local homesteaders came. No big deal—but it made the facts of that story a little less accessible.

On the other hand, what can go wrong when local historians fail to "zoom" their attention from foreground materials to broader reckonings? I'll take for my illustration a collective research project that is now in progress, and thus "open-ended." Recently our historical society has rediscovered the work of an important but forgotten early photographer, Ole Hedlund, who between 1909 and 1912 took thousands of beautifully detailed, long-focus photographs of the epic railroad construction of James J. Hill's Oregon Trunk Line up the Deschutes River canyon (for a time, racing Edward Harriman's "Des Chutes Railroad" team on opposite sides of the river), ultimately emerging from the canyon and into Central Oregon at Madras on February 15, 1911. Hedlund photographed the railroad work from every angle—tunneling, track-laying, and bridge-and-trestle building; the machinery involved; the workmen, mainly Greek and Italian immigrants, and their camps along the route. The photos are awe-inspiring.

But as long as we gaze on those sharply focused scenes just as foreign images imposed on the local landscape, important historical dimensions can be missed. To do our interpretive part as serious local historians, we need to look at them (and in a sense look *through* them) with our wide-angle lens, trying to understand how part of their meaning may be regional, or national. The machinery—was it used elsewhere in the West by Hill and Harriman? Those mostly nameless workmen—where had they worked before coming into Central Oregon? How were they treated on the job, here and elsewhere? Were they in some way "organized," if not unionized? Did they move on to other railroad projects elsewhere in the West? Did they eventually settle down along the way, becoming US citizens? And behind it all, what were the national political and economic forces driving such extravagant railway projects in the Northwest?

We won't fully understand our priceless Hedlund photos until we've wrestled with such "panoramic" historical questions. Which is to say that we're going to have to do some serious reading, in the abundant scholarship on American railroads, labor management, economic conditions, and related topics at the turn of the twentieth century. (We might well begin with Gunther Peck's *Reinventing Free Labor,* and Larry Hoeg's *Harriman vs. Hill: Wall Street's Great Railroad War.*) But our "labors" in books and monographs should bring us rich rewards, yielding deeper understandings of how our Hedlund photos document national as well as local historical circumstances.

To put it another way, professional/academic historians and local history workers can learn much from each other's efforts. What I have crudely called the "wide-angle" and the "close-up" perspectives characteristic of the work of each group are not easily reconciled or synthesized in the work of historical research and interpretation—but they need to be. Doing so involves engaging history in *dialectical* terms, actively playing one perspective against the other to see what lights up in our subjects thereby.

This being a book about episodes in the history of a particular locale (one not very well-known at that), I'm eager to recommend the dialectical approach (or if you prefer, the zoom button) to my fellow local historians, and I hope they will find useful examples of its interpretive value in these essays. And my own recent immersion in the work of our field—often literally hands-on, time-consuming, highly social, exasperating and gratifying by turns, irresistible—leads me here to offer some additional wishes for the field itself, wherever its practitioners happen to work:

- that they strive to be *inclusive* in their coverage of local topics, not concentrating on one prominent set of human actors (say, homesteaders) to the exclusion of others who also played their part (say, early businessmen and professionals; women in general).
- that they try in every phase of their work to keep firmly in mind the proposition that history is *ongoing*, an open-ended continuum, meaning that along with the heroic doings of the old-timers and town fathers and town mothers, the contributions of more recently arrived folks, even latecomers, need to be recorded and studied. For example, the recent settlement in Central Oregon of Latino families is extensive. Latinos are becoming an important part of our collective latter-day history, and their contributions deserve to be written into the historical record.
- that local historians will give serious attention to matters of *natural history* as they pertain to the human stories of their localities. Geology, topography, climate and weather, water and the lack of it, soil conditions, native (and introduced) plants and animals, and other environmental factors underlie and shape the human activities that make up the stuff of history, and they are especially important when what's being studied is the human story of particular homelands. "What was the weather like back then? What weeds were they fighting?"

- that the history enthusiasts in every community will endeavor to share their enthusiasm (and knowledge) with schoolkids from the primary grades upward and look for ways to collaborate with teachers in the cause of making local history come alive for students, as an indispensable (but widely neglected) part of their cultural heritage.

- that historians of homelands will take conscious pride and satisfaction (whether their academic counterparts recognize them or not) in their multifarious ways of "doing" history—historical society and museum work (including care and display of artifacts and archiving of written records and photos), historical reenactments of all sorts, tours and talks, "history pubs," displays, "History Day" poster contests in schools, and so on. Writing and reading are not the only means of advancing the cause of historical awareness!

As was the case with its predecessor, *New Era,* most of the essays in this book were conceived and written as independent explorations, but with an understanding that they would eventually make up a book of interrelated pieces on Central Oregon history. Again, as with *New Era,* my intent has not been to attempt a systematic history of the region, as desirable as that might be; rather, my hope has been that by sorting through that rich history from various angles, I could help my readers to gain a dexterous "purchase" of their own on it, one fortified by an awareness of possible regional and national meanings in the cavalcade of local events.

These essays are organized chronologically, proceeding with topical interlinkages from Lieutenant Henry Larcom Abbot's neglected 1855 explorations through Central Oregon to episodes from the homesteading, railroading, and community-building era from 1870 to 1930 and concluding with a particular event—the death of a young Army Air Corps lieutenant named Robert Cranston in the crash of his fighter plane near Madras in 1944—in which national and local history tragically intersect. Along the way, I offer what I hope are useful examples of alternative ways of engaging our history in writing and performance—historical fiction, historical reenactments in the form of skits, excursions into folk customs and regional linguistics, and so on.

My ultimate hope is that, over and above their diversity of subjects, approaches, and tone, these essays will seem to talk to each other, as "words marked by a place."

Acknowledgments

The work of historians, on any level, is a collaborative endeavor, and it's a pleasure to acknowledge here the help and support of many generous people whose contributions surely mark the best parts of this book. The historical coverage of "middle Oregon" is still very much an early work-in-progress, as is the story of the region itself; but there are clear signs, I think, of a growing historical self-consciousness here, manifesting itself in the vitality of our historical societies and museums, in school and civic programs, in extensive media attention to local historical doings and discoveries. And I want to count the help and encouragement I've received from people such as the following as another sign that, in these parts, history really does matter.

My heartfelt thanks to my fellow directors of the Jefferson County Historical Society over the years, notably Elaine Henderson and the late Steve Rankin; George Aguilar, Kelly Cannon-Miller, Gordon Gillespie, Steve Lent, Loren Irving, coworkers in the keeping of Central Oregon history; Eliza Canty-Jones, editor of *Oregon Historical Quarterly*; Kim Stafford, William Lang and Marianne Keddington-Lang, Leon Speroff, and Alice Parman; Joanie Cooper and Shaun Shepherd of the Home Orchard Society; at OSU Press, Tom Booth, Mary Braun, Marty Brown, Micki Reaman, and Susan Campbell, editors and enablers par excellence.

Thanks also to Tony Ahern, Susan Matheny, Holly Gill, and Tom Culbertson, of the Madras *Pioneer*; Jane Ahern, editor of *The Agate*, the local history journal of the Jefferson County Historical Society; Mike Ahern, Jefferson County commissioner; Royce Embanks, mayor of Madras; Joe Krenowicz and Helen Houts, Madras/Jefferson County Chamber of Commerce; and Tom Brown, Rick Donahoe, Zack Harwell, Professor Gene Cranston, Ursula Le Guin, and the late Dell Hymes.

And my far-flung but ever-supportive family: Kate Ramsey, Tim Watson, Leo Ramsey Watson; Sophia Ramsey, Martin Bland, Henry and Madeleine Bland; John, Monica, Samantha, and Willa Ramsey; Jim and

Diane Ramsey; Patty Moore Howard and Nancy Moore; and, as always, my
wife and stalwart partner-in-everything, Dorothy Quinn Ramsey.

JWR
Madras, Oregon
Midwinter 2017

One
Henry Larcom Abbot in Central Oregon, 1855

In the rains of early October 1855, a young army engineer named Henry Larcom Abbot and a party of seventeen men and sixty worn-out pack mules were struggling westward through heavy brush and fallen timber in the hills south of Mount Hood. They were guided, more or less, by a young Indian named Sam An-ax-shat. This was not one of the loose gangs of gold-seekers and soldiers of fortune that were prowling through the interior wilds of Oregon in the 1850s and 1860s. Abbot and his party were "official": their mission was to scout out possible railroad routes from San Francisco Bay north to the Columbia River, both east and west of the Cascade Range, as part of an ambitious Pacific Railroad Survey authorized by the secretary of war.

They'd been in the field northbound since leaving Benicia, near San Francisco, on July 10. The survey, with Lieutenant Robert S. Williamson in command, had gone quite well; but now Williamson and the expedition's military escort were exploring west of the mountains, and Abbot's appointed task—to find a better wagon route around Mount Hood than the notorious Barlow Road—had been turned on end in recent days by news from a settler in Tygh Valley that the Indians on both sides of the Columbia had risen up and were burning missions and killing Indian agents and settlers. So the possible route over the mountains to Oregon City that the party was supposed to survey had become, in the face of what seemed to be dire danger, their only route to safety. As Abbot later wrote, "Encumbered with a large number of jaded animals and considerable baggage, we suddenly found ourselves among hostile and well-armed Indians, to whom our train would render us a tempting prey" (Abbot, *Pacific Railroad Survey Reports*, vol. 6, p. 96; hereafter *Reports*). He added that they had only five rifles among them. And their guide was a young Indian who spoke no English, and Abbot had only begun to learn Chinook Jargon.

1

Not an auspicious arrangement, but Abbot's immediate challenge was to pick and angle his way up and down through long stretches of blowdown and underbrush, while Sam An-ax-shat scouted out the faint Indian trails that might lead them on to the Willamette Valley and safety. The going was hard enough on foot and on mule-back, but they were trying to proceed with a two-wheeled cart, which carried their fragile surveying instruments, including glass barometers and thermometers, sextants, and the like, and also an odometer to measure their daily mileage. The odometer's mechanism made a clicking sound, and Sam An-ax-shat named the cart the "chik-chik." Watching their constant struggles with it, whether behind a mule or wrestled by men, Sam soon rendered an ultimatum to Abbot in emphatic Chinook Jargon: "Mamook memaloose tenas chik-chik!" ("Kill the little cart!" *Reports*, p. 97).

But we must now briefly leave Lieutenant Abbot in his mountainside lurch in order to get a firmer grip on the main elements of his story and the historical events and forces that were shaping it out in Oregon Territory in 1855. It's a story that seems to connect meaningfully with regional and national history at almost every turn, both during Abbot's adventures with the Pacific Railroad Survey expedition and right on through the rest of his long, consequential life—he died in 1927, at ninety-six. It's surprising, given what he accomplished early and late and the notable Americans he associated with, that he is so little known.

In Central Oregon, three minor landmarks bear his name—Abbot Butte and Abbot Creek, west of the Metolius River, and Abbot Road and Pass along his route around Mount Hood. (During World War II, an Army Corps of Engineers encampment south of Bend was known as "Camp Abbot," but the resort complex that was created on the site in the 1970s was named Sunriver.) That he and his explorations are even this much recognized today is the result of efforts by the late Robert Sawyer, early editor-publisher of the Bend *Bulletin* and one of the pioneers of Central Oregon historical research. After Abbot's death, Sawyer contacted his family in Massachusetts and was given his personal journals for the 1855 expedition, which he edited (with extensive notes) and published as "Abbot Railroad Surveys, 1855" in *Oregon Historical Quarterly* in March and June of 1932 (hereafter *Quarterly*).

Portrait of Henry Larcom Abbot at West Point

Part of the appeal of Abbot's Oregon story is that it follows the archetype of the tale of the clever young man going forth into the wide risky world and proving himself—"Little Jack," *le petit Jean* in French folklore, and so on. But another source of this appeal is that we can read Abbot's 1855 Oregon narrative in three different versions, each recounted by him but under very different circumstances: his carefully edited "official" report, as published by the government in 1857 in volume 6 of the *Pacific Railroad Survey Reports*; his field journals, as found and edited by Robert Sawyer, which informally record his adventures day by day in the field, as they came; and a little-known memoir he wrote as an old man, published as "Reminiscences of the Oregon War of 1855," in the *Journal of the Military Service Institute* in 1909 (hereafter "Reminiscences").

The official 1857 *Reports* will be our main text, of course, but these other, lesser-known accounts are fascinating on their own terms, and will come in handy to illuminate Abbot's story as we follow it. In general, he was a very capable writer, and his vivid descriptions in the *Reports* of the natural features of Central Oregon and how he reacted to them deserve to be more widely known.

Henry Abbot graduated from West Point in 1854, second in his class. Hoping to receive an appointment that would send him out on the western frontier, he initially signed up for artillery duty, but one of his West Point advisers told him that his best chance for frontier service was with the Corps of Topographical Engineers, and that it might not be too late to reapply. For Abbot's career (and for Oregon history), it was good and timely advice. Later in 1854, he was invited to serve with an expedition being organized as the final component of the Pacific Railroad Surveys, funded by Congress in 1853 for $150,000 (the 1855 survey was budgeted at $46,000), and authorized by Secretary of War Jefferson Davis (soon destined to become president of the Confederacy).

The official purpose of the Railroad Surveys was "to ascertain the most practical and economic route for a railroad from the Mississippi River to the Pacific Ocean"; the Corps of Topographical Engineers was put in charge, under Captain (later General) George McClellan. There were in fact five survey expeditions: the North Pacific Survey, from St. Paul to Puget Sound, led by Washington territorial governor Isaac Stevens; the Central Pacific Survey, from St. Louis to San Francisco, led by Lieutenants John Gunnison and E. C. Beckwith; two "southern" missions, one leading from Oklahoma Territory to San Diego under Lieutenant Daniel Whipple, the other from Texas to San Diego under Lieutenant John Parke; and finally the 1855 Pacific Coast Survey, with Lieutenant Robert S. Williamson in charge and Lieutenant Henry Abbot second-in-command.

Coming as they did just before the upheavals of the Civil War, the Railroad Surveys were a remarkably farsighted, successful venture by the government. The Central Pacific Survey led straight on to the Union Pacific-Central Pacific transcontinental line, completed in 1869; and by the 1880s all of the nation's transcontinental railroad lines were operating in the West on routes first surveyed and recommended in the 1853–1855 surveys. As for the Williamson-Abbot 1855 survey of possible routes from central California to the Columbia River, Abbot's hurried southbound reconnaissance in late 1855 through the Willamette Valley and the mountains of southern Oregon mapped the way for the construction of the "Oregon and California" line in the 1870s and 1880s (later the Southern Pacific). And although Abbot's unequivocal declaration that "no railroad could be built in the valley near the Deschutes River" (*Reports*, p. 91) would be refuted only a half century later by James J. Hill and Edward Harriman in their famous "railroad race" up the Deschutes, it's only fair to recognize that what made that extravagant episode possible was abundance of capital and plutocratic ambition beyond anything imaginable to Abbot, or any-body else, in 1855.

When Abbot revisited Oregon in 1896 as a member of a federal "national forests" commission, he duly noted that in southern Oregon he rode in comfort in a railroad "parlor car" through the mountains where he and his survey party had struggled to find their way (and avoid hostile Indians) only forty years before ("Reminiscences," p. 442).

In addition to providing crucial engineering information on possible (and impossible) railroad routes through the American West, the Pacific Railroad Surveys made important pioneering contributions to the mapping of the West and to knowledge of the region's geology, botany, zoology, and ethnography (Abbot was keenly attentive to Native languages and customs as he encountered them). The twelve volumes of the *Survey Reports*, hefty and well edited, were published by the US government between 1855 and 1861. Beautifully illustrated with engravings and lithographs (in lieu of photographs) by skilled artists like John Mix Stanley, Gustav Sohon, and John Young, they constitute a neglected national historical treasure.

The survey expeditions were of course preceded in the previous decade by the well-known expeditions of Captain John Fremont. The flamboy-ant and ambitious Fremont was himself a member of the Army Corps of Topographical Engineers, which supported the first two of his four explo-rations, but overall he proceeded with neither the sponsorship of Congress and the secretary of war, nor the specific railroad-route-finding instruc-tions that guided the surveys. His second and most successful expedi-tion, in 1843, usefully mapped the main route of the Oregon Trail out to the Columbia River, and then, in the fall of that year, found its way south through Central Oregon east of the Cascades to Klamath Lake, where (on his own dubious initiative) Fremont and his party headed off into Nevada and, eventually, survived the first crossing of the Sierras in midwinter and reached safety at Sutter's Fort on the Sacramento River.

Like the expeditions to follow, Fremont's undertook extensive map-ping and scientific observations along the way, which were subsequently published; in particular, his field notes and the superb maps of his cartog-rapher Charles Preuss were available to Williamson and Abbot when they came through Oregon in 1855, roughly following Fremont's route west of the Deschutes in reverse. Like them, Fremont saw fit to use a two-wheeled cart to carry his navigational and scientific equipment, but before heading south from The Dalles, he donated the cart to the Methodist mission there—and almost immediately, now carried on mule-back, the equipment was broken. As a result, his efforts to calculate longitude along the way were very uncertain, and Henry Abbot seems to have taken special pains both before and during his expedition to correct Fremont's inaccurate readings. It's amusing to consider that whereas Fremont decided to dispose of his "instrument cart" before heading south, and as a result lost most of his instruments early on, Williamson and Abbot persisted in dragging their cart with great trouble and difficulty all the way to Mount Hood—even though, as Abbot's field notes make clear, the delicate instruments carried on it were often damaged in transit and had to be repaired. But Abbot's dogged attachment to his cart pales to nothing compared with Fremont's insistence on dragging a four-hundred-pound wheeled howitzer all the way along his 1843 route until, finally, it had to be abandoned on the snowy slopes of the eastern Sierras.

Abbot's superior, Lieutenant Robert S. Williamson, was six years older than Abbot and graduated from West Point in 1848, fifth in his class. By the time the 1855 survey was being organized, Williamson was already an experienced western explorer. He evidently went out to California on US Army Corps of Engineers orders soon after graduating from West Point. As an officer with Captain William Warner's party exploring the Pit River country in northeast California in 1849, he and the main detachment had been encamped at Goose Lake in late September when Warner and a small advance party were killed by Indians near what was later named Warner Valley.

Remaining in California, Williamson subsequently worked on the western phases of the two "southern" railroad surveys, concentrating on southern and central California; and then returned to Washington, where he helped prepare volumes 3 and 5 of the *Reports*, published in 1853 and 1854. By late 1854 he and Abbot were sharing quarters and working together in the capital to prepare for their expedition the following year, and on May 5, 1855, they left New York City by ship and arrived in San Francisco via the Isthmus of Panama on May 31. Once in California, they spent six weeks collecting and organizing the men, animals, and gear they needed, and when they finally set forth from their advance camp at Fort Reading, they were without exaggeration a small army—upward of 130 men and an unspecified number of horses and mules. The basic survey party numbered twenty-six, and their military escort out of Fort Reading consisted of twenty well-armed "dragoons" and eighty regular soldiers, plus several civilians as packers and hunters.

The core survey team, in addition to Williamson and Abbot, was made up of Dr. J. S. Newberry (for whom Newberry Crater is named), geologist and botanist; Dr. E. Sterling, physician for the party and naturalist; H. C. Fillebrown, assistant engineer; C. D. Anderson, curiously identified as "computer," apparently meaning that he kept track of and calculated scientific data; Charles Coleman, "chief of train" (packmaster); and John Young, draughtsman and cartographer. Regular army officers from Fort Reading in charge of the military escort were Lieutenant George Crook (soon to make his mark in the Civil War, and later in Indian campaigns in Oregon and elsewhere in the West) as quartermaster and commissary, and Lieutenants J. B. Hood and H. C. Gibson.

The size of the escort clearly indicates concern on the part of the expedition's leaders about the likelihood of hostile encounters with Natives as it traveled north into Oregon. Since Fremont's unescorted and relatively trouble-free journey in 1843, a decade of uprisings, killings, and reprisals had ensued in the Northwest, beginning with the Whitman Massacre in 1847 and its aftermaths, leading up to the Columbia River treaties earlier in 1855 (to which most Natives reacted with resentment) and, most recently, intermittent violence along the Umpqua and Rogue Rivers. Undoubtedly, while planning his itinerary, Williamson must have had vividly in mind the killing of his commanding officer, Captain William Warner, and his party in Pit River country in 1849. The dragoons and regular troops were already in place at Fort Reading, and it must have made good sense to take them along, in spite of the logistical problems (especially forage for the pack animals) they would cause.

So they set off on July 28, in an impressive caravan that must have stretched out over a quarter of a mile, attended in the midsummer heat by dust and flies. The two-wheeled cart soon revealed itself as a nuisance—on August 4, near Pit River, Abbot noted that "when attempting to run over a mesquite bush, it turned completely over, so that the mule lay on its back, struggling violently in the thick underbrush" (*Reports*, p. 62). On the same day, the train was overtaken by Lieutenant Philip Sheridan, who had been sent out from Fort Reading to replace Lieutenant Hood; Hood returned to the Fort for other duties. (Like Crook, the diminutive and feisty Sheridan

would soon go on to national fame as a Union general in the Civil War.)
Three weeks later, as the expedition reached "Klamath Country," their anxi-
eties about meeting hostile Natives appeared to be confirmed, in Abbot's
tense journal notes for August 21: "Separated from party. Indians calling.
Many Indians entered camp. Cleaned pistols. Extra guard. Expected attack.
Indians driving off horses" (*Quarterly*, p. 16).

But the crisis passed, and soon over open country they reached the
southern boundaries of the Deschutes Basin, which for Henry Abbot
was to be his main area to explore and survey (although, regrettably, he
never ventured east of the Deschutes River). When the party reached the
Deschutes headwaters, around modern-day Sunriver, it began to divide
temporarily into smaller detachments, to better cover the enormous and
(except for Fremont's maps) uncharted territory ahead. The comings and
goings, departures and reunions of Williamson and Abbot and their teams
are complicated, but by pausing to outline them here we can most effectively trace their overall survey of the interior of Oregon on either side of
the Cascade Range, and also gain some insight into Abbot's perplexities as
he tried to fulfill his part of the mission.

Williamson had already, in fact, begun to go off the main track for day
trips. But on August 24, he, Fillebrown, Young, Dr. Newberry, and Sheridan
with the dragoons left the main party near today's La Pine, heading west,
and became the first known explorers of the Three Sisters/Broken Top
range, camping at Green Lakes. (Because Williamson did not write up
an account of his separate travels for the 1857 *Reports*, and seems to have
left no private journals of them, what he encountered is unknown, except
for Abbot's cursory summary in chapter 4 of the *Reports*.) In Williamson's
absence, Abbot and the rest of the party moved on to Camp 40, which they
named "Depot Camp" (on Whychus Creek, near modern Sisters), and there
the parties reunited on September 3.

On September 6, Williamson set off for the mountains again, with
Sheridan and the dragoons, Fillebrown, and Young the artist, with instruc-
tions for Abbot to proceed with the main party, exploring the country
between the Cascades and the Deschutes River as far as Fort Dalles, where
he was to obtain provisions enough for the remainder of the survey and
return with them to Camp 40, where the two groups would rendezvous.
This time, Williamson seems to have explored the country between Mount
Washington and the Santiam lava fields, making him probably the first

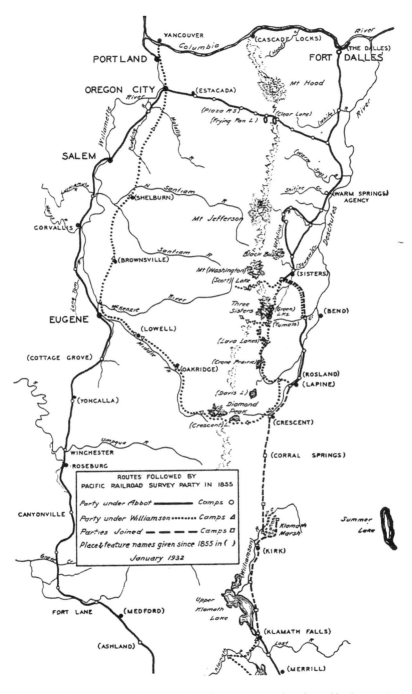

Map of Pacific Railroad Survey explorations through Oregon, 1855, based on Abbot's narrative (prepared by Robert Sawyer)

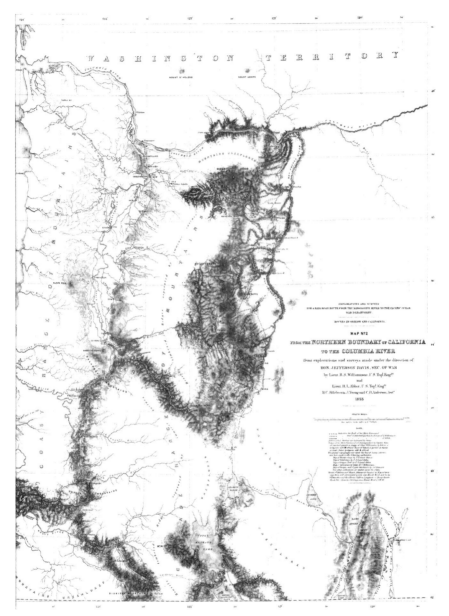

Official map of 1855 Pacific Railroad Survey, published in 1861

Anglo to see what would become the eastern approaches to the McKenzie and Santiam passes. He probably made other local excursions while waiting for Abbot to return from Fort Dalles, which he did on September 23.

Abbot's trip had been uneventful for the most part. Crossing Tygh Valley northbound, they stopped at the "rancho" of a Mr. Evelyn, who hospitably served them potatoes from his own garden, a welcome respite from military rations, especially as they had been showing signs of developing scurvy (*Reports*, p. 87). At Fort Dalles, Abbot and Dr. Newberry traveled down the Columbia Gorge as far as the Cascades Rapids (Bridge of the Gods), marveling at the force of the river and observing Indians fishing with spears and nets. At the fort, he wrote letters to his parents and his fiancée Susie Everett for mailing (somehow) home to Massachusetts; and he began to learn Chinook Jargon, which officers at the fort were using, he noted, as a sort of "court language." Jargon would soon become more than a linguistic amusement to him. Abbot also shrewdly sought out a Wasco man, Billy Chinook, who had traveled with Fremont in 1843. Chinook emphatically refuted rumors going back to Fremont's travels that there was a viable north–south route along the eastern base of the Cascades. Headed south again, at Tygh Valley Abbot met a half-blood named Domenich who told him about a good, well-traveled Indian route around Mount Hood, for wagons at least—a possible improvement over the notorious Barlow Road, which emigrants had been using reluctantly since 1846 as an alternative to rafting their wagons down the Columbia.

By the time of Abbot's return to Camp 40, Williamson had decided to divide the survey party again—this time more drastically. His plan was for Abbot to lead the main party back north once again, with instructions to explore the rumored route around Mount Hood that Abbot had heard about in Tygh Valley, and so on to Oregon City. Williamson, meanwhile, resolved to travel south with Crook, Sheridan, and the dragoons as far as Diamond Peak, where they would strike a new wagon road (modern Willamette Pass), then go north across the McKenzie River and so on between the Willamette and the eastern Cascade foothills to Oregon City, where the two parties would regroup for the long march back to Fort Reading and a possible secondary survey in search of a route through the northern Sierras.

So, with Williamson on his way over the mountains, we can resume our tracking of Abbot through Central Oregon. In the *Reports*, he offers this ironic comment on the division of their forces on September 24: "Not anticipating any Indian trouble, we considered my party [minus the dragoons and troops] strong enough for the mission at hand." As for the mission itself, he notes that on his marches to Fort Dalles and back, "I had already seen that no railroad could be built in the valley near the Deschutes River" (*Reports*, p. 91). Consequently, he decided to send Charles Coleman and most of the company (with the instrument cart) straight on east of Green Ridge and across the Metolius River (near Fly Creek), and so on across the eastern plains of what is now the Warm Springs Reservation as far as "Nee-nee Springs" (now Nena Springs and Creek), on the east side of the Mutton Mountains, where they would wait and try to rehabilitate their worn-out, underfed animals.

Meanwhile, Abbot set off with Anderson, Dr. Newberry, and eight men, with twelve lightly loaded mules, into the canyon of the Metolius, apparently determined to find out if there was possibly a pass over the mountains south of Mount Jefferson. It proved to be probably the wildest and most challenging leg of the trip so far, especially when they tried to climb up out of the canyon to approach the base of the mountain itself. Going ahead of his companions in search of a route, Abbot came to an impasse in the form of a sheer precipice, and in the *Reports* he remembered his feelings of awe and unease:

> A more desolate spot cannot be conceived. No sign of life was visible. Rough masses of dark lava piled around like the waves of a stormy sea. Fir-clad mountains reared their inaccessible summits on every side, apparently cutting off retreat; while Mt. Jefferson, without one intervening ridge, towered high above all, ragged with precipices and capped with glittering snow. It was a spot where, in all probability, no human foot had ever before intruded, for even the wild children of the forest abandon it to the fiends and demons of their traditions. (*Reports*, p. 93)

Despite his struggles to survey the lower Metolius Canyon and the formidable southeastern approaches to Mount Jefferson, Abbot was clearly much taken with that stretch of country, and fifty-four years later he fondly (and prophetically) celebrated "the Mpto-ly-as [Metolius] River, which heads near Mt. Jefferson, and whose canyon presents scenery so

Survey lithograph of Cascade Range skyline by John Young, 1855

magnificent that it will surely become some day a point to be visited by lovers of nature" ("Reminiscences," p. 437).

The next day (September 28), the party was thrashing its way back down the west side of the Metolius, across the river from Castle Rock (still a little-known wonder on the lower river). Then it took up the well-beaten "Fremont" trail north to Seekseekwa Canyon, where Abbot and Anderson made a side trip down to look at the Deschutes River; then on to a camp on Shitike Creek at or near Warm Springs (again Abbot hiked down from here to inspect the Deschutes, where the Highway 26 bridge is now); and so on to their rendezvous with Coleman and the others at Nena Springs.

On October 3, Abbot and the reunited party stopped once again at Evelyn's place at Tygh Valley and learned the very bad news about the rumored general Indian uprising. Evelyn himself was about to leave his farm, he said, for the safety of Fort Dalles. Now the possible Indian trail to the valley around the south side of Mount Hood must have seemed much less important to Abbot as a possible railroad or wagon route to survey than as an escape route, pure and simple. But who could guide them?

The half-blood, Domenich, who had told Abbot earlier about the way, declined to come along, and the Tygh leader Kuckup (in Abbot's transcription, "Kok-kup"; later chief of the "Warm Springs" Sahaptin-speaking population on the reservation) said that he didn't know about it. Abbot's prospects looked grimmer than ever—until Kuckup produced a young Indian, Sam An-ax-shat, who claimed that he knew the way, at least most of it, from family trips after huckleberries. After "a formal and ceremonious council" with Kuckup (who was given a red handkerchief for his help), Sam was signed on as a guide, "with strict orders to be obedient to me" (*Reports*, p. 96). In his 1896 memoir, Abbot recollected that "he was about eighteen years old, very intelligent, and I have little doubt that we owe our lives to his fidelity" ("Reminiscences," p. 438).

Up front, Sam's wages were very generous—two dollars a day, plus eight dollars for his return to Tygh Valley. But as the party left Evelyn's on October 5, Abbot must have been vexed by two interrelated issues: (1) Sam knew no English, and his new boss knew only as much Jargon as he had idly picked up at Fort Dalles; (2) Sam *was* an Indian, young and untested, however well recommended by Kuckup. So be it—the risks ahead of Abbot probably seemed less scary than the risks immediately behind.

Survey lithograph by John Young of Abbot's party at Tygh Valley, October 1855

At first the going was relatively easy, in a southwesterly direction, up through the open country around today's Wapinitia, and so on west in the vicinity of Indian and Beaver Creeks and their stretches of meadows, reaching modern-day Bear Springs, just east of Highway 26, on October 6. From there they crossed Camas Prairie and came to Clear Creek, finding increasingly dense forest cover and brush as they gained altitude. Their way was becoming maze-like, with trail-forks that led off promisingly only to end in huckleberry fields—where, surprisingly (at least by today's seasonal reckoning) the berries were still plentiful and juicy on the bushes.

The real problem, beyond Sam's uncertain trial-and-error route-finding, was the growing impassability of long stretches of blowdown, fallen pines, and fir laid across each other at random like giant jackstraws, obliterating whatever Indian trail they were trying to follow. In a journal note, Abbot growled (on behalf of everyone who's ever struggled through blowdowns): "Poets and our primeval forests"—which, in the more genteel language of the *Reports*, became, "We were all fully convinced that wandering around 'forests primeval' [the reference is probably to Longfellow's *Evangeline*] and among the Cascade Mountains, are two essentially different things" (*Quarterly*, p. 119; *Reports*, p. 98). It was also now raining, and there was less and less forage for the pack mules; and because the train was often strung out because of the trouble with route-finding, Abbot worried about their vulnerability to Indian attack from the rear. At night he set up regular watch duty.

Somewhere on October 6, probably around their camp on Camas Prairie (Sam called it "yaugh-pas-ses," meaning "cranberries" in Wasco Chinookan), Abbot decided to follow his guide's advice, "much against my will," and "kill the chik-chik." His long-suffering companions must have cheered, at least silently; the wooden spokes of the cart's wheels were duly salvaged as "picket-pins" for the mules, which were, for lack of feed and sometimes water, increasingly prone to wander off overnight.

Things must have looked brighter the next day, when they followed Clear Creek to Clear Lake ("wat-tum-pa"; just west of Highway 26), where they camped, and Coleman managed to kill some ducks for fresh camp meat. The following day (October 8) brought them through a prairie-like meadow ("lua-hum lua-hum"; Dry Meadow today) and, two miles farther west, to "a beautiful mountain lake"—identified by Sam as "ty-ty-pa," but Abbot initially followed the Anglo impulse to rename the Western landscape and christened it "Oolallee," after the Jargon word for huckleberries, which were abundant. The same renaming impulse has long since given the lake, on USFS maps, a prosaic Anglo name for its shape: Fryingpan Lake. Here one can get, as Abbot did, a fine view of Mount Hood through the trees; and because it was "raining furiously" the next day, he decided to rest his men and animals with an extra day at "[this] little camping place, which will be long remembered" (*Reports*, p. 99).

Back on the trail on October 10, and reenergized, the company logged probably its most strenuous day—southwest to Black Wolf Meadow (some USFS maps show their route as "Abbot Road," No. 58) and around and up on High Rock, from whose summit they were able to survey, more or less, their way northwest. From High Rock they descended past Linney Butte and skirted around the northern rim of Roaring River Canyon, within the southern boundary of today's Salmon-Huckleberry Wilderness. Taking frequent compass headings, Abbot noticed something strange in the vicinity of High Rock: extreme compass deflections, as much as 34 degrees, apparently indicating a mass of iron in or near the rock, but unexplained to this day. Finally, overtaken by darkness, the exhausted party had to make a waterless, forage-less camp in the timber. At length Sam found a small seep-spring—enough water for the men, "but none for the suffering animals, and their cries from hunger and thirst were incessant through the night" (*Reports*, p. 100).

The next day, October 11, they arose before light and straggled on, down into ravines and up onto ridges, reaching a place Sam called "the Stone House" (Abbot surmised that there was a cave nearby, but the name remains a mystery), but then pushing on until they stopped for the night at the site of former USFS Plaza Ranger Station near the head of the south fork of the Salmon River. And after another lay-by day, in incessant rain, they forged on due west to the summit of Squaw Mountain. Their deliverance was at last in view: "The blue Willamette Valley, marked by a line of fog rising from the water, lay before us, and the word 'settlements' shouted down the line, inspired every one with new life" (*Reports*, p. 101).

Two more arduous days, now descending, and they reached the "settlements," southeast of modern-day Estacada, and heard hair-raising reports of Indian uprisings east of the mountains. They set up one last camp for several days on Clackamas Prairie, courtesy of a settler there, Hugh Currin. Back in the timber, a mule loaded with "a valuable pack" had strayed, and

Abbot sent Sam back to find and bring back both in three days. Which he did, another testament to both his skill in the woods and his reliability. After his return, there was an ugly confrontation at Currin's with a posse of angry, fearful white settlers that Abbot chose to omit from both his journal and the official *Reports*, but recounted in his 1909 memoir. It reveals much about the widespread anti-Indian hysteria in Oregon in those anxious days—and also much about Abbot's feelings for his young guide:

> The neighbors in this vicinity were panic-stricken by the appearance of my train, for they had believed the [mountain] chain to be impassable, and a delegation soon presented themselves and coolly suggested that, in the interest of the public, my guide should be then and there killed to prevent him from bringing over a war party. It is needless to record my answer; he started on his return that night, fully warned. ("Reminiscences," p. 439)

Elsewhere in both his journal and in the *Reports*, as we have seen, Abbot says that "we all owe our lives to the fidelity of this Indian." Historically, it might be argued that the threat of Indian attack that Abbot felt he was under while crossing the mountains was not as grave as it seemed in the woods. But what matters most here is that he believed that Sam had saved their lives—and now, "back in civilization" so to speak, in the face of a threatening and no doubt armed gang of settlers, he unflinchingly returned the favor. It is also indicative of the very real threat Sam was under that he headed back into the timber and over the mountains *that same night* (October 15, 1855), taking with him his pay: $38 dollars, provisions, and Abbot's gift of a military blanket.

As we watch Sam depart from Abbot's ongoing story after ten days of intense companionship, who can resist speculating about the rest of *his* story—another enterprising and capable young man at the end of his first big adventure? The cultural and historical gulf between the two men is wide, and we'll probably never know how it went for Sam after he returned to Kuckup's camp on Tygh Prairie. Presumably, he eventually relocated to the Warm Springs Reservation, where Kuckup became the first Warm Springs chief (there is a fine meadow near Mount Jefferson named for him). But no records of Sam under the name of "An-ax-shat" have been found on the tribal rolls. Although he was at the right age to serve with the Warm

Springs scouts in the Paiute Wars of the 1860s, under Dr. William McKay, his name does not appear in the military records (see Clark and Clark, "William McKay's Journals 1866–7"). There is one tantalizing possible hint of Sam on file: one of the signers of the 1855 Columbia River Indian Treaty (dated June 25, at The Dalles) was a Dog River (Hood River) Wasco leader named "Ash-na-chat" (sometimes printed as "Ash-ha-chat"). Given the variations of Indian names as phonetically transcribed, this could very well be a form of "An-ax-shat" (or vice versa), but the signer would probably be an older relative, maybe father or grandfather, not young Sam himself. So we're left wondering—how did he fare, and what stories did he tell about guiding Abbot over the mountains, and about killing the chik-chik?

On October 19, Abbot and his crew, now traveling over the easy last leg of the Barlow Road, reached Oregon City, where they found a new set of unwelcome surprises. Abbot had been expecting to regroup with Williamson—but Williamson had left only a few days before for Vancouver, and by now was ship-bound for San Francisco, leaving instructions for Abbot to finish the surveying southbound along the Willamette Valley's west side and on through the Umpqua and Rogue River valleys and over the Siskiyou Mountains into California and so on to Fort Reading. That the active hostility of the Native groups in the Rogue River country was likely to be an issue in their return to California, Williamson and Abbot had known from the start, and they had been counting on the escort of dragoons and regular troops that Williamson had taken with him into the valley on September 24—but now Abbot learned from Williamson's memo that, as of October 10, all of the dragoons and most of the regulars had been commandeered by Major G. J. Rains of the 4th Infantry stationed in Vancouver, and sent under Phil Sheridan to assist army units already fighting Indians along the Columbia.

Williamson had protested Rains's action in a polite letter, pointing out that the escort had been specifically assigned to the survey by the secretary of war (oddly enough, he fails to mention that Abbot's part of the survey was still in the field, but expected soon); but Sheridan and his company were already "deployed" by the time Abbot arrived.

Abbot promptly wrote his own, much stronger, letter of protest, invoking the secretary of war's original orders, emphasizing the extreme jeopardy the major's actions had put him and his men under for their march through Rogue country, where the Indians had only recently resumed their attacks on settlers and troops, and imploring Rains to send the dragoons (and Phil Sheridan) back. Without waiting for a reply (remember, this was a young second lieutenant, only a year out of West Point), he took himself off to Portland, where he met with territorial governor George Curry. Curry was sympathetic, but unable as a civilian to countermand Rains's order. Instead, he noted that a volunteer militia had been called up to deal with the Indian crisis in the south, and issued a general order for all volunteer officers in the field there to do what they could to provide the survey party with safe passage through the "war zone" along the Umpqua and Rogue.

With this less-than-ironclad assurance, Abbot and Lieutenant Crook (the only other officer left with the survey contingent) organized the march south. But before briefly following them along the survey's final leg, we need to pause here to consider Lieutenant Williamson's decision to leave Oregon City before Abbot's arrival. Abbot's official account of the situation he found when he came out of the woods is, in both the *Reports* and his journal entries, tersely matter-of-fact; but it's hard not to question Williamson's judgment in leaving before Abbot showed up—especially knowing as he did that his junior officer would have to deal with the loss of the military escort, and somehow figure out how to get the survey party through the southwestern war zone. And what if Abbot and his party had somehow come to grief in crossing the mountains? Was Williamson's need to get to San Francisco to plan for the survey's possible second mission into the Sierras (now, given the lateness of the year, very unlikely) so urgent as to justify leaving Abbot to deal, when and if he turned up in Oregon City, with all these contingencies?

A personal factor might have been at work in all this: Williamson's health. Soon after he and Abbot reached San Francisco in May 1855, Abbot noted in his journal (excerpted by Robert Sawyer in the Bend *Bulletin* in June 2, 1943, and not included in his *Oregon Historical Quarterly* text of the journals) that his chief had taken ill and "was too weak and sick to attend to business." Whatever his ailment was, he recovered in time to lead the survey party north in early July, and Abbot makes no further note of his being ill while they are together in the field. But when the two of them returned to Washington in January 1856, Williamson became very ill again (the malady is not identified), and as a consequence he was unable to write up his own portions of the *Survey Reports*, let alone take charge of editing the whole volume—which Abbot did for him. Williamson did see action in the Civil

War, and then returned to California to serve out his military career as an army engineer there; but his death in 1882, after twenty years of ill health, was reportedly caused by tuberculosis.

Whether his incapacitating illnesses just before and after the 1855 survey were early episodes of TB is unknown. As is, finally, whether his abrupt and puzzling departure from Oregon City in October 1855 was prompted by recurrent illness. Probably the fairest interpretation of Williamson's actions is that they must indicate that he had great confidence in his young second-in-command—and, as it turned out, that confidence was very well founded.

Leaving Oregon City on October 23, Abbot and Crook and their company traveled south on mostly good roads on the west side of the Willamette River. They passed through Salem (conferring there with local surveyors), Corvallis ("a long street"), Eugene ("a dirty place"), and eventually, near Roseburg, caught up with the Oregon volunteers, under a Major Martin, who promised them an escort to Fort Lane (north of Jacksonville). As West Pointers, Abbot and Crook must have enjoyed some comic relief with the hastily mustered, untrained Oregon Mounted Volunteers, despite their impatience to catch up with Captain A. J. Smith and his regular troops. In his *Autobiography*, Crook recalled that "a motlier crew has never been seen since Old Falstaff's time" (pp. 26–27). Abbot tried to teach them some rudiments of military dressage, but his efforts to get the company off on an early morning start got nowhere over the question of breakfast. To Major Martin's exhortations, one of the volunteers replied, "Major, when I'm going into battle I likes to have my belly full of beans." Abbot adds, "There was nothing more to be said, and we waited for the beans" ("Reminiscences," p. 440).

Abbot and Crook must have had some serious misgivings about how effectively their party would be protected by such an escort; but fortunately, just as they reached the "front lines" and began to see for themselves burnt-out farms and dead livestock and wounded soldiers in retreat, they caught up with Captain Smith and his company of regulars at Grave Creek and were promised a proper escort of thirty-five soldiers through to Fort Lane and beyond. On November 6, having passed through the mountains without incident, they ferried across the Klamath River and headed for Fort Reading. There the faithful Crook was redeployed to Fort Jones, near Yreka, and so Abbot had to take on full command of the survey party and Crook's

troops. It was hardly the first time he had had to step up unexpectedly to
new responsibilities; on November 15, he led his caravan to Fort Reading.

On November 21, Williamson came up from San Francisco, having
already decided that the "second mission" into the Sierras was unfeasible
because of the season; soon orders came from Washington instructing them
to return to the capital without delay, to prepare their survey's *Reports*. They
sailed from San Francisco on December 20, and when en route down the
Pacific coast they met a northbound ship and exchanged mail and newspapers, they found an article in the New York *Herald* mistakenly reporting
the massacre of Abbot's party on Mount Hood ("Reminiscences," p. 442).
They reached New York on January 12, 1856, and after a brief furlough
with his family in Massachusetts, Abbot returned to Washington and, in
the concluding words of his *Reports* narrative, "immediately entered upon
office work" (*Reports*, p. 111). In doing so—shifting abruptly from a saddle
to a desk-chair—he must have felt both relief and a bit let down after such
adventures.

With Williamson unable to contribute because of his extended illness,
the monumental "office work" of writing much of and editing all of the five-
hundred-page volume 6 of the *Pacific Railroad Survey Reports* (its maps
would not be published until 1861) fell to Abbot, but by the spring of 1857
it was mostly done. In his prefatory letter to the secretary of war (now John
F. Floyd) he modestly acknowledges that

> the preparation of this report has devolved upon me, in
> consequence of the severe and protracted illness of Lt. Williamson;
> and it is due to myself to state that I have performed the duty with
> extreme reluctance, partly because it was not originally designed
> for me by the Department [of War], and partly because it properly
> belongs to the officer by whose foresight and professional ability
> the expedition has been brought to a successful termination.
> (*Reports*, p. 3)

Later, in the introductory section of the volume, Abbot highlights
what was probably in his view his own most important contribution to the
Oregon survey: "A new pass south of Mt. Hood. This pass was discovered
by the detached party in my charge" (*Reports*, p. 34). Despite his tribula-
tions while finding his way (with Sam An-ax-shat's help) around Mount

Hood, he had concluded from his observations that if cleared of fallen timber the route would be much preferable for emigrant travel to the Barlow Road, offering better forage and water and much more passable terrain. But because he had no time in Oregon to promote his new "road," and later was preoccupied with the editing of the survey volume, the idea went nowhere; and for the apparent lack of a better alternative, emigrants kept on struggling over the Barlow Road, enduring the terrors of Laurel Hill and all.

On May 3, 1857, Abbot mused to his family in a letter, "It will be two years day after tomorrow since I sailed to California. How many scenes I have gone through since. They would make up a life for many persons" (*Quarterly*, p. 130). Perhaps this confident young man intuited that his recent wilderness exploits were only the prologue to what was going to be a very long and historically eventful life. *That* should be, as they say, another story—but it will have to suffice here to outline its main headings:

- 1857–1861: With General Andrew Humphreys, pioneered hydrological surveys of the lower Mississippi River, leading to early flood control measures.
- 1861–1865: Saw active service with the Union Army in the Civil War; wounded in the first battle of Bull Run, later in command of "siege artillery" forces in major Civil War battles; ended the war as a brevet brigadier general.
- 1866–1895: Served in the United States and abroad with the Army Corps of Engineers, contributing to the design of US coastal defenses; helped to establish the US Army Engineering School of Practice in New York City; retired from the army as a brigadier general.
- 1896–1897: Became a member of Presidential US Forestry Commission (with Charles Sargent, Gifford Pinchot, John Muir, and others)—the commission's report led to the establishment of the national forest system and the USFS.
- 1897–1915: Served as a principal engineering consultant first to the French and then to the American Panama Canal projects; crucial advocate of the "two-lock" Panama canal route over the "no-lock" sea-level route in Nicaragua.
- Authored several books and scores of articles on the Panama Canal and a wide range of engineering and scientific topics.

Soon after his return from Oregon, Abbot married his fiancée, Mary Susan ("Susie") Everett; they had two sons and two daughters. Mrs. Abbot died tragically young in 1871, soon after the birth of their second son Henry—who died in 1881 in an accident at the family farm in New Hampshire. Abbot never remarried; his older son, Frederic, graduated from West Point himself and had a long and illustrious career of his own with the Army Corps of Engineers.

The spacious trajectory of Henry Larcom Abbot's life might qualify as an illustration of H. L. Davis's wry description of Oregon as "the place where stories begin that end up someplace else" ("Oregon," in *Collected Essays*, p. 52). But, all things considered, what a rich Oregon beginning it was, for Abbot, and what a signifying American life story to follow.

Two
"A Visit from Sam Anaxshat," from *Maudy's Year*

"A Visit from Sam Anaxshat" is an episode from a children's novel-in-progress, *Maudy's Year*, based on the girlhood experiences of my maternal grandmother, Ella McCoin Mendenhall, and her sister (my great-aunt) Minnie McCoin Helfrich. Their parents, Julius and Sarah Osborn McCoin, homesteaded in the 1880s on the northeast flanks of Gray Butte, about fifteen miles west of Prineville, the first town in Central Oregon.

In addition to raising horses and cattle, and planting what became a large fruit orchard, Julius took up freighting, hauling wool, meat, and grain from Prineville to The Dalles and coming back with merchandise for settlers, including large barrels of beer and whiskey. His freight runs took upward of two weeks round-trip. While he was away on one of these trips in late spring of 1888, Sarah suddenly became ill—probably with pneumonia—and died at the ranch, attended only by Minnie (age nine) and Ella (seven) and their brothers Numa (twelve) and Walter (four).

Julius never remarried, and when Numa began to "work out" as a sheepherder, it was up to Minnie, Ella, and Walter, in their father's absence, to take care of everything on the ranch and also to go to school when they could. Their few neighbors around the butte (including a family of relatives) helped out, but basically the McCoin children grew up looking after each other and the place.

My grandmother, Ella, died young, like her mother. But my Aunt Minnie lived to be 101; and she was a spellbinding storyteller. The stories she told about her childhood were vivid revelations of early homesteading life, by turns funny, frightening, terribly sad, shocking, earthy. Years ago I determined to try to find a way to catch their historical essence in writing—and one way to do that seemed to be historical fiction, with Laura Ingalls Wilder's wonderful Little House series as an inspiration.

In this selection from *Maudy's Year*, I've invented "Sam Anaxshat's" visit to his friend's Joshua Speaker's place—but of course Sam An-ax-shat was a historical figure, as documented in the 1855 narrative of Henry Larcom Abbot (see chapter 1 in this book). And whatever else happens in this segment of *Maudy's Year* is based on Aunt Minnie's anecdotes and on local homestead circumstances that she loved to tell about. The story that Sam Anaxshat tells to Maudy Speaker and her family is adapted from a traditional Wasco-Wishram Chinook narrative, probably known to the historical Sam and included in my anthology of Native American traditional literature from the Oregon Country, *Coyote Was Going There* (Ramsey, pp. 81–84).

Pa was able to stay home for most of that September, except for one short run to Bakeoven to pick up what was left of the freight of a wagon that had busted an axle and tipped over, spilling groceries, furniture, and whiskey barrels down a dry wash. Maudy and Mame and Perry each told him a version of their adventures while he was gone, and Pa, being Pa, listened patiently to it all, including the arguments, whether at the breakfast table or in the horse barn or at night before bed. He let on like he wasn't surprised that they had managed so well. "I can see that you're all three good hands—your mother would be proud," he'd say, looking them over carefully. Then, grinning, "I reckon I'll keep you on the payroll!"

Well, of course Perry and Mame would swell up like blowsnakes under such praise, especially if there was someone else around to hear it. Maudy liked it too, of course—when Pa said you'd done good at something then it was like telling the whole world. But as they settled back into their usual routines, she could feel something odd about him, a kind of absent-mindedness, like his thoughts weren't really fixed on what he was doing or saying. Sometimes out in the fields, or mending fence, he would look off into space for a minute or more, and at night, after she and Mame and Perry were bedded down, she knew that he would be sitting up alone at the kitchen table by the coal-oil lamp, his galluses down and boots off, his whiskery chin in his hands. It was all about Mama, but Maudy didn't know what she could do.

There was plenty to do around the place, it being September. The days were bright one after the other, but not heavy-hot as in July or August, and the nights were turning off cold. Sunsets, what they could see around Mowich Butte, were flaming red now, as if the clouds and the sky itself reflected a bonfire. Pa said he could smell smoke from fires burning over in the Willamette Valley, and the children all sniffed and declared that they could, too. All the nesting birds, so busy around the house in summer, the bee martins, wild canaries, sparrows, and bluebirds, had reared their last nestlings and left. Yet it wasn't really fall; it hadn't frozen the water in the log troughs, not yet.

The far end of the barley field that had been left to ripen for seed grain and horse feed turned light-orange, and Pa worked all one week, in the mornings when it was cool and the grain wouldn't shatter out, scything it and then cradling it into bundles ready to be forked into the wagon. Maudy loved to watch him swing the big crooked scythe back and forth through the grain, and then the cradle with its long wooden fingers that made up the bundles. It looked, she thought, like Pa was doing a kind of slow dance by himself in the field, but every time he whirled toward the standing grain, and then whirled back, a new gap of stubble opened up in the standing barley. Bewildered at losing their tall cover, mice scurried underfoot, and Perry and Ben followed along to chase them.

When it was all cut and cradled, Pa hitched up Bess and Dick to the hay wagon and, starting and stopping them with only his voice, drove them back and forth across the field while he pitchforked the shocks of grain on—carefully, so as not to knock out the fat hard barley kernels. Once, when Maudy was fetching him a jug of cold water, he forked up a shock only to find a big rattlesnake curled up under it, asleep. Maudy told Mame and Perry that they had to wear their shoes in the field after that. And after he'd taken several loads down to the Ogilvies to be thrashed in the fanning mill, Papa reported that they had actually pitched a great big rattler off with a load and run it through the machine—stopping everything, all the belts and gears and shafts, until Peter Paul Ogilvy could crawl back inside the works and pull it out in pieces.

"He didn't much like the job," Pa said, laughing. "Not at all until I promised him my old pocketknife."

"Ben and me, we'd have done it for free, Pa!" said Perry.

"Sure enough, Perry—I'll know who to ask next time around!"

Eventually Papa and Uncle Rob went together and took all their feed grain to the grist mill on Crooked River, at Prineville, and after a couple of weeks they brought it back ground up fine and put up in neat cotton bags, with ears that stuck up like a cottontail rabbit's. Pa and Uncle Rob grumbled some about how much ground grain they had to give back to the miller to pay for the grinding, but he ran the only mill in the country, so they had no choice.

Maudy was at the stove, canning. As hot as it was in the garden, where Perry and Mame were supposed to be picking beans, and corn, and the last of the gooseberries, it was sweltering over the stove, steam rising from the canning vat and the jars. She felt like she was fit to be canned, herself! Anyway, she would soon run out of jars—Pa said they'd put up too many jars of string beans in their first canning spree last month, but Maudy wasn't sorry, really—beans were better than corn, anyway, and easier to fix. Pa thought they were doing a fine job, but it did rattle him a little when he discovered that since Mama died they'd just been putting the used-up jars back in the root cellar without washing them out. It took Maudy a whole morning just to scour the mold out with boiling water, and she guessed she'd learned a lesson. Pa called it "acting kid-like."

After the vegetables came applesauce and pears, from the orchard, just a little dab of each, a few jars, from the young trees. But when Pa tasted the fresh applesauce, he declared it was the best ever—even though, Maudy noticed, he put some sugar on it, and had to spit out some pips that had gotten through. Maudy couldn't help wondering how much applesauce they'd have to can when the trees were full grown.

One clear night it froze hard, and when she looked out the next morning, early, Maudy saw that all the remaining stalks and vines in the garden were lying flat: Jack Frost had gotten them. Perry came in from his chores with a platter of ice from the troughs, which they peered through at each other, making faces, until it melted, and the biscuits began to smell like burning.

Pa came in blowing on his hands, and announced that the first freeze last year was on September 25, so they were ten days to the good this year. He went to the calendar and put a check by October 5. "Now then," he continued, sitting down to his plate, "who knows what happens around here after it freezes?"

"No more garden, no more canning!" Maudy said.

"Wrong, Maudy," Mame broke in. "There's potatoes to dig."

Perry said eagerly, "You're going hunting with Mr. Spoonlicker and kill a buck deer, Pa?"

"Well, you are all right so far, but what else? What's crunchy, and comes out of a big black pot?"

"Cracklings!" Perry and Mame shouted together, but Maudy thought, oh no, butchering and rendering. What a mess to clean up—she'd helped her mother at it, before.

"One more thing. Let's see, where do children go when it's time for them to learn to spell, and do sums, and sit still?"

"Up in the mountains?" Perry asked hopefully.

"No, silly," Mame said. "He means—*school!*"

"Right, Mame. Mr. Sturtevant told the directors he figures on opening the school October 15. Perry, you'll be going this year, too, on account of nobody at home."

"Well, can Ben come too?"

"We'll see." Pa was proud to be one of the directors of New Age School District No. 2; Uncle Rob Ogilvie was another, and the other directors were some men who lived along the road to Prineville and had mostly mean kids. Maudy hoped things would be better this year, with Mr. Sturtevant, the new teacher.

Digging the spuds was fun, once you got into it. Pa had to take some horses down to Spoonlickers to be reshod, so just the three of them were digging. Mame and Perry took turns pulling up the big dark green vines, now wilted and turning black from the frost; if you pulled slow and easy, with both hands, you could bring up four or five small potatoes with the roots. Some vines were so big, Mame and Perry had to pull them out together, like a tug of war, and then they would fall over in a pile, giggling and scuffling. Maudy came along behind with a little spade, and carefully dug into each hill to find the biggest spuds, which she put in gunnysacks. The ground was dry and cloddy on top, but down under it was moist and sweet-smelling. She always wondered how far down to dig—was she missing a giant Blue Victor spud by stopping too soon? As it was, some were as big as a quart jar, with queer bulges and knobs like noses that made them laugh. They were all dirty on the outside, and then you rubbed the clinging dirt off and they were a kind of purply blue; and then if you scraped the skin off with your fingernail, of course, they were as white and clean inside as fine paper.

Mame ran to the house and got a little salt and a paring knife, and they sat down and ate raw potatoes right there in the field, and no apples ever tasted better. Then they started dragging them in out of the field in the gunnysacks, and when Pa got home at supper time, the potato crop was all harvested, and Maudy had fixed fried potatoes, sliced the long way, with just about the last of the salt pork.

Mame was very attached to one of the young shoat-pigs to be butchered. She had named him Skookum and used to ride on him around the pig-lot until he scampered and squealed. Mame didn't want Skookum killed—she said she wouldn't eat him, and she didn't want anybody else eating him, either. Pa tried to reason with her, but things got more and more out of hand, until the morning Mr. Spoonlicker arrived with his long knives and whetstone to help with the butchering, and Pa discovered that he was missing one shoat-pig out of the lot of seven. Skookum!

"Mame! You, Mame!"

Mame went out to the pig-lot, dragging both hind feet. Pa was looking at the pig-lot gate. "Now Mame, where's that shoat-pig?"

"I let him out last night." Maudy, listening, wondered how her little sister could be so naughty, and so brave. Mame got a spanking then, while Pa as always whistled seriously between his teeth. Mame didn't cry a bit, until Pa asked her how long she thought the pig would last running around loose in the hills, with coyotes, and cougars, and Indian hunters looking for meat. Then she cried, and told Pa she was sorry, and could they start looking for Skookum right now? Pa said no, and told her to go back to the house.

Perry sang, "The coyotes are eating ba-con!" until Mame punched him in the nose, and by the time Maudy got it broken up, the butchering had already begun. She didn't like it, either, and was glad to stay in the house until she was called. First they killed the poor hogs, just how she didn't want to know, and then each one was lowered with ropes from a tripod into the big three-legged iron hog-vat with a fire under it, full of boiling water, and then, once the hair was loosened, Pa scraped it off with a sharp scraper, and he and Mr. Spoonlicker cut the hog open and cleaned it out, saving more of the innards than Maudy thought was necessary.

Now they were cutting up the carcasses on clean boards laid across the troughs, like a table, and Pa came in and told Maudy they were ready for her to come out and begin the rendering. She tried not to look at the blood on the boards, on the grass, and on Pa's and Mr. Spoonlicker's aprons—she went right to the little rendering pot and built a fire under it. When it was hot enough, she began to drop in the white pieces of fat Pa cut up for her. They sizzled and splattered and threw up a strong smell like bacon frying that at first made Maudy hungry, and then not hungry at all. When she knelt down to feed the fire, the wood smoke made her eyes water, and when she turned the melting pieces with a forked stick, she felt like an old witch, with the greasy smoke in her hair.

All that day and most of the next, she worked by that stinking old vat. Every so often she would fish out the rendered-out cracklings, bubbling hot and golden, and put them in a basket made of screen-wire, so that the grease left in them could drip out into a bucket. Then she gave some of the crisp cracklings to Perry and Mame, who gobbled them up like candy—no doubt spoiling their suppers. Maddy had no appetite for them. Everything—her hair, her clothes, her skin—smelled like rendering. Maudy didn't think it was fair for her to have to make lard for the Spoonlickers, too, with all those kids to do it, and when she was filling up the tin pails and crocks with the stuff, she put most of the yellowish leavings in their containers. Then she felt mean, and poured it out, and gave them some of the best lard. Not that they would notice, she thought. Not that Pa notices what awful nasty work this is for me to do.

Pa and Mr. Spoonlicker, meanwhile, were cutting up the pork meat and hams, to be hung up in cotton bags in the barn and cooled out. In about a week, Pa would take each piece of meat and rub a tasty mixture of salt-brine and brown sugar all over it; then he would hang it all up in the smokehouse, which looked just like the outhouse except that there was a long dirt-covered trench leading to one side of it, and in the mouth of this tunnel Pa would build a smoky little fire of willow wood. The good-smelling smoke followed the tunnel into the smokehouse where the meat was hanging, locked up to keep the varmints out; smoke leaked out of the cracks of the little house, as if it were catching fire. Once when it was empty Perry had wriggled into the tunnel and gotten himself stuck, and squalled and howled until Pa had to tear up part of the tunnel to get him loose. When Pa carried him into the house, Mama had said he smelled like a Christmas ham, and they'd all laughed and teased about that for days.

Well, Maudy thought, washing herself up on the back porch, *I* smell like an old tub of rancid lard. Not fit to bait a trap with. But when she opened the kitchen door, she saw to her surprise that the table was all set, and that Mame, back in Pa's good graces after letting the pig loose, was serving up from the stove. Even if it was pork ribs, Maudy felt some better. Pa caught her under her arms and whirled her around, before dropping her on the kitchen bench.

"Here now, Sobersides, we *render* to you the seat of honor!"

Oh, it was a fine dinner, and when the dishes were done and put away afterward, Pa shooed Mame and Perry out of the kitchen and told Maddy she could draw water for a bath all her own. "Can't have you starting school smelling like a frying pan, can we?" he joked. Imagine, she thought, a bath just for yourself, with no one else waiting to get in! While Maudy was tempering the water in the tin tub, Pa went to the back of the house and came back with something in his hands. He smiled at Maudy, but his eyes were sad. "Brought you a little of your mother's fancy bath-salts, child." He handed her a tiny jar with pink grains inside, and then turned abruptly and went out. On the jar was a label showing a fine lady with a parasol; Maudy knew the lovely smell—roses—even before she removed the stopper.

So then there was school, beginning October 15. New Age School was a funny little building with front steps and a narrow porch, where the teacher stood to ring the handbell to call the scholars in from recess or noon and to wave goodbye to them when school let out at 3:30 or thereabouts.

All three of them were eager to go, but Mame was the eagerest, fussing about her clothes and school-gear, and chattering. "Maudy, I'll bet Mr. Sturtevant won't blow *kisses* to us when school lets out, the way Miss Newsom did. I'll bet he doesn't take any guff off those mean Proctor kids, either!"

"Well, let's hope so, but remember, he's from Portland, and he don't look very strong, either. Huddie Proctor's as big as he is, anyway."

The school was north of the Speaker place about two and a half miles, just off the road around the butte, on a corner of the "school section" that the government had set aside from homesteading claims. Papa explained that on the government maps in The Dalles there was always one school section marked for every township, or thirty-six-square-mile area, but of course a lot of ground hadn't even been claimed for homesteading yet, so New Age School was the only one for miles around. Last year there were twenty-one scholars in six grades, and the ones who came the farthest—when they came—were the Proctor kids, from over on the Prineville Road, along Scabby Canyon. Huddie was the oldest, about thirteen, and then Nate, a year or so younger, and then Nell, who was exactly Maudy's age, and the worst bully of the bunch. Really, the only reason they hadn't been expelled last year was that their father was a director of the school. As it was, poor Miss Newsom took sick with the collywobbles in early April—nerves, probably—and school ended three weeks too soon.

When it turned real cold, they would ride Dick and Bess to and from school, but at the beginning they just got up early and walked, carrying their lunches in an old Indian basket with a rope handle. Perry had been told to tie Ben up to keep him from following, and now Perry was stumbling through the sagebrush, very unhappy.

"Perry, you're too little to go into the grades," Mame told him over her shoulder. "The teacher will have to find you a special little place. Probably right by his desk!"

Perry began to bawl. "I . . . don't . . . want to go to school! I want to stay home! I hate Mame!" He threw a rock at her. "I'm a-goin' home!" He was running.

"Perry, you come back here right now. You know that Pa's gone to Grizzly for lumber and there's nobody home." Maudy ran back and got him by his shirttail. "Don't you mind Mame." He stopped struggling. "And you Mame! I'll tell both Mr. Sturtevant and Pa, see if I don't!"

Mr. Sturtevant was showing Peter Paul Ogilvie and one of the Spoonlicker boys how to put up the new American flag on its pole when they arrived. The schoolhouse smelled rank inside, and Mr. Sturtevant said he had found a big packrat's nest under his desk, full of buttons and tin cups and pencils, and the pages of a McGuffey's Reader. "No doubt we can expect to be visited by educated packrats," Mr. Sturtevant joked.

When he had them all lined up on the benches according to grades, big children at the sides, little ones (including Perry) at the front, and scholars the age of Mame and Maudy in the middle, Mr. Sturtevant had them say the Lord's Prayer together, and then he told them that he was new to Central Oregon, having come clear from Minnesota originally, and that he hoped they would be able to teach him some things about the wildlife in this beautiful country, while he was teaching them book-learning. Maudy noticed that the Proctors hadn't arrived yet.

"Well, teacher, you're liable to have better luck educatin' that packrat than some of us hombres. Like me, for instance." It was Joe Swenson, a follower of the Proctors. Mr. Sturtevant turned around and smiled at him. It was a pleasant, even smile, but it lasted a long time, until even Joe began to fidget. "Everybody in school will learn the best he can, young man," Mr. Sturtevant replied, "and those who won't—including packrats—will be made to leave. But be assured"—now he smiled broadly, and crossed his arms—"that I will fight to educate everybody!"

Mr. Sturtevant was reading them a story about Abraham Lincoln teaching himself to read when the door flew open with a crash. It was the Proctors, Huddie, Nate, and Nell, and Mr. Proctor bringing up the rear, as if he were herding calves. "Howdy teacher—I reckon we're a little late, but these here roughnecks of mine wouldn't have come at all if I hadn't headed them off at the Prineville Junction and run 'em on in." Huddie and Nate were eyeing Mr. Sturtevant, as if for size. "Now, they're good kids, and bright, too, but we've never had no teacher in here who would give 'em half a chance. Always makin' teachers' pets"—Mr. Proctor's hard little eyes flicked around the schoolroom—"and playin' favorites. How do you stand on teachers' pets, hey, Teacher?"

Mr. Sturtevant folded his arms again and smiled. "I don't allow animals of any kind in my school, Mr. Proctor, neither teachers' pets, nor bullies. Now then, if your children will just find seats, please, we'll proceed with our lessons. Scholars, say good-day to Mr. Proctor, who is one of our school's directors!"

Maudy thought maybe Mr. Sturtevant *would* make it through the term; at least it was a good beginning. But when she saw the Proctor boys and Nell and Joe Swenson whispering together after school, gesturing back toward the schoolhouse, she knew that there would be some mischief sooner or later. Did the teacher really mean it, about no pets?

Pa came home from Grizzly and announced that he was going deer hunting with Mr. Spoonlicker and his boys, up and around the butte. "At least you don't have to render venison, Maudy," he laughed. "Perry, if you think you can keep up, you can come along, too."

"Oh yes, Pa, I'll be the tracker!"

"Pa, I want to come along too!" Mame whined.

"No, Mame, you and Maudy are my scholars now, remember, and besides, it's not fitten' for lady-folks to go hunting."

"Well, why *not*? I could shoot a gun, too!"

Pa just laughed. "I hear that when a little Indian boy makes his first kill, his dad has him cut the buck open, and then splashes him all over with warm blood—would you like that, Mame?"

"Oh boy, will you do that to me, Pa?" asked Perry.

So the menfolk were up and gone before Maudy and Mame even woke up. There was no trouble to speak of at school that day—the Proctor boys were absent, probably deer hunting, too. On the way home, Maudy and Mame were arguing about the chores as usual, until, as they came up the lane, they realized they were being watched! A row of dark faces looked out at them from the porch—Indians! There must have been seven or eight of them, men and boys. Some had guns, and their dogs began to bark fiercely, and Ben—tied up in the barn—joined in.

"Land a' Goshen, Maudy," Mame whispered, "What do they want with us? Will it be a massacree?"

"No, silly, the Indians on the Warm Springs aren't that kind. They just want something." But Maudy felt her arms stiffening: she hoped they wouldn't ask for too much. When would Pa come home?

While the others sat watching on the porch, expressionless, an old Indian stood up and came crippling down the steps. He was little and skinny, not much bigger than Maudy; he was wearing a very big black hat with beads around the crown, and his long gray braids hung down over his shoulders. Like the others, he wore moccasins, and his old blue coat looked like it had once been part of a uniform. He limped up to Maudy, his black eyes fixed on the girls like agates. "Lordy!" whispered Mame.

Then the old Indian whipped off his big hat, and grinned at them until his brown face was nothing but wrinkles. "Say something to him, Maudy," hissed Mame. Maudy was trying to remember some words in the Chinook Jargon that folks used when they dickered with Indians.

"Klahowya!" she managed.

"Klahowya," answered the old man, very deep in his throat.

"Uh, nesika kah klatawa?"

"Oh, nesika kah momook mowich, klona moolock, klonas *moosmoos*! Nesika skookum *hunters*!" The old man laughed, and all of his party on the porch laughed too.

"I think he said they were going deer hunting," Maudy whispered. "But there was something about cows, too . . ."

"Oh no," interrupted the old Indian. "That was a joke, young ladies. Can we talk your talk now?" As they stood there, open-mouthed, he held out his hand. "Your father, Joshua Speaker, he knows me—I am Sam Anaxshat, and those are my boys." He pointed behind him with his chin.

Mame recovered first, as always. "Pleased to meet you, Mr. Anaxshat, I'm Mame Speaker, and this here is my sister Maudy." They shook hands with Mr. Anaxshat, and then, after he made a funny clicking sound deep in his throat, all the other Indians trooped off the porch and shook hands, too. Some of them looked pretty fierce, Maudy thought, but it was all very friendly. The dogs sniffed around and wagged their tails.

"Is your father at home?" the old man asked.

"No sir," Mame answered, "he's gone deer hunting, too, behind the Butte."

"But he should be home any minute now," Maudy added emphatically.

"Kloshe—good. S'pose we stay here tonight, okay? Just traveling through to the Ochocos—our old staying place down below, big barn, many horses, the man there say we couldn't stop there one more time. My folks been stoppin' there *ahhhhkutte*, many years now, but the man says no." Maudy realized he was talking about the Ogilvies. Mr. Anaxshat looked very solemn, and then he laughed. "Hee hee, man's wife, she telling him what to say to us, from the house—oh my yes, hyas klootchman, cultus wahwah, in't?"

The other Indians laughed, and Maudy giggled in spite of herself. "Well, I'm sure it's okay for you to put your horses in the corral there—" Mame chimed in, "Yes, and you'll always be welcome up *here*, Mr. Anaxshat!" She grinned up at him, and he shook her hand, then Maudy's. "Okay, young ladies, thanks."

While they were taking care of the horses, Mame bustling along as hostess, Maudy wondered what do to about eating and sleeping. Did they expect to be fed? Just then there was a terrific racket of dogs barking and men yelling: Pa was home! She ran outside—Pa had a sleepy-looking Perry on his neck, and spraddled across the horse he was leading was a fine buck deer, a four-point. Pa and Mr. Anaxshat shook hands and slapped each other on the back, like old friends, then Pa shook hands with all the others. "Sam, it's good to see you up here, your boys too! They leave the gate open at the agency?"

Mr. Anaxshat grinned. "I see you killin' Indians' deer again, Joshua."

"Oh, just a little camp-meat. How about sharing the liver with us?" Maudy tugged at her father's sleeve and whispered, "Pa, how can I set places for all of them?"

"Now Maudy, simmer down—they'll do their own fixin'. But you might offer to brew some coffee for them."

As they shuttled back and forth between their chores, Pa cleaning out the deer and the Indians making their supper over a fire by the troughs, Perry and Mame reported that they were cooking with pots and pans just like white people. "Well, what did you expect, sillies, that they'd eat everything raw?" Maudy teased. But when she took out their share of the deer liver, Mr. Anaxshat cut off a little bit with his pocketknife and smacked his lips over it loudly. "Mmmm—kloshe muckamuck!" he said, "That means *delicious*, in't?" He winked at Maudy. "I been to school, many times. We thank you. S'pose after supper, you come out with coffee, okay? One time I come by here, years ago, your momma give us coffee with sugar and milk. Where is your momma?"

"She died last June, Mr. Anaxshat." It seemed strange to be confiding in the old Indian, but he looked wise and kind, and Maudy talked on. "Perry and Mame and I, we have to shift for ourselves now when Pa is gone freighting, and lots of folks think we can't possibly make it, but Pa does, and *I* do! And we all miss Mama terrible, but Pa misses her most of all, I think. He's sad deep down, you can tell, and—"

He held up his hand. "She good woman, your momma. Too bad, too bad." Then he added gently, "Indian folks they think of their dead ones all the time, too, but they do not name them, not to keep their spirit around.

Folks die, and we must live, young lady." He looked intently at her, and Maudy pondered what he was saying. Then he grinned and said, "You bring out the coffee after supper, and maybe I tell a story or so."

So, after they'd eaten, they all put on their coats against the silent chilly evening air, and walked out to the Indians' fire. Maudy carried the big coffeepot, and poured out as much steaming coffee as she had cups for; the Indians took turns drinking. They're really very polite, she decided; I wish they were in school in place of the Proctors.

Perry and Mame sat down between Pa and the old Indian. They were eyeing his ragged blue coat, and finally Mame piped up. "Mr. Anaxshat, Perry wants to know about your nice jacket."

"Oho!" He put his hands in the coat's pockets and looked very proud. "George Crook give me this coat, right off his back. That was when we was fightin' Paiutes in the Ochocos, ahhhnkuttee!"

Pa explained, "He means General George Crook, kids, in the Snake Wars in the 1860s. Sam was a famous scout with the Warm Springs, and interpreted for all the bigwigs."

"You bet," said the old man. "Me and Donald McKay, we were the war chiefs then—chased those Snakes clear to Californee! And then we took care of the chipmunk eaters, too!"

"He means the Modocs," Pa explained. "Captain Jack and Sconchin Jim, all that."

"Uncle Sam give me a fancy paper with my name on it for fighting that war, but I swapped it for a pony. You want to hear how we yelled going into battle?" He threw back his head and gave out a long howl that turned into a scream at the end, and echoed up on the butte. Perry and Mame stared; even the young Indians looked impressed.

Pa threw a stick into the fire and asked, "Sam, who was the first white man you ever met? Elip Boston?"

"You, Joshua."

Pa laughed. "No, I mean *really* the first."

"Hmm. S'pose young army fella, name Henry Abbot. Comin' through with horses and mules, a few soldiers, when I was about this one's size." He poked one of the older boys. "Before the agency, even. Nike tillikum, we all livin' on Tygh Prairie then. Henry Abbot comin' through, stay with my folks. Big talk about Indians killin' white men all along the Columbia River. Hee hee! Henry Abbot, he got pretty scared, want to get to the fort at

Oregon City, so he hire me as guide around Wy-east, what you call Mount Hood. You know that way, Joshua?"

Papa nodded.

"Well, I *didn't*—mainly just knew about it. Was lost maybe half the time, Abbot and his boys lost all the time. They had a little chickchick—a cart, like—full of wheels. Told them how far between places. Kept hanging up in the brush, until I say, 'Henry, we won't get around this mountain until you kill the chickchick!' But he said he couldn't do it, it belong to Uncle Sam, until one day they all got mad at it in a blowdown and took their axes and *mamook memaloose chickchick, tklope tklope*—just chopped it all to pieces and left it in the brush!" The old man laughed and laughed.

"Those fellas were scared crazy, all right—thought Indians were going to jump them from behind, maybe at night—didn't trust me as an Indian, *had* to trust me. Well, we came out of the woods after seven days, right near Oregon City. Henry Abbot, he shook my hand hard and say, 'Sam, you saved our lives, but if I bring you into the town here they'd kill you, maybe. The chief in Washington owes you a medal, Sam'—and he gave me his gun and his blanket, and some dollars. I ain't seen that medal yet. Henry Abbot, hmm—brave young fella, but he was all the time scared. Never did find out why he was comin' through with that chickchick—just lost, I s'pose, trying to find himself. Old-time white-eyes, they was always lost, in't? Abbot never came back this way."

"I never heard tell of him before, Sam," said Pa.

"Tell us a story, a real Indian story, Mr. Anaxshat, like you said," Mame pleaded. Before he could reply, a coyote howled up on the butte, and then another. He looked across the fire at Maudy.

"Old Man Coyote wants to tell it himself, you see. His heart is sad tonight, but not as sad as it once was. People get over one sadness, and then they get another." The Indian's singsong voice became tight, husky, and his speech, broken before, became smooth. It felt like Maudy was thinking the words of the story to herself, as he told it.

"Once Coyote and Eagle live together, and their women both took sick, and died, first Eagle's, and then Coyote's. Coyote cried and cried, and carried on, until Eagle said, 'Straighten up, you Coyote! If you come with me, and do what I say, and keep out of trouble, maybe we can get our women back.'

"So they put on new moccasins and walked and walked, until one evening they came to a big river. In the river was an island, and on the island was a big lodge, and a canoe. 'There,' said Eagle. So Coyote yelled and yelled, 'Hey, you, come over and get us!' but nobody came. Eagle made a flute out of a tule stem, and played on it in the water. Right away that canoe came across the river by itself, and they jumped in, and it took them over to the island.

"How did it do *that*?" interrupted Perry. "Shhh!" said one of the Indian boys, and Mame poked Perry in the ribs. Mr. Anaxshat went on.

"Well, Coyote and Eagle they went into the lodge, what was mostly underground. It was very dark. The only person they saw was an old frog woman sitting along one wall. 'Coyote, you watch her,' said Eagle. On the other wall was the moon. Pretty soon someone yelled, 'It is night, all come in!' and people began coming into the lodge, old people, men and women, little children. Coyote saw Eagle's woman, and then he saw his own woman.

"When the room was full, the old frog woman hopped five times clear across the room, until she was beside the moon. Then—gulp—she swallowed the moon, and all the people dance and talk in the dark until dawn. Then the voice, it call out, 'It is day,' and that old frog took the moon out of her mouth and hung it back on the wall. Then all the people left the lodge again.

"'Now Coyote,' said Eagle, 'can you do what the frog woman did?' 'I think so,' said Coyote. So Eagle showed him how to make a wooden box, as large as he could carry, and they lined it with every kind of leaf and every kind of grass. Then they killed the old frog woman, and Coyote put on her skin, and took her place on the floor. Eagle said to do everything just so, and hid with the box.

"After sunset the voice says again, 'It is night, all come in!' and the people came in and filled up the room. So Coyote began to jump across the lodge, toward the moon, but he was so clumsy he almost didn't make it in five jumps, and the people talked to themselves about it in the dark. 'Is this the old frog?' they said, 'or is it someone alive?' Then when Coyote tried to swallow the moon, its edges stuck out of the corners of his mouth, and he had to cover them with his hands."

Mr. Anaxshat bent over and held his hands over his mouth, elbows out. He looked so comical, everybody laughed, and he did too. Then he went on. "Well, all night long Coyote sat there, just about choking to death, his woman and Eagle's woman and all the other people laughing and dancing around him, until that voice said, 'It is day.' Coyote pulled the moon out of his mouth and put it back on the wall, and the people began to leave. But Eagle, he put the box right in the doorway, and when they had all walked into it, he put the lid on and tied it up. 'Now, brother, we have done it,' Eagle said, and threw the moon up in the sky, where it stuck. Coyote took off the frog skin, and they climbed back into the canoe, with the box, and crossed over the river.

"They were going home, and Eagle carried the box. It made a sound like a big swarm of flies, mmmmmmm. On the third night, Coyote thought he could hear voices coming from it, and on the fourth night, when he put his ear against it, he heard his woman's voice. He laughed out loud to hear her voice, but he said nothing to Eagle, who was asleep. Coyote listened by that box all night.

"On the morning of the fifth and last day of their trip home, Coyote said to Eagle, 'Eagle, you must be tired. I will carry the box for you now, you have carried it a long way.'

"'No,' Eagle answered, 'I will carry it all the way home, I am chief!'

"'But how will it look, then, when we get home, for the chief to be carrying the load?'

"So Eagle let Coyote take the box on his back for a little while. It was very heavy. As he went along behind with the box, Coyote kept laughing because he could hear his woman's voice; he thought she was saying, 'Let me out!' When Eagle got out of sight, he untied the string and began to loosen the lid. But oh! The lid flew off with a bang, knocking Coyote down, and Coyote's woman, and Eagle's woman, and all the other dead folks flew out in a cloud—*fffwwweeee*—and went out of sight to the west.

"Eagle heard the bang of the lid and ran back, but he was too late. The dead folks were all gone, the box was all empty, except for the grass and the leaves in the bottom. Eagle got pretty mad. 'Look what you have done with your mischief, Coyote! If we had gotten these dead folks all the way home, they would be alive with us again, and people would not have to die forever, but only for a season, like these plants in the box. Now trees and grass will die only in the winter, but in the spring, they will turn green again. So it could have been with your woman, and mine, and all the folks who die. The people who are coming will know about it.'

"'Oh, let's go back and catch them again!' said Coyote.

"But Eagle said, 'No, we can't reach them now; they are where the moon is, way up in the sky.'"

Mr. Anaxshat's voice trailed off. "K'ani k'ani," he said quietly, "there's no more to tell. People aren't meant to live forever, they say; that's why we must be sorry for each other, take care of each other while we can."

The fire was almost out, just flickering red; but while they'd been sitting there in a circle around it, the full yellow moon had risen behind the house. And now it shone brightly down on everything tall, the house chimney, the gateposts, the junipers beyond the corral, the flanks of Mowich Butte. Its rays touched all their faces the same, Indians and whites, and their eyes gleamed back at it like animals'. Maudy wondered. Mr. Anaxshat's story was very sad at the end, what with her mother and all, but somehow, the way he told it, it made her feel happy, happy and wild. When Pa got up and shook his old friend's hand without saying anything, Maudy amazed herself by running to him and kissing his tough old cheek. "Thank you for the wonderful story, Mr. Anaxshat," she said. "Klahowya!"

"Klahowya, young lady. We see you again, you bet!"

Next morning, the Indians were gone on their way to the Ochocos, not a trace of them but their tracks, running east. It was Saturday, no school, and it looked like a lost day. Until, that is, Mame came in from the hog-pen. "He's back! Oh, he's really come back!"

"Who?"

There, standing on wobbly legs, his hide filthy, his eyes running, all his ribs showing, but alive, was Skookum the pig! He grunted hungrily at Mame, but that was all they ever found out about his mysterious travels to escape the smokehouse and the lard bucket.

Three
Our Homestead Orchards

I

As a boy, riding after cattle in late August or September on our old summer range in the hills below Blizzard Ridge, I always contrived to swing by the little homestead orchard along Kibbee Creek. Likely there would be cows and calves to count or gather, there to eat the wind-fallen apples; my own ulterior purpose was to pick two or three off a low branch for a snack, lustrous red, unlike everything else in so dry and sparse a country, amazingly juicy and sweet. Years later (and years ago from now), I wrote a poem about that taste—

"MEMORANDUM"

Lunching in a dusty office, eating from a green sack,
     the taste
the taste of an apple has carried me away,
away to autumn on horseback in the hill country,
red cattle staring in a meadow, the cheatgrass
white and stiff, and in the woodpeckered trees
     apples
apples for the grabbing, cheek or pocket sized,
crimson tasting, too wild for anything but bird or boy.
I learned in joy, and learn another way
how things will stay, and serve . . .
that homestead orchard, sixty years unpruned,
windfall dropping on the settler's grave,
to show the sweet and random bounty of the earth;
     this taste

this taste revived along my tongue to show,
how far in apple eating I can go.
(*Love in an Earthquake*, p. 61)

When I was young, the sharp tang of those apples was all that mattered
to me; now I think of that orchard and others like it in historical terms, as
astonishing living relics of homesteading days, a century ago or more. Now
I know that they were from an Astrakhan tree, with its own rich and nearly
forgotten horticultural history, including being carried out to Oregon over
the Oregon Trail by Henderson Luelling in 1847. But still, at the heart of
my historical reflections is the simple eating of an apple—and the perpetual
wonder of actually tasting what someone, some homesteader, with certain
purposes in mind, planted and later smacked his lips over, so long ago. On
the level of sensory experience, at least, it is a kind of time travel.

II

Historically, the portion of Crook County now incorporated in Jefferson
County was one of the last areas in the United States to have been settled
by homesteaders (1890–1920), and like their forebears dating back to the
days of Johnny Appleseed, many of them sensibly planted fruit trees as part
of "proving up" and gaining legal title to their homestead claims. Many
of them also planted Lombardy poplars for shade and windbreak, so that
today, more than a century later, many homestead sites in eastern Jefferson
County are hauntingly marked by tall sentinel poplars. And on many of
these sites stand equally ancient apple trees, some of them still bearing fruit
after years of total neglect.

These pioneer orchards (typically just a few trees, but in some
instances as many as a hundred) are a living part of our local historical
heritage, linking us to the aspirations, know-how, and food preferences of
our ancestors on this land. What varieties are there among these gnarly
old survivors? Some of them are now-forgotten "heirloom" varieties like
Astrakhan, Sheepsnose, Winter Banana, Grimes Golden, and so on, with
other rarities yet to be identified. And why—for what reasons of cultivation, taste, and cooking—were they chosen by the settlers? Why did they
plant their trees in these particular sites on their homestead properties?
Where did they get their tree starts, or seeds? And how can we now, in

the twenty-first century, protect and conserve the homestead orchards of Central Oregon?

Implicit in these historical questions is a deeper and more urgent issue, about the conservation of our food resources. In *Forgotten Fruits: Manual and Manifesto: Apples* (edited by anthropologist and ecologist Gary Paul Nabhan), it is claimed that during the last half century, 80 percent of the apple varieties unique to America have essentially vanished from view, in large part because of the advent of chain supermarkets and their policy of marketing only a very narrow range of "popular" fruits—for apples, for example, the photogenic but vastly overrated Red Delicious. The *Manifesto* also notes "a dramatic loss of traditional knowledge about what apples grow best in a particular locality," and emphasizes the crucial importance of "abandoned orchards" as sources for recovering these lost varieties and the know-how necessary to cultivate them.

The *Manifesto* refers to comments by well-known nature writer Verlyn Klinkenborg to the effect that abandoned orchards are an "archive of diversity," offering us a chance to reidentify and preserve apple varieties that have been forgotten or given up for lost. Klinkenborg adds the interesting point that the horticultural variety of long ago must have been based on an equivalent diversity of taste in our forebears—now mostly lost, but perhaps recoverable (Klinkenborg's essay, "Apples, Apples, Apples," appeared in the *New York Times*, November 5, 2009).

So for all these historical and ecological reasons for inquiry (and for the fun of a grownup treasure hunt over rough ground), the Jefferson County Historical Society undertook in August 2012 to collaborate with the Home Orchard Society of Portland in mounting the first Central Oregon "homestead orchard tour." It was a great success, in part because 2012 was a bumper year for local fruit crops (2014 was another), and at the time of our visit to the old orchards around Gray Butte, the trees were loaded with ripe or ripening apples. We prepared for the tour by scouting out the orchards a week before the actual tour with our Home Orchard Society guests, Joanie Cooper and Shaun Shepherd of Portland. These enthusiastic and expert "fruit detectives" carefully mapped the old trees, took samples and cuttings for future study and identification and, on their return for the tour itself, greatly enhanced both our understanding of the lore and life cycle of fruit trees and our appreciation of the living historical legacy of our forgotten homestead orchards.

III

Perhaps it will help characterize these sites for what they are, and suggest something of their diverse charm, if we make a quick verbal tour of six of them—noting as we set out that these are only six out of an unknown number of them still holding on in scattered locations throughout Central Oregon, mostly on public lands.

SIX PIONEER ORCHARDS

The Cove Orchard (approximately 1,745 feet elevation)

Any account of pioneer orchards in Jefferson County needs to begin with the first one—the once-celebrated Cove Orchard, deep in Crooked River canyon west of Culver. The original homesteader of The Cove, William Clark Rogers, probably planted some fruit trees soon after he settled there in 1879; his successor, T. F. "Ferd" McCallister, acquired the place in 1888 and established a real orchard, with apples and peaches, which thrived in the mild microclimate of the canyon bottom. William Boegli, later the first judge of Jefferson County, worked for McCallister as a boy and bought the place in 1905, developing what became the first sizeable commercial orchard in Central Oregon, with eleven acres of irrigated apples, pears, apricots, peaches (his Crawford Yellow variety was highly prized), plums, grapes, and nuts. In its heyday about 1920, The Cove Orchard supplied

Boegli's Orchard at The Cove on Crooked River, 1920s

markets in Prineville and Bend once or twice a week, hauling the fruit up
the arduous grade out of Crooked River Canyon; later (in 1940) Boegli
sold The Cove to the Oregon State Highway Commission and it became a
much-loved state park, the site of many picnics and campouts (and informal fruit-pickings), until it was flooded in 1964 by completion of the Round
Butte Dam and creation of Lake Billy Chinook.

It's historically regrettable that the throngs of fishermen, water-
skiers, and pleasure-boaters who flock to the lake every summer are mostly
unaware that two hundred feet below the surface of the water, not far from
the main bridge, The Cove and its neat fields and buildings lie unmarked
and forgotten. And in terms of the renewed interest in heritage fruit varieties today, it's too bad that the identities of most of Bill Boegli's fruit trees
are unknown.

The Clark Orchard (about 3,600 feet elevation)

Across Blizzard Ridge on the Old Ashwood Road (on east from its intersection with Wilson Creek Road, which leads on to the "new" Ashwood Road),
along a grade leading to the southeast edge of the ridge and the final descent
into Ashwood, lies the Clark Place. It is marked nowadays by its surviving
orchard—located where the grade makes a sharp switchback across a gully
(on the south side of the road). Jim Clark and his family settled here in the
1890s; he was a descendant of the Clark emigrant train of 1851, which was
attacked by Indians along the Snake River, with several fatalities. Eventually
the Clark party reached the Deschutes River and camped at what is now
Pioneer Park on Bend's north side. According to Evada Power in *Jefferson
County Reminiscences*, after the Clarks established their Blizzard Ridge
ranch, they "kept travel" (took in and fed travelers),

> and Mrs. Clark's skill with sourdough became known far and wide.
> Her biscuits were the kind that melted in the mouth and always
> kept a hunger for just one more. To late comers [along Ashwood
> Road] with their one and two-room cabins, the Clark homestead
> with its wall-to-wall rag carpet, three bedrooms and hospitable
> board seemed like an oasis in the desert. Many a weary traveler
> made it a point to stop at the Clark Place at meal time, finding
> replenishment of body and spirit. The orchard set out by the Clarks
> is a well-known spot on the Ashwood Road. (p. 44)

Nowadays all of the Clarks' buildings are long gone, but many of their fruit trees survive on the south (uphill) side of the road, above the switchback, somehow managing to bear fruit every year, including the ubiquitous Yellow Transparent and Blue Pearmain apples, as well as Green Sweet, Rambo, Wealthy, White Pippin, Canada Baldwin, and other apple varieties as yet unidentified, and plums, apricots, and pears. (Note: the Clark Orchard is on private land, owned by the Fessler family of Madras.)

The McCoin Orchard (about 3,800 feet elevation)

Julius and Sarah Osborn McCoin (my great-grandparents) homesteaded here on the southeast flank of Gray Butte in the spring of 1886, at the head of a gully with a good spring. Julius set up as a freighter between Prineville and The Dalles and sometimes Shaniko, driving big twelve-horse wagons loaded with wool, meat, hides and other produce going out, and merchandise (notably big barrels of whiskey) coming back. According to family tradition, early on he began returning home with fruit-tree starts (presumably from The Dalles) to plant in the protected draw below his house, until his orchard—apples, pears, plums, peaches—numbered over one hundred trees, of which over seventy survive today.

In the late spring of 1888, while Julius was off on one of his freight runs, Sarah took sick and died suddenly, leaving three of their children still at home—Minnie (age nine), Ella (eight), and Walter (four). Taking stock of his family's predicament, Julius decided that, with capable Minnie in charge, his kids had gumption enough to run the ranch during his absences, sometimes for up to two weeks, and in fact he never remarried.

Whether the McCoins actually sold fruit commercially from their big orchard is doubtful; more likely, they simply offered the overflow to their neighbors around Gray Butte, Opal City, Haystack/Old Culver, and Lamonta. When the McCoin property was sold in the early 1930s to the Federal Resettlement Administration program, the house and outbuildings were torn down and the orchard abandoned. But in the 1970s, two USFS/National Grasslands range specialists from Prineville, Duane Ecker and Harry Ketrenos, rescued the surviving trees by systematically pruning them and clearing out brush. Fruit identified include Roxbury, Northern Spy, Yellow Transparent, Melon, Olympia, and Astrakhan apples, and some pears and plums in the lower orchard.

Julius and Sarah McCoin Orchard on Gray Butte, 2017

Embedded in the trunk of a tree in the center of the orchard is a rusty pitchfork, its tines protruding through the bark at waist level—a reminder of the days when the McCoin place was a working homestead ranch.

Today the McCoin Orchard is a much-visited scenic spot, and the trailhead for the popular Gray Butte Trail is just south of the McCoin homesite in the poplars. Recognizing the growing popularity of and interest in the site, and the Cyrus homesteads and orchards around the butte to the north, the Crooked River National Grasslands division of the US Forest Service commendably filed for and received official recognition for them in the National Registry of Historic Places. To reach the McCoin Orchard, turn off Laurel Lane at the Scales Corral onto Road 500 and follow it, bearing left, about two and a half miles uphill to Road 17—left on Road 17 to the orchard and Gray Butte Trailhead.

The Cyrus Horse Camp Orchard (about 3,400 feet elevation)

This very popular campsite and meeting place for riders (administered by the National Grasslands in collaboration with local saddle clubs) is located on the site of the 1882 homestead of Enoch and Mary Cyrus. In 1882, the Gray Butte country was so sparsely settled that Mrs. Cyrus recalled that for their first seven months on the place, she didn't see another woman. But within a few years, they built a two-story, four-bedroom house here and farmed about five hundred acres with their five sons and two daughters. Enoch Cyrus was a very innovative farmer, introducing barbed-wire fences to this part of Central Oregon, pioneering a strain of hard winter wheat (which was known as "Cyrus wheat"), and innovating new machines for harvesting grain, including a reaper-binder. The Cyruses typically ran 1,500 to 3,000 head of sheep, planted huge vegetable gardens, and kept up an orchard of apples, crabapples, peaches, and pears. Only the apples survive today, including Yellow Transparents and several varieties of fall apples as yet unidentified.

In 1900, Enoch and Mary left the Gray Butte ranch and became homesteaders again in the Cloverdale area between Redmond and Sisters, where they could practice irrigated farming, and they launched a new crop for Central Oregon—seed potatoes. In the heyday of potato farming in Deschutes and Jefferson Counties (1945–1975) the Cyrus spud cellars around Cloverdale were a prime source of seed potatoes. After his parents moved, their youngest son, Dean, ran the Gray Butte place (with time out for a few years after 1910 speculating in the boom state of Florida), and eventually he sold the place to the Resettlement/Marginal Lands program in 1934.

From Laurel Lane, turn off at the Horse Camp sign just east of Gray Butte Cemetery (another historic site worth visiting), and follow Hagman

Homestead orchard tour at Omer Cyrus Orchard, August 2012

Road uphill and southeasterly to the Horse Camp. The orchard lies just south and uphill from the camp.

The Omer Cyrus Orchard (about 3,400 feet elevation)

Omer Cyrus, Enoch and Mary's middle son, homesteaded here about a half mile west of his parents' place, in 1900. His house and buildings—torn down in the "relocation" work of the 1930s—were in the grove of trees just west of and below his orchard. A dedicated pioneer photographer, he worked in a studio next to his house until his eyesight deteriorated to the point that he couldn't tint photos or use his equipment. Omer's main orchard, situated on a north-sloping hillside with no obvious source of water, is remarkably well-preserved, with still-vigorous small trees bearing copious fruiting of "summer apples" (mainly Yellow Transparents), Jonathans, and, as identified by Shaun Shepherd of the Home Orchard Society in 2012, a very rare variety known as Esteline—also Purple Siberian crabapples, and a few pears. As in the McCoin Orchard, the survival of this orchard and Enoch Cyrus's owes much to the timely interventions of Duane Ecker and Harry Ketrenos in the 1970s.

The Omer Cyrus "Barn Orchard" (about 3,200 feet elevation)

Located below and about one-quarter of a mile northwest of the main Omer Cyrus Orchard, this cluster of old trees was recently rediscovered in the course of the preparation of the National Historic Sites application for the McCoin and Cyrus homestead sites mentioned above. Apparently, Omer Cyrus's barn must have overlooked the orchard, which covers roughly seven acres and includes numerous trees, about twenty-five of which are still living. Most seem to be apples and crabapples and red pears; some appear to be volunteers, grown from seeds of fallen trees. Identification of varieties is under way. Unlike the McCoin and main Cyrus orchards, this one is heavily overgrown with sagebrush and junipers, to the point of being nearly invisible until you are standing in it.

IV

Reflecting on old orchards like these and others like them in the "outback" of Central Oregon, it's impossible not to wonder how they have managed to survive at all. Cultivated fruit trees have fairly predictable lifespans—for any individual tree, of course, much depends on circumstances of soil, moisture, climate, and human attention. In general, apples have the greatest longevity. There are cases of apple trees living, and bearing fruit, for well over a century, but as a general rule their span of life approximates our own mortal span. Pears come close; apricots and peaches typically have shorter lives. When the local climate and moisture conditions are factored in, and also the many decades of total human neglect and unrestricted competition from junipers, sagebrush, and other rangeland vegetation, the stubborn persistence of so many of our local trees seems all the more astonishing. Many have died along the way, of course; intermixed with living specimens, their brittle branches and broken trunks tell a tale of the fierce struggle to grow. And here and there one finds—especially in wet years—long-dead hulks with green branches asserting new life, lurking somewhere deep in the old heartwood still.

H. L. Davis, Oregon's only Pulitzer Prize–winning fiction writer, seems to have held a low opinion of the early homesteaders he encountered as a boy around The Dalles, Antelope, and elsewhere in north Central Oregon. But in one of his short stories, "Homestead Orchard," the plot turns on this incredible capacity of fruit trees to survive abandonment in a parched landscape. The orchard in question appears to have dried up since the homesteader who planted it moved away, nothing but dead and dying trees—but when water from a nearby spring is rerouted their way so as to provide for a roving band of sheep, the apples and apricots burst into bloom overnight, and bees appear out of nowhere to pollinate them. Horticulturally, such a magical re-quickening is probably impossible, fictional license on Davis's part—but it works symbolically to underscore the reconciliation of the returned homesteader and his alienated son. And it seems to express Davis's own admiration for the tough avidity of the trees themselves. Like the gritty protagonists of his best fiction, they knew how to adapt and hold on.

On the score of particular locales, a few orchards as already noted were blessed at the start by being established in sheltered microclimates offering moderate temperatures and some protection from killing frosts at blossoming and fruit-setting times. Did the homestead orchardists in such favored locations discover this, through a year or two of close observation, before planting? But such lucky settings excepted, the local climate is in general undeniably severe, even harsh—hard freezes possible any time between late October and May; strong chilling and withering winds, especially in late winter and spring; and relatively short growing seasons, especially above 3,000 feet, where most of the trees are located.

And underlying all other challenges in this "high desert" land, here in the rain shadow of the Cascade Range, is the lack of moisture. The overall average annual precipitation in Jefferson County, for example, is about eleven inches a year. That's plenty dry, but for about twenty years, when these trees were still maturing or reaching their early prime, between about 1918 and the end of the 1930s, all of Central Oregon was in the clutch of a cruel drought. At its worst, this ultimate dry cycle brought a total of 5.43 inches of precipitation for Jefferson County in 1924, and 4.69 inches in 1930. With irrigation still decades away, historically, and seeming a hopeless pipe dream to the area's dry-farmers anyway, this was the local dustbowl time that led to wholesale abandonment of homesteads, tax defaults, and the federal relocation and reclamation programs that converted about seventy thousand acres of Jefferson County farmland into "marginal lands" for grazing. The conversion included most of the orchards described above. In many areas of the West, according to Susan Dolan in her excellent book *Fruitful Legacy: A Historic Context of Orchards in the United States* (2009), the Resettlement Administration Civilian Conservation Corps crews that actually did the work on the land usually cut down and burned all orchard remnants they found (p. 102). Why that didn't happen here is unknown, but whether by local bureaucratic decision or by accident, it's something in our history to be grateful for.

In the early decades of homesteading here, roughly 1890 to 1910, a wet weather cycle seems to have prevailed, producing bountiful grain and hay crops and stories about wild bunchgrass up to a horse's belly in the high eastern range country. So, no doubt, the more exuberant homesteaders, taking one weather cycle for the norm, planted fruit trees with the same optimism that they planted their wheat and barley crops. All too soon, only the trees were left.

Why the settlers tended to select certain apple, pear, peach and other varieties and not others is an interesting question, but hard to answer. In the later waves of homesteading around the arrival of the railroads in 1911, no doubt newcomers saw for themselves what kinds of fruit trees were thriving and chose accordingly. For apples, it also came down to practical choices about how the fruit was to be used. For early eating and applesauce, "summer" varieties like Yellow Transparent and Astrakhan were obvious selections, being pickable by mid-August or a little later. For keeping (as in a cellar), the choice led to once-popular fall and winter apples like Jonathan, Rome Beauty, Duchess of Oldenburg, Winter Banana, and Northern Spy—pickable in September and October, and keepable (if not wormy) through winter—some varieties (Jonathan, notably) were favored for eating "out of hand"; others (Rome Beauty and Pearmain) were kept for baking and pies.

The historical truth behind the legend of Johnny Appleseed is that through the beginning of the nineteenth century, apples were mainly used for making cider. Johnny's random seeds produced trees of unpredictable and generally unknown identities, but for the making of hard cider in quantity that didn't matter. There doesn't seem to have been much cider-making in pioneer Central Oregon, and the great majority of surviving trees are of known grafted varieties—presumably ordered as bare-root stock from nurseries like R. H. Weber's The Dalles Nurseries and mail-order outfits like Stark's and R. Shumway, and brought up here by freight wagons and, later, by train.

One of Henry David Thoreau's last essays before his death in 1862 is titled "Wild Apples," and though it begins with an eloquent tribute to the apple, calling it "the most civilized of all trees" and "the noblest of fruits," Thoreau underscores his own preference for what he calls "wild apples"—grown up from random seedlings scattered by deer and cattle in the woods around Concord—over the "civilized" grafted varieties popular in his day like Baldwins, Pearmains, Porters, and so on. (Although he does concede, "I have known a Blue Pearmain tree, growing on the edge of a swamp, almost as good as wild"; Thoreau, p. 205)

In his preference for wild apples, Thoreau celebrates the crabapple, *Malus coronaria*, as the wildest and most aboriginal American fruit of all, and laments that in his time it didn't grow in Massachusetts: he finally got to see specimens in bloom on a railroad trip through Michigan in May 1861. But out here in Central Oregon half a century later, settlers almost invariably planted a few crab trees, mostly of the grafted Purple Siberian variety (which Thoreau probably wouldn't have approved of), and the survivors are still producing copiously nearly every year. What was their use or purpose? A reasonable guess is that they were cultivated here as elsewhere for crabapple jelly and pickling—and if cider was to be made, crabs would be a welcome spicy addition to the mix, too.

If there was a body of handed-down know-how and family lore about the siting and cultivation of fruit trees that settlers brought with them to Central Oregon, it doesn't seem to have survived in family traditions; and yet, visiting their sites, one guesses that many of them did draw on such lore, adjusting it as necessary to local conditions. In the case of my great-grandfather Julius McCoin, who came out here from Kansas in the early 1880s, there are records indicating that his father-in-law, William F. Osborn, did have an extensive orchard in that state. So maybe Julius came to Gray Butte with fruit-growing savvy and ambitions already in his head. But I don't know of similar family lineages for our other early orchardists, the Cyruses, the Clarks, and so on.

In *Fruitful Legacy*, Susan Dolan identifies what was *the* authoritative American fruit-growing handbook from the 1850s on into the twentieth century—Andrew Jackson Downing's *The Fruits and Fruit Trees of America*, which first appeared in 1845 and went through many widely circulated editions. (Downing, also notable as a landscape architect and as one of the instigators of Central Park, was killed in a steamboat explosion in 1852, but his brother Charles carried on with the book.) I'm not aware that Downing's guide was in any local homesteading family's library, but possibly some of his precepts were put to use out here on the frontier, "second-hand" as it were. For example, he strongly opposed extensive regular pruning, believing (probably incorrectly) that pruning shortens the life span of trees, and encourages "biennial" rather than annual fruit production (which apples and pears tend to grow into as they age). So trees cultivated according to Downing's advice tended to be large specimens in maturity (no dwarf varieties in those days), and to allow for this growth, he recommended that they be generously spaced—at least thirty feet apart. As a matter of fact, that corresponds pretty closely to the rough spacing of trees in some of our old orchards, but that may be more attributable to common sense, given our climate and precipitation, than to Downing's authority.

Let's suppose you've filed a homestead claim in 1906 somewhere in the hills east of the Deschutes and Crooked Rivers. Say that you've been able to make what seems like an auspicious claim—the land is hilly, but there's a good spring, a wet-weather meadow with lush grass, and a couple of relatively flat, level stretches between the hills that might become grain or hay fields—or the site of the small orchard you hope to establish, as part of your "proving up" as an entryman. Where to plant the young trees on your new domain?

There is a striking uniformity to the way our homesteaders puzzled out the location of their orchards, suggesting to me that in fact they did have access to a body of practical know-how, maybe partly family lore and partly local wisdom, that guided them. Nearly all of the surviving orchards I know about are situated, first of all, below a spring of some sort, with indications of a subsurface water flow if not a flowing stream. This seems self-evident as a strategy, especially in so parched a climate—but the orchards are also mostly planted on north or northeast slopes. This seems at first notice horticulturally illogical—north slopes get less sun and more shade than south slopes, for one thing; for another, the worst winds and storms in this country tend to come out of the north. But here are the McCoin and Cyrus and Clark trees, for example, carrying on in their northerly exposure; clearly it has worked for them, and other orchards likewise, over the years. If this is by conscious design, what is its rationale?

Would that the McCoins and Cyruses and their kind could answer our questions. But a probable explanation goes something like this, and it has a lot to do with the crucial need to protect the trees against killing frosts in this region's always uncertain springs. On an incline, air movement is constant down the slope, preventing the static pooling of air on level ground that in freezing temperatures is certain to kill blossoms and germinated fruit buds. But why *north* slopes, especially? Perhaps because the cooler air flows over them year-round serve to acclimatize and "toughen" maturing trees, conditioning them to bloom and bud later, avoiding the killing frosts that regularly cancel fruit set on trees in these parts that are located on flat or south-tilted ground. So, at least, I've heard knowledgeable nurserymen explain the north-slope pattern here and elsewhere.

In the long years since the homesteaders left their trees to fend for themselves, the fruit has faithfully ripened in season, falling off to be eaten by deer and cattle—and occasionally to be harvested by local families who held on through the Depression and knew where, and when, to go for fruit that was now as wild and free-for-the-taking as huckleberries in the mountains. One of these gleaners was my uncle Max Mendenhall—a bachelor grandson of Julius McCoin and a neighbor of the Cyruses—who lived "off the land" pretty extensively—venison and trout for meat, a big vegetable garden (especially cabbages for sauerkraut), and huckleberries and "wild" apples for fruit (mostly to be canned). For the last, Max kept a close eye each summer on certain trees in his itinerary of abandoned orchards and picked what he needed for a year's supply of canned applesauce. I wish I could reproduced his recipe—I doubt that he ever wrote it down—but I do know that he was very fussy about getting exactly the right blend of "red" and "yellow" apples; and to the eye and the tongue his applesauce was invariably a splendid creation—deep pink, somewhat chunky in texture, and rich and zesty in flavor. Whatever dreams those homesteaders had for their trees, this always seemed to me like a long-in-coming, half-wild fruition—out of a Mason jar.

I remember discussing apples once with Uncle Max and another uncle, Cecil Moore, who as a dedicated rockhound knew our backcountry and its forgotten roads as well as anybody, and who in later years established a commercial "wild plum nursery" on some land he owned near Opal City. He was also a close friend and helper of Larry McGraw, the founder of the Home Orchard Society. Somehow our conversation got around to the topic of "the most delicious apple," and after each of us had weighed in with a favorite, we realized that we were talking about the same tree—a vigorous specimen with big red fruit, variety unknown, in a forlorn, half-dead little settler's orchard in the hills east of Hay Creek Ranch. Max and Cecil had sampled this wonderful apple on separate deer-hunting trips up there in the 1940s; I had found it in the 1970s in the course of exploring an alternative route to our summer range, Sky Ranch. Each of us had meant to go back the next September for another taste, but we didn't.

We agreed that it was by far the best apple we'd ever eaten, but what variety was it? Or—could it have been a sport, grown a la Johnny Appleseed from a seed into one of those unique ungrafted wonders that have shaped and enriched the history of fruit culture, like the Baldwin, the Spitzenburg, Northern Spy, and McIntosh? And—remembering this now years later—is it still alive, and bearing fruit? Thoreau, that great lover of the wild apple, has the perfect spur-to-action for all such speculation on the part of apple prospectors: "Who knows," he asks, enticingly, "but that this chance wild fruit, planted by a cow or a bird on some remote and rocky hillside, where it is as yet unnoticed by man, may be the choicest of all its kind?" ("Wild Apples," p. 195). Who knows, indeed, and I'm not likely to be very easy to live with until I can relocate the site of that old tree next summer, and—let's hope—pluck some samples.

Four
The Railroad Era and Its Legacy

When the towns of Madras, Metolius, and Culver celebrated Railroad Day in February 2011, they were commemorating a century of railway's influence on local history. The arrival of Oregon Trunk tracks (and on them, a locomotive pulling two cars full of dignitaries) in Willow Creek Canyon just west of Madras at midmorning, February 15, 1911, was a truly momentous event, unlike any other in these parts.

The story of the crazy, epic rail line race between the crews of James J. Hill (Oregon Trunk/Great Northern) and those of his archrival Edward Harriman (Des Chutes/Union Pacific) has been told often, most recently by Dr. Leon Speroff in *The Deschutes Railroad War* (2006), and Walter Grande, in *The Northwest's Own Railway* (1992). For America's two mightiest rail moguls to go at it head-to-head and damn-the-cost up the canyon of the Deschutes River, from 1909 to 1911, created a great spectacle of plutocratic ambition, egomania, engineering derring-do, and conspicuous waste, something never to be repeated in America.

Certainly both Hill and Harriman had plausible economic motives for trying to build a line from the Columbia into Central Oregon in the first years of the new century. Both were on record as wanting to connect their recently completed Northwest rail networks (Harriman on the Oregon side of the Columbia, Hill on the Washington side) with their lines in California. And along the way, in the interior of Oregon, there were untapped resources to be opened up—cattle, sheep, and wheat, and seemingly unlimited timber. But rational analysis probably won't explain why the railroad war ensued.

At bottom, Hill and Harriman had faced each other as rivals and adversaries over twenty years of railroad skirmishing across the Midwest and West, and they seemed not to like each other overmuch. Then too, there is the odd fact that in the years just preceding the Deschutes campaign, Harriman had come to be widely disliked by Oregon politicians and editors (despite his traveling widely in the state and even keeping a vacation retreat on Klamath Lake), whereas Hill was lionized. One reason for the antipathy to Harriman was that, having consolidated his network of routes in Portland in 1900, and having given intermittent assurances that he intended to move on into Central Oregon, he did not follow through. To Oregonians between 1904 and 1909, increasingly impatient to open up the central hinterlands, this seemed like bad faith, a kind of trifling with their hopes. So they turned increasingly to the older, gruff, bearlike Hill, who expressed from time to time a noncommittal interest in building a line into the interior but, cagily, made no promises.

Oregonians in their impatience also briefly flirted in this period with a far-fetched scheme called the People's Railroad, which would have required an amendment to the Oregon State Constitution, to allow the state to build its own railroad lines. The idea soon evaporated.

Meanwhile, behind the scenes, Hill's lieutenants in St. Paul and Portland, notably his right-hand engineer and route-finder, John F. Stevens, were very busy laying the groundwork for the route into the interior. Stevens, a remarkably capable man who had recently returned from several years as a top-level engineer on the Panama Canal project, was as skillful at cloak-and-dagger corporate and legal intrigue as he was at engineering canal and railway routes. He traveled through Central Oregon in the summer of 1909, disguised as a Scottish angler named "John F. Sampson," checking out possible rights-of-way along the Deschutes as he fished, photographed, and hobnobbed with locals—when possible, buying up land strategically. Working as Hill's secret agent with complete carte blanche, he crucially managed to buy the Oregon Trunk Line and its unused properties and rights in a secret meeting at midnight in a Portland city park, on August 15, 1909 (Speroff, p. 78). Talk about high intrigue.

Despite their rivals' secrecy, Harriman's forces were increasingly aware in 1909 that something was afoot, but did not react decisively until Stevens openly announced soon after his midnight meeting in the park that "the road will be built as fast as can be reasonably done with men and money. The project is a personal one, and I have no objection to saying that J. J. Hill as an individual is financially interested to any extent necessary to carry the road through successful completion" (Grande, p. 278). The mention of Hill's interest was of course what Oregonians most wanted to hear. Even before this formal announcement, the Bend *Bulletin* had declared, on July 28,

Oregon Trunk and Des Chutes Railroad lines at North Junction, 1910 (Hedlund photo)

1909, that, given what it was gleaning from both sides, "It looks like war"—
and then added gleefully, expressing the feelings of most Oregonians, especially in places like Madras and Bend, "And we hope it is!" At last, after all
the wild rumors and even wilder speculations, the railroad would come to
Central Oregon—even *two* of them, running a race to Madras!

The story of that incredible race, with the Oregon Trunk crews mostly
on the west side of the river and the Des Chutes Railroad on the east, is
worth following in detail but beyond the scope of this essay. Readers are
urged to study it, in the books already mentioned by Speroff and Grande.
All the way up to North Junction, with an estimated eight thousand workers involved (Grande, p. 287), both sides resorted to dirty tricks and out-
right sabotage of each other's efforts, ranging from exploding black powder
caches and rolling rocks on each other's camps to constant legal harassment
over property rights. Once the Oregon Trunk even sent Des Chutes chief
engineer George Boschke a fake telegram telling him that the Galveston,
Texas, seawall that he had recently built to protect that city was in danger
of collapsing, and imploring him to came back to save it. Confident in his
engineering, Boschke refused the bait (Grande p. 290).

The unexpected death, on September 9, 1909, of Edward Harriman
may have somewhat diminished Jim Hill's personal drive to win the
upriver race, but for both sides it went right on. Even after various legal

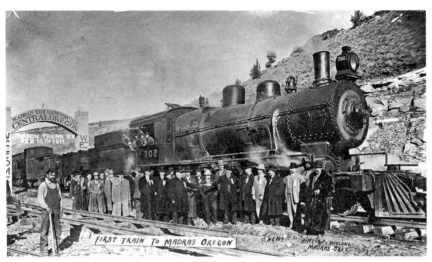

Railroad Day in Madras, February 15, 1911 (Hedlund photo)

maneuverings and federal interventions led to a mandatory sharing of the Des Chutes' line on the east side of the river between North Junction and South Junction (much to the advantage of the Oregon Trunk because of route difficulties on their side), Hill's team stubbornly opted to resume its original line from South Junction up the Deschutes to Mecca and then on up to Willow Creek Canyon, and Madras—a challenging and costly stretch of about twenty-three miles that would require several tunnels, two very large trestles and numerous small ones, and many deep cuts and culverts.

Never mind—if anything, the pace of the Oregon Trunk's work accelerated through the later months of 1910, and on February 15 of the next year, Locomotive 702 came puffing and snorting out of Willow Creek Canyon and stopped under an elaborate welcome arch that proclaimed Madras "The Gateway to Central Oregon." Railroad Day in Madras drew a wildly enthusiastic crowd of several thousand from all over the area. The speeches that day, including remarks by John F. Stevens and Ralph Budd, chief Oregon Trunk engineer (and later president of Great Northern), did not overtly emphasize the celebration as a victory for Jim Hill and the Oregon Trunk, and in fact the Harriman side was represented by an official from the Southern Pacific, but clearly everybody knew that Hill and the "OT" had won; it was their day. Meanwhile, the Des Chutes Railroad crews worked away on their more sensible route, across Trout Creek to Gateway and around the eastern rim of Agency Plains to their designated depot site overlooking Madras, arriving there in early May, and strutting their stuff by bringing in the first circus ever to appear in Central Oregon, on May 11. They completed their big steel trestle over Willow Creek Canyon in June.

Meanwhile, regular Oregon Trunk train service to Madras began soon after Railroad Day; thanks to easy terrain and the efficiencies of the Harris track-laying machine, which could lay over two miles of track on a good day, the OT was able to begin service at Metolius on March 1, Culver on April 11, and Opal City on April 23. At Opal City the track-laying paused for six months until completion of the Crooked River Bridge, and then resumed in September, with service opening in Redmond in early October and in Bend on November 1, preceded by *their* Railroad Day celebration

Early construction of Oregon Trunk bridge over Crooked River, 1910 (Hedlund photo)

on October 5. This time, James J. Hill was in attendance as guest of honor (having been conveyed from Opal City by a train going *backward*, because there was no way as yet to turn around in Bend). Hill's old rancher friend Bill Hanley, who had been urging him to build into Central Oregon, came up from Harney County for the festivities, and Hill's droll remark to him that day wonderfully underplays the urgent corporate and personal motives that had driven him and his crews up the Deschutes—"I was building the railroad to come and see you" (Grande, p. 301).

The cost of the race? For the Hill side, over sixteen million dollars; for Harriman's side, about nine million. The fundamental duplicative waste-fulness of it all must have been blatantly obvious to everybody from the corporate level down to the immigrant laborers hammering and blasting and clearing in the Deschutes canyon. John Stevens revealed later that he foresaw that the race up the canyon would be extravagantly wasteful, and so on his own he approached a high Harriman executive about working out some sort of collaboration, but was rebuffed (p. 62). Later, in the 1920s, after the dust and the excitement had settled, Oregonians came to realize that one unhappy consequence of the race was that capital was used up on it that could have been spent by both railroads on further extensions through the territory—notably, from Bend on south to Klamath country and so on to California (a job that was not completed until 1931).

Endorsing a proposal to further consolidate the two lines on April 5, 1922, the Portland *Journal* declared that the "more than 100 miles of two tracks, side by side, never should have been built in that canyon," and went on, predictably, to blame Harriman more than Hill:

> It is just to say that the Harriman interests were chiefly responsible for this crime of the Deschutes. Urged by then Gov. Chamberlain and others to build a railway into Central Oregon, Mr. Harriman steadfastly refused to do so. James J. Hill came along after the trip of John F. Stevens through the country, and set about to build the line. Harriman rushed in with his own line and ushered in the gloomy chapter of the wasted millions, with most of the Central Oregon territory still unserved by a railroad.

But in the rapturous year of 1911 and on through to the end of World War I, Central Oregonians saw only shining advantage in what had come up the Deschutes into their lives. The bright future for exporting livestock, for example, was prefigured a few days after Railroad Day, when a shipment of six hundred sheep headed for Portland. The lumber mills in Bend and Prineville (after that town built its own rail connection to the main line at O'Neil Junction) soon began to ship out huge quantities of lumber. Dryland wheat farmers on the Agency Plains were soon hauling their wheat sacks down to track-side warehouses at Mecca, Vanora, Gateway, and Madras, instead of paying exorbitant freight-wagon costs to get their crops to market via Shaniko (as high as forty cents per bushel to Portland, at a time when the market price of wheat was less than a dollar a bushel). If they had a new invasive weed to contend with in their fields, apparently brought in by the railroads' mules and horses, they named it Jim Hill Mustard and discovered that it was delicious as greens, boiled or raw.

On the score of merchandise and building materials, the local economic gains were really dramatic. Barbed wire cost $7 per hundredweight before 1911 and $4 afterward; cement in the pre-railroad days ran about $15 a barrel but was $4.25 by rail; lime (for mortar) ran $7.50 per barrel before and $1.75 after; the cost of a bundle of roofing squares fell from $8 to $1.75—reductions that greatly spurred the erection of stone and brick buildings. And farm machinery (and for that matter, automobiles) could be rail-freighted directly FOB to Madras much more cheaply—25 to 30 percent less (*Guide to Willow Creek Canyon Trail*, p. 4). As for Madras—if it lost its substantial (and unruly) rail-construction population, and also their camp followers, when the Oregon Trunk and Des Chutes forces moved on, the town now known semiofficially as "the Gateway to Central Oregon" entered the new railroad era confidently, with new stores opening every month and a new "railroad addition" selling lots near the Oregon Trunk depot on the west side.

Then there was the new opportunity for human transportation in and out. The first passenger train to Madras, on March 1, 1911, brought in 135 visitors, substantially more people that the town had accommodations for—homestead seekers, business speculators, salesmen of every kind, and tumbleweeds. The full trip to Portland via The Dalles took about eleven hours, the northbound run leaving Madras late at night and arriving at Portland's Union Station early enough in the morning to permit a day's worth of business. One-way fares ran around seven dollars. And it quickly became a trendy adventure for local farming families to take the train to

Portland: a couple of episodes from my family history will illustrate what this new mobility meant.

In the early summer of 1913, my paternal grandfather W. H. Ramsey took members of his own family (including my father, age eight) and some relatives newly arrived from Missouri on a leisurely tour of the Willamette Valley and the coast. They went cross-country by wagon and buggy, around Mount Hood over parts of the Barlow Road and on west over the Coast Range to Siletz Bay, and then came back by way of Sweet Home and the Santiam wagon road. They were gone over two months. In contrast, two years earlier, in 1911, my maternal grandfather Joe Mendenhall of Opal City took *his* family (including my mother, age five) to Portland and on to Yamhill County to visit relatives. They went, of course, via the Oregon Trunk (which had reached Opal City only a month before) to Portland, had their photo taken in a famous studio-set aeroplane "flying over Portland," and were back at their homestead south of Juniper Butte in about ten days. O brave new world! (Such early travel by rail was not without risks. A few weeks after the Mendenhalls came home from their adventure, an Oregon Trunk locomotive jumped the track along the Deschutes River near Dant, killing the engineer and eight passengers. The victims, including a storekeeper from Warm Springs, were scalded to death by steam.)

Inevitably, the corporate extravagance that had brought two railroads to town came under sober review by both companies. Always eager to encourage homesteading and productive farming along its lines, the Oregon Trunk noted with alarm early on that, although a lot of people were traveling into Central Oregon, not many were staying. An informal survey of exiting passengers revealed that some were disenchanted about finding good homestead land still open and dubious about making a go at farming in such a dry, austere country; others were put off by the frontier rawness of towns like Madras. In the words of one disgruntled visitor, Madras was just a place of "graft and gab" (Schwantes, "Problems of Empire Building").

As early as 1918, looking no doubt at massive maintenance and repair costs on the numerous wooden trestles along the OT line from South Junction to Metolius, especially on the last leg, from Mecca to Madras, the two companies jointly proposed that the OT section be abandoned and that the two lines share the Harriman route to Metolius. Hearings on the proposal, which would be decided by the Interstate Commerce Commission, were held through 1923—during which time the OT had to spend $225,000 on upkeep along the section in question (Grande, p. 315).

As noted above, newspapers in Portland, Salem, and Bend all endorsed the principle of abandonment and consolidation, but (predictably) in what had just recently become Jefferson County, and especially in Madras (the new county seat), the proposal drew indignation and outrage. The *Pioneer,* representing wheat farmers, Indian ranchers on the Warm Springs Reservation, and business interests in Madras, cried "Betrayal!" But in 1923 the ICC approved the closure of the line of track that had culminated so grandly just twelve years before in Railroad Day. Under the headline "Deserted Rails," the *Pioneer* offered an obituary:

> Thus dies a great conflict. The day of railroad competition is not passing. But that era of rivalry in railroad construction has now reached its zenith, and the trend of the gauge is now downward. No longer, in this age of the motor car, will the golden spike mark the entrance of steam transportation into unexplored and unexploited virgin lands. A Central Oregon railroad has been abandoned. (August 19, 1922)

In a year when the county's farmers were already struggling with a severe drought and falling wheat prices, the closure must have seemed like a cruel insult laid on top of economic injury—especially coming in part from "our" railroad, the Oregon Trunk. Nonetheless, the downtown Madras Depot was quickly dismantled and sold to the Oregon Electric Line in Eugene; twenty-three miles of salvageable ninety-pound steel rails were torn up for use elsewhere; the dream of Vanora (a few miles below Pelton dam site), of becoming the industrial center of the Deschutes Valley, evaporated with the strokes of a few distant pens; and the regular train whistles echoing up Willow Creek Canyon and the winter-morning start-up clatter from Mecca that my dad heard as a boy growing up on the west rim of Agency Plains were silenced forever.

In fact, the 1923 closure was more insult than injury here. Rail service into and out of Madras continued unabated, except now it no longer came right into town but operated out of the Union Pacific Depot complex on the south edge of Agency Plains—where, as the farm depression worsened and ran on into the Great Depression, the already sizeable UP hobo jungle there absorbed the OT jungle in town. And of course the closure meant nothing to the legions of Portland fishermen, who could still ride upriver with their gear on OT "fisherman's specials," get off at otherwise inaccessible fishy places like Tuskan and Sinamox, catch their limits of redsides, and be picked up and carried home—a delightful amenity (imagine it now!) that lasted to World War II and never to my knowledge operated officially any farther upriver than North Junction.

And if our farmers mainly bore the inconvenience of the closure, there were compensations. Even in the construction era, and on to 1923, there was along the tracks always a good supply of scrap lumber, timbers, iron hardware, even sections of lightweight rail used with "Swede cars" for clearing rubble off the right-of-way during its initial construction. Farmers being by nature opportunistic, about scrap metal especially, every farmstead acquired a stockpile of cast-off Oregon Trunk matériel—if nothing else, big bolts, nuts, spikes, and flanges, and sections of hexagonal steel star-drill rods, perfect for prying up rocks and digging fencepost holes. We still rely on several of these authentic "Jim Hill" relics around our ranch.

Probably the most ambitious scavenging job carried out by local farmers came in the late 1930s, when the few hard-cases still farming learned that the OT would let them salvage the timbers (some of them gigantic—8" by 18" by 28'—cut and milled on Grizzly Mountain) on the big Pelton trestle, directly east uphill from today's Pelton Park. So a crew of them (including my dad and his older brother Leslie) assembled at the site, armed with wrenches, prybars, and sledgehammers, and went to work, letting the timbers fall into the ravine a hundred feet under them, to be retrieved and divided later.

After a few days of this strenuous and dangerous labor, most of the farmers decided that they had pried loose all the timbers they needed—and, perhaps more important, that their dismantling of the trestle had advanced to the point where it was becoming unstable. But one of the crew, a stubborn fellow true to his Missouri roots, declared that *he* would carry on with the work by himself until he'd harvested all the timbers he wanted. But the next morning, as he tiptoed out on the rickety skeleton of the trestle, it began to shake itself to pieces in front of him. Luckily he managed to scramble back to safety. He, and my dad and uncle, were after the biggest timbers to build A-frame machine sheds to house their big pull-combines in the off season, and at least two of these distinctive structures still stand on the Agency Plains, monuments to their builders' grit—and to the bounty of the Oregon Trunk.

When I was growing up here in the 1940s and 1950s, the railroad through our country—by then shared by the Union Pacific and the Spokane, Portland & Seattle Railway—was something that we relied on, but the boom-era romance of it had long since faded away. During World War II, heavy equipment to build Madras Army Air Field near the Union Pacific Depot came by rail, and during the peak years of the war long troop trains, brightly illuminated at night, ran over our rails, carrying soldiers from Fort Lewis to the Bay Area for deployment in the South Pacific. We still hauled our truckloads of dryland wheat in sacks to the grain warehouses at the depot, to be eventually loaded by hand on railcars (fiendishly hard work!) and carried off—I wondered, where to?—to be ground into—what, exactly? Every year my mother and I would visit the depot to pick up the shipments of baby chickens she had ordered; and once my brother Jim and I were taken to meet the train and claim two newborn Guernsey calves for our 4-H projects.

I never missed an opportunity to wave at the engineers of passing locomotives (or the brakemen, or the hoboes—whoever would wave back), but I came along too late, I guess, to aspire to become an engineer myself. I did have, however, one boyhood railroad fixation. One of my uncles worked intermittently for the Spokane, Portland & Seattle Railway out of Culver and Metolius as a section hand, and when I discovered that he regularly rode on what was called a "speeder," I suffered my first vehicular obsession. A speeder was a kind of go-cart on rails, a lightweight frame with two bench seats and four flanged wheels driven by a one-cylinder motor, no steering wheel, and just a throttle between you and the open road, or rather, track. It was commonly used for short-range track inspections and getting workers to and from jobs; if overtaken by a train, you just stopped and manhandled the little thing off the tracks. My uncle always pleaded "company policy" in response to my wheedling to ride on one, so I never did—but until I discovered cars I yearned mightily for my own private speeder.

Nowadays the local Burlington and Northern track crews ride over their routes in style in big pickups with retractable rail-wheels. That's progress, no doubt, but I wish they still had the little speeders in their shops, so that elderly children might borrow them on occasion for joyrides from horizon to horizon on Jim Hill's shining rails.

🌀

More than a half century before the railroad boom, a young army engineer named Henry Larcom Abbot spent the summer of 1855 exploring the possibilities of a railroad route through Central Oregon for the US War Department. Abbot's view of the country was probably colored by his fears about Indian uprisings while he was in the field, but at any rate his judgment as an engineer looking for possible rail routes was unequivocally negative:

> The Deschutes valley is mostly a barren region, furrowed by immense canyons, and offering few inducements to settlers. Its few fertile spots, excepting those in the immediate vicinity of Fort Dalles, are separated from the rest of the world by almost impassable barriers, and Nature seems to have guaranteed it forever to the wandering savage and the lonely seeker after wild and sublime scenery. . . . The route down the Deschutes Valley to the Columbia River is considered utterly impracticable for a railroad. (*Reports*, pp. 29 and 45)

A century and a half later, the "wild and sublime scenery" is still magnificently around us (and for natives, *in* us), but Abbot would surely be flabbergasted by the human developments along his 1855 route. So, for that matter, would Jim Hill, John Stevens, Edward Harriman, and their indomitable crews, but it is important to recognize now that what has happened in Central Oregon in the century since they came is a direct consequence of their bold vision and their reckless, wasteful, heroic campaign up the Deschutes. The trains of the Burlington Northern and Santa Fe and the Union Pacific still cross the Willow Creek trestle and the Crooked River Bridge daily, in testimony to what, and how well, they built. It's a legacy well worth celebrating.

Five
The Birth of Jefferson County: Part One

At the outset of 1914, the good people of northwestern Crook County, including the upstart communities of Madras, Culver, Metolius, Opal City, Lamonta, Grandview, Grizzly, and Ashwood, had plenty of issues to think about. True, the railroads had recently arrived and were boosting the local economy; and the burning topic of women's suffrage had been settled statewide in 1912—but what women were going to do with their new voting powers was still an open question, and would they actually run for office?

Then there was the perpetual matter of Prohibition. By 1914 it was not so much a question of *if*, as *when* alcoholic beverages would be banned. On a "local option" law dating back to 1904, some Central Oregon precincts had already voted to become "dry" (Kutcher–Agency Plains and Mud Springs, for example, but not Ashwood or Madras), before a legislative vote brought Prohibition to all of Oregon in 1916. And, starting around 1912, there was growing interest on the part of our region's farmers in irrigation. Dryland crops of wheat and barley had been good in the early years of homesteading, but the possibility of irrigated farming with water somehow conveyed from the Cascade uplands was actively percolating in people's minds from Redmond to Gateway, with meetings and hearings a regular distraction in 1914.

But the number one public issue in 1914 was whether the growing (and increasingly uppity) population of western Crook County was going to separate from Prineville and the rest of the county and become a new Oregon county, or maybe two. Crook itself had been carved out of Wasco in 1882; Wasco had been created by the territorial government in 1854 as an abstract entity that stretched from the Cascades to the Rockies, making it over time the mother of Eastern and Central Oregon counties. Soon after the country along the Deschutes Basin started to populate with homesteaders and others after the turn of the century, complaints began to mount against the county government in Prineville. As the county seat, it was said to be physically too distant from the new western population; it was uninformed about and probably indifferent to "westside" concerns; county taxes were being unequally spent, especially on roads, and so on. To one faction around Bend, the remedy was to leave the county boundaries alone and move the county seat to Bend; but increasingly the westside separationists were calling for the creation of two new counties, north and south, the arrangements to be worked out in tandem so that the two units would be born as geopolitical twins—a charming notion that might have sweetened Central Oregon history if it had come to pass.

The initial response in Prineville to all this agitation was to plan and build an impressive new county courthouse, the idea being, apparently, to awe the westsiders and consolidate the county status quo. But after the foundations were quarried from local basalt and laid, the contractors wrangled and then quit, giving the opposition a new set of complaints to register—arrogance! incompetence! waste! The courthouse project was eventually rescued by an intrepid Englishman named Jack Shipp, but the grand opening of the building in 1909 did not placate the westside secessionists, not at all, and by 1912 they were formally alleging serious and possibly fraudulent irregularities in the county's bookkeeping. Audits were called for, hearings were held, and so on.

So it went, acrimoniously, to late 1913, when forward thinkers in the West decided that the time had come to bring the cause of separation to a vote. It's probably not coincidental that the state legislature had passed a "county separation" bill earlier that year, which stipulated that new counties could be created out of existing ones if 65 percent of the voters in the proposed new unit voted in favor, and at least 35 percent in the existing unit did likewise. If these requirements were met, then the governor would appoint two temporary commissioners and a judge, who would then select a temporary county seat. The permanent county seat and elected county officials were to be items on the ballot for the next general election (i.e., 1916). This measure had originally been passed by the legislature in 1911, but vetoed by Governor Oswald West (for reasons unknown), reintroduced and passed again in 1913, again vetoed by West, but this time his veto was overridden by the legislature, and the measure became law.

How to bring separation to a vote? It appears that the organizers decided to use Oregon's recently established "initiative and referendum" system, which had been adopted through an amendment to the state constitution in 1903 and, despite recent successful uses such as women's suffrage and the direct primary (or maybe because of them), was still a controversial tactic. (See, for example, a skeptical editorial in the Culver *Tribune*, October 17, 1912.) This tactic was the brainchild of William S. U'Ren, a Milwaukie lawyer and progressive activist, whose brother, Charlie, happened to be mayor of Madras in 1914. The "Oregon Plan," as it used to be labeled in textbooks, called for the circulation of petitions, to be signed by supporters of the measure in question; if enough signatures were obtained (generally 50 percent of the registered voters in the affected area) within a specified time, then the measure would appear on the ballot.

By May 1914, copies of the petition were being circulated all across the would-be county—but before this coordinated effort could be launched, the text of the separation measure had to be prepared, and also the new county's proposed boundaries. This latter task must have been especially challenging, reminding us that such homely entities as counties, even their physical shapes and dimensions, didn't just grow like trees, they had to be planned or, more accurately, schemed out, negotiated by people with personal and often conflicting interests in what was being created.

This was certainly the case with the drawing of the county's boundaries—private land was involved, after all, and competing economic interests in Crook County and on the west side. Very little is known today about who actually participated in the work, or about the disputes and horse-trading that must have attended it. One tantalizing clue is given by Howard Turner (probably an active participant in this as in everything else pertaining to the separation cause). In his long rambling essay, "Madras," in *Jefferson County Reminiscences*, Turner remembers that

> the boundary was a sticking point for a long time, but finally early in 1914 a group came to an agreement in Prineville where it should be. J. H. Haner, then interested in timber holdings and also in Crook County . . . had much to do with the establishment of the boundary, especially along the southeastern part and along Grizzly Mountain, it being thought that the high points should be the line, and too considerable timber was allowed to remain in Crook County. (p. 134)

Mr. Haner seems to be unknown today, but he may well be chiefly responsible for the fact that the southern county line runs well *north* of the summit of Grizzly Mountain, in fact not far from the community of Grizzly, meaning that the butte's rich north-slope stands of fir and pine were retained for the tax and commercial advantage of Crook County. This "Grizzly exclusion" is in fact part of a striking stair-step pattern that marks this eastern portion of the county's south boundary. It begins with a six-mile northern jog just west of the butte, then runs eight miles due east, well past the butte and its timbered eastern flanks, and then six mile due north again, turning east again near Awbrey Butte and running twenty-two miles to the Wheeler County line. The jogs follow surveyed township and section lines; it's hard to avoid the conclusion that they were intended (as Howard Turner hints above) to retain substantial timber resources for Crook County. On the Jefferson County side of this line, the forested land quickly turns sparse and scrubby as you go north. One wonders, what did the westside separationists get out of such a concession?

While the negotiations were going on, the Culver *Tribune* reported on July 23 that the in-progress boundary was thought to run close to the settlement of O'Neil (north of Redmond), which, if adopted, would have given Jefferson County a strip seven miles wide running all the way to the non-negotiable western boundary of the Cascade crest, including Terrebonne, Crooked River Ranch, and Black Butte Ranch. Were representatives of (future) Deschutes County interests involved in this phase of the work? Was this desirable piece of real estate also traded off in the boundary negotiations in Prineville in spring 1914?

No telling what happened, but it's probably just as well that our county's other boundaries were, like the west line, not open to negotiation—on the north, a straight line marking the southern margin of Wasco County, and on the east, the western edge of Wheeler County (created in 1889, along with Sherman), marked by a curving stretch of the John Day River and then a straight surveyed line, no jogs or stair-steps.

By the end of May 1914, the separation petition was apparently completed and ready to be circulated. Addressed "To the County Court of Crook County," it began, "Whereas it appears to be expedient and desirable to form a new county, to be known as Jefferson County, out of that portion of Crook County lying north of a line beginning at the southeast corner of

Township 11 South, Range 19 East"—and so on through a legal description of county lines as they exist today (*Pioneer*, May 28, 1914).

In June and July, volunteers carried copies of the petition through the northern and western reaches of Crook County, seeking signatures from registered voters. Their packets also contained small outline maps of "Jefferson County," and pamphlets suggesting why and how the new county would bring lower taxes and greater efficiency than was the case with Crook County (opponents of separation were of course claiming just the opposite). Apparently the same canvassing for separation went forward in and around Bend, Redmond, Laidlaw (Tumalo), Terrebonne, and Sisters. By July 16, according to the Bend *Bulletin*, the north-end petitioners had reached their goal, with over eight hundred signatures collected; the article also noted that the process was going more slowly in the southern precincts, but by September 1 the Bend *Bulletin* reported that both campaigns had reached their goals.

With their cause gathering momentum, the north-enders scheduled a series of community meetings across the countryside to promote victory

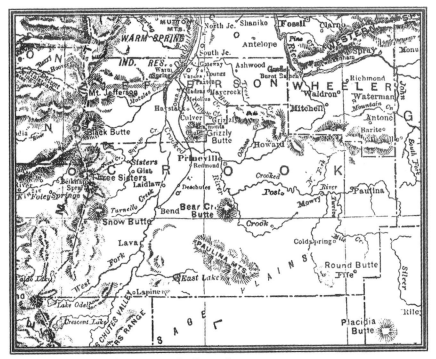

Crook County in 1915, after creation of Jefferson County

for separation in the November 3 election. The schedule of meetings, on Friday and Saturday nights through October, would be ambitious even today, but in 1914, roads and transportation being what they were, it seems astonishing, unlike anything in the history of Central Oregon since then. In Gateway on October 15, the measure's proponents encountered three carloads of opponents from Prineville; on October 22, at Grandview, the Prineville opposition didn't show up, having been turned back by impassibly muddy conditions on the Grandview grades—a sweet moral victory in itself for the westsiders of Culver and Grandview, who had been complaining for years about Crook County's lack of attention to these same roads! The next night at Grizzly, five carloads of supporters mixed it up with a delegation over from Prineville, almost to the point of fisticuffs. And at the Culver session on October 29, the Prinevillians were joined by fellow anti-separationists from Trout Creek and Lamonta, but were shouted down by the home folks (*Pioneer*, October 15, October 22, October 29, 1914).

And so it went, in a crescendo of local excitement, to the election of November 3. When the votes were counted, the westsiders celebrated a great victory—in the "new" precincts, the vote was lopsidedly affirmative, 1,040 to 320 (Ashwood alone voted against the separation, 86 to 65), far beyond the 65 percent of voters required, and in the rest of Crook County, nearly 48 percent also supported separation, well above the required 35 percent minimum. Maybe the rank and file in and around Prineville were tired of the endless complaints and accusations from the westsiders and were ready to cut them loose, if that's what they wanted? The Madras *Pioneer's* headline on November 5, 1914, ran: "Three Cheers for Jefferson County! Everybody, Even Some Anti-Divisionists, Rejoice Over Results of Recent Election!"

An odd detail in all this: the two top Crook County officials at this time were Guyon Springer, county judge, and Frank Elkins, sheriff. Springer was a homesteader in the Haystack area, and Elkins had a farm on Agency Plains. You have to wonder what they thought about the separation movement while in office—both stepped down after the election. As for the cause of separation in south Crook County: it failed in 1914, having lagged behind the northwest campaign from the beginning, possibly because of strong business ties between Bend and Prineville. Deschutes County would not gain its independence until 1916, the last Oregon county to be established.

Now the "plot of separation"—which up to the 1914 vote had moved along with remarkable harmony between advocates from Madras, Culver,

Metolius, and other communities—began to thicken. With the great common goal of attaining county-hood essentially in hand, stresses and differences appeared in the alliance, especially on the issue of locating the county seat. It was understood that the governor would officially proclaim the existence of Jefferson County by the end of the year and announce his choice of a temporary judge and two commissioners, who would then confer and select the county seat. What Governor West (who had chosen not to run again and would be succeeded by governor-elect Withycombe) expected from the westsiders in the way of nominations and recommendations is unknown, but a group centered in Madras organized a "convention" at Metolius to be held November 14, made up of delegates from every precinct in the new county—one delegate for every fifty voters in each precinct, so somewhere around thirty participants. The main purpose was to select a slate of candidates to recommend to the governor.

But a few days before the meeting, the Culver *Tribune* announced that Culver would not take part in the convention, apparently on the grounds that it was thought to be manifestly a pro-Madras operation, aimed at getting men appointed who would be sure to vote for Madras for the county seat (Culver *Tribune*, November 12, 1914). The convention went forward anyway (oddly enough, a Culver man, O. C. Young, was listed as temporary secretary of the sessions). It was an all-day affair, and at the end three men were nominated for county court: for judge, S. K. King of Madras; and for commissioners, Roscoe Gard of Agency Plains (Kutcher Precinct) and Lorenzo Thomas of Lamonta. The fact that these men were known to be Madras-for-county-seat advocates would seem to confirm de facto the suspicions in Culver about the convention—except that if all the Culver delegates *had* attended and voted, the outcome might have been different (*Pioneer*, November 19, 1914).

In any event, the recommendations were duly communicated to Governor West, and on December 17, 1914, he announced his appointments to the first Jefferson County Court. Roscoe Gard was on the list for commissioner, but in place of S. K. King and Lorenzo Thomas, the governor named J. M. (John) King for commissioner and William Boegli for judge. John King was a recently arrived but well-known farmer whose land was on the Culver side of Gray Butte, but he was registered in Opal City, and Boegli was a former schoolteacher and owner of The Cove Orchards, who maintained a residence in Culver. In response to questions about these

(Left) Oregon governor "Oz" West, 1914; (Right) Mrs. and William Boegli of Culver, first judge of Jefferson County, 1914–1916

substitutions, the governor noted that a county seat battle was already brewing, and he was only interested in appointing competent officials, who could take care of that issue "at home." He added, "We took one man from each list" (*Pioneer*, December 17, 1914).

Besides the slate endorsed by the Metolius convention, what other lists was he talking about, offered by whom? It's highly unlikely that these other lists of nominees came out of the convention, but a *Pioneer* article notes, without explanation, that the governor did indeed receive three slates—one from the convention; one from Metolius recommending J. M. King for judge and H. J. Chenowith (Grandview) and S. S. Black (Ashwood) for commissioners; and one from Culver recommending William Boegli (Culver) for judge, and D. E. Blanchard (Lamonta) and H. L. Priday (Cross Keys) for commissioners (*Pioneer*, December 17, 1914). How these additional slates were produced, and what authority they carried, is unknown, but whatever maneuvering lay behind them, they also reached the governor's desk—and Culver's nomination for county judge, William Boegli, received that crucial appointment from the governor.

The *Pioneer's* editorial reaction to this turn of events was surprisingly moderate, given what must have been strong disappointment and anger in and around Madras; the Culver *Tribune*, predictably, declared that Culver was "well satisfied with the Governor's appointments." The *Oregonian* reported in its coverage, however, that the appointments "caused sur-prise to a great part of the residents of the county," and added this hint of possible mischief behind the scenes: "A few who had been in touch with the Governor's office had a fair idea of who would be the appointees" (*Oregonian*, December 17, 1914).

The Madras partisans didn't wait long to vent their suspicions. The Portland *Evening Tribune* reported on January 27, 1915, that Howard Turner and Lewis H. ("Turk") Irving, en route to Salem to lobby for a bill that would lower the vote requirement for relocation of county seats from 60 percent to a simple majority (the effort failed) had made sensational allegations against Culver leaders and ex-governor West on the matter of the latter's appointments. According to Turner and Irving, they had it on good authority that Culver had opted out of the Metolius convention in November on the advice of Culver town founder (and Portland real estate agent) J. C. Cockerham, because he and Governor West were old friends and Culver could be sure that the governor would look after its interests. Supposedly Cockerham had boasted that "he had more influence over Gov. West than all the Democrats in Jefferson County put together."

The allegations were heatedly denied in Culver; in response, Turk Irving published a letter in the *Pioneer* (February 3, 1915) insisting that he and others had been told by L. B. Howsley of Culver about Cockerham's boast, but added that his chief grievance was against ex-governor West—who, as far as is known, said nothing about the controversy. And so it passed—but not without adding more resentment, suspicion, and ill will to the rivalry rapidly developing between the new county's two leading towns.

As mandated by the state-county separation laws, the new county court's first item of business was to select a temporary county seat. Before the court met in Metolius on Monday, December 28, Madras, Culver, and Metolius all filed arguments outlining their claims on gaining the seat of government (*Pioneer*, December 31, 1914). Maybe these documents were duly reviewed during that historic first session, but what mainly hap-pened—over two days—is surely one of the most bizarre, truly goofy epi-sodes in the history of local government anywhere. The three towns aspiring to become the county seat each had, at least temporarily, an advocate on the court—Judge Boegli for Culver, Commissioner Gard for Madras, and Commissioner King for Metolius—so, on the first ballot, each man voted accordingly. And then they did it again, and again, and yet again, with recesses, into the evening of December 28, and then again through much of Tuesday, December 29 (with more recesses), for a total of 280 fruitless ballots, until late Tuesday afternoon John King abruptly switched his vote to Culver, giving it the prize.

Judge Boegli's young son Willis was apparently an eyewitness to part of the spectacle, and years later remembered how it went: "Dad would say 'Culver,' and Mr. King would say 'Metolius,' and Mr. Gard would say 'Madras'. . . . And finally Mr. King, who actually lived closer to Culver than he did to Metolius, said 'Culver.' So Culver became what all the Culverites would call the county seat" (Boegli, unpublished ms).

As far as we know, King—who later served as county judge himself—never explained why after so long he shifted his vote and broke the deadlock. Maybe he had cows to milk and feed on his farm; maybe his civic stubbornness was a little less rigid than that of his colleagues. Maybe (as was rumored in Madras) he held out so long for Metolius to show that the court really did deliberate seriously and fairly on the county seat issue, before casting his deciding vote, according to a Culver plot, for Culver. It's likely that, after a century, we'll never know—but the "marathon vote" became an essential part of Jefferson County's distinctive and sometimes peculiar early history, an exercise of prolonged and obstinate balloting that surpasses anything in the annals of Congress, or the election of popes. The absurdist comedy of it all seems not to have been appreciated by the weary participants, especially not die-hard Madras partisan Roscoe Gard, who, when asked by Judge Boegli to switch his vote to make it unanimous for Culver, replied testily, for the record, "Absolutely not!" (Boegli, unpublished ms).

So Culver became the first but officially temporary seat of Jefferson Country government, and county business proceeded there, in a flat-roofed two-story building that had been rapidly built for the purpose. But bad feelings had been stirred up, and battle lines were being sketched out in Madras and Culver, aiming at the next general election, in November 1916. Which town would win the permanent county seat?

Six
The Birth of Jefferson County: Part Two

As the year 1915 began, mapmakers were busy redrawing the maps of Oregon to show the newly established boundaries of Jefferson County—and in the temporary county seat of Culver, the fledgling county court was meeting regularly to take care of business.

Judge William Boegli and Commissioners John M. King and Roscoe ("Bob") Gard had plenty to do to get the infant county on its feet and walking—separating records, assets, and responsibilities from Crook County and hiring first-time county officials such as School Superintendent Lillian Watts (who occupied the post for the next thirty-five years) and County Inspector of Weights and Measures W. H. Lucy. They were also making up budgets, with a wary eye on the separationists' campaign promise in 1914 that the new county would actually *save* taxpayers' money; and pursuing long-deferred road projects like the road between Madras and Ashwood (past Hay Creek Ranch and over Blizzard Ridge), and the grades and bridge at Trail Crossing in the Crooked River Gorge.

Maybe because there was so much to do, and all of it for the first time, the court seems to have gotten past the bad feelings and suspicions stirred up by the protracted face-off over locating the temporary county seat and worked together fairly harmoniously. A hint of underlying discord appears, however, as early as March 1915, in the court minutes for the third day of that month. Two bids for construction of a county jail had been presented, one by William ("Bill") Barber of Culver, and another by a group of Madrasites. The Madras bid was summarily voted down by the Boegli/King alliance, over Roscoe Gard's "yes" vote, and then Boegli and King voted to accept the Culver proposal (Culver *Tribune*, March 5, 1915).

Looming just ahead—especially in Madras and Culver—was the stipulation laid down in the 1914 election, and reemphasized in Governor West's "Jefferson County" proclamation, that both the appointed court officials and their selection of a county seat were *temporary*, to be revisited in a county-wide vote in the next general election, early in November 1916. In anticipation of the challenges to come, the Culver *Tribune* printed an extended comment it had obtained from Oregon attorney general George Brown. Brown's remarks were apparently written to convey his informal opinion, not as a formal declaration. He wrote,

> Does Culver, the present temporary location, have to petition the same as the other contenders? The statute is not clear on this subject, but apparently it does not contemplate that the place at which the county seat is located shall be named in any petition for the removal of the county seat. The language of Section 2877 is that the petition shall set forth the names of the towns or cities to which the county seat is proposed to be removed. Apparently, therefore, the town or city at which the county seat is located, becomes a candidate for such location without the filing of a petition. (*Tribune*, February 2, 1916)

The obvious practical question that goes begging in Brown's statement is *how does* Culver, the temporary seat, take its place on the ballot alongside the petitioning candidates, Madras and Metolius? If not by filing its own petition, then by a simple stroke of the county clerk's pen, or what? And if Culver were not to appear on the ballot, and thus not be "votable," how could it hope to prevail in the election and retain the county seat permanently? The attorney general acknowledged that the statute on county seat removals/relocations was "not clear"—but there is no evidence that the *Tribune* or the Culver-based county district attorney, W. P. Meyers, or anybody else, sought further clarification beyond Brown's equivocal statement. Instead, they seem to have let themselves be assured by what Brown did say—that it appeared that it would not be necessary to file a petition—and proceeded from there. In hindsight, it looks like a huge miscalculation, and one suggesting very limited and inexpert legal counsel.

It's likely that reservations about use of the initiative and referendum process, and its reliance on initiative petitions, had some influence on Culver's tactics in 1915–1916. Back in October 1912, approaching the general election of that year, the *Tribune* pointedly warned its readers that the "much talked about 'Oregon System' is still on trial," and capable of

William U'Ren, adviser of the "Madras for county seat" faction

generating bad ballot measures in the name of "power to the people" (Culver *Tribune*, October 17, 1912). The editorial noted that there were no less than thirty-eight "Oregon System" measures on the statewide ballot that year, a very mixed bag indeed (most failed)—anticipating wholesale abuses of the system in our own time.

But such reservations, which were widely held, back then, especially among conservative voters, had been suspended in Culver, Madras, and elsewhere in 1914 in order to bring about the separation of Jefferson County from Crook. Earlier efforts to do the job through legislative action in Salem had failed; and William U'Ren's initiative system was ready for the purpose at hand, and it worked. But would it "work," politically and legally, to bring to a vote either confirmation or relocation of Jefferson County's seat of government in 1916?

Evidently there were no such questions in Madras and Metolius as 1915 moved on into 1916. No doubt this confidence, at least in Madras, was based on the fact that its leaders had retained William U'Ren himself (whose brother, C. P. "Charlie" U'Ren, was mayor of Madras) as counsel. It might be argued that this "local" connection made Culverites all the more suspicious of the Oregon System, especially on the issue of county-seat relocation! In any event, the petitions for both Madras and Metolius were circulated throughout the county, with this text for Madras (signed by M. C. Mason, Perry Henderson, and A. W. Ashley, of The Madras for County Seat Club):

AN ACT

Section 1: That on and after the 1st day of January AD 1917, the City of Madras shall be the County Seat of Jefferson County;

Section 2: On or after the 1st day of January 1917, all the County offices and the circuit and county courts shall be at Madras, and all County business required to be done at the County Seat shall be in Madras. On or before said 1st day of January the County shall remove all the County records, books, office equipment and other County property from Culver to Madras, and shall provide the necessary office rooms, furniture, and equipment at the City of Madras for doing and carrying on all the business of the County that is required to be done at the County Seat.

Section 3: All laws in conflict herewith are hereby repealed."
(Culver *Tribune*, March 30, 1916)

According to Oregon statutes, the Madras and Metolius campaigners were required to obtain signatures on their respective petitions amounting to at least 8 percent of the votes cast in the last general election. This requirement must have posed a puzzle: the last general election would have been in 1912, but at that time, of course, it was all Crook County, and the total votes cast then would have been big enough to have made it difficult in 1916 to meet the requirement, especially with two competing petitions in play. Perhaps the requirement was adjusted—with the approval of the secretary of state?—so as to be based on the total votes cast only in the precincts of what became Jefferson County.

What is definite is that the petition drive did succeed, with the Madras proposal gaining 552 signers, and so the relocation effort went forward in summer and early fall 1916—alongside, it should be noticed, on the national level, the presidential campaign of incumbent Woodrow Wilson and the GOP candidate, Charles Evans Hughes, justice of the US Supreme Court.

Before moving on to the county seat campaign and the 1916 vote and its aftermath, it's instructive to digress briefly on other instances of controversies in Oregon over locating seats of government. When Oregon itself was still a territory, in 1849, a fierce serial battle broke out over whether Oregon City, the original territorial capital, or Salem, should be the seat. At one time the territorial government was literally divided between the two towns, with most of the legislature meeting in Salem, and the governor and most of his appointees holding forth in Oregon City. The conflict was not officially resolved until a statewide vote in 1864 made Salem the capital.

On the county level, both Umatilla and Union Counties have had county-seat wars. In Umatilla County, a heated battle raged in the 1860s between Umatilla, the original seat, and Pendleton, with the latter making off with the county records and hiding them in a farmhouse, then giving them back, until voters chose Pendleton as county seat in 1870. In Union County, when the state legislature created the county in 1864, it also presumed to designate La Grande as the "temporary" county seat (sound familiar?), but in 1874, after a county-wide vote had selected Union as the permanent seat, its citizens raided the courthouse in La Grande and carted the paraphernalia of government back to Union. Ten years later, another county vote chose La Grande, and everything was hauled back again, this time for good (see Corning, *Dictionary of Oregon History*, pp. 65–66).

Then there is the bizarre case of Klamath Falls, which has always been the county seat of Klamath County, but in exactly the same years as Jefferson County's birth and growing pains, there were actually two courthouses and two rival judges in Klamath Falls. What must have been a bureaucratic two-ring circus, with impeachments, recalls, lawsuits, injunctions and court orders abounding, wasn't settled until the Oregon Supreme Court intervened in 1920 (Janine Robben, "The Courthouse Blues," *Oregon State Bar Bulletin*, Feb/March 2005). The situation taking shape in Jefferson County in 1916 was certainly contentious and complicated, but not to this

First Jefferson County courthouse, Culver, 1914–1916

dysfunctional degree, as things played out. As these other episodes suggest, it could have been much worse here, much more disruptive, than it was.

In the months leading up to the November 7, 1916, election, the "removal" proponents, especially in Madras, kept up a relentless campaign against Culver's right to retain the county seat and for their right to replace it. The editor of the Madras *Pioneer* led the way with regular front-page editorials and colorfully slanted "pro-Madras" news reports on how things were shaping up. In one issue (October 19, 1916), for example, somebody's remark that Culver wasn't even really a town, just a railroad siding, was quoted; in the October 12 issue, Madrasite A. P. Clark was quoted to the effect that "Madras and Metolius are the only contestants in the field that are worthy of any consideration in the minds of the voters." Clark went on to say that "Culver is a nice little town composed in the main of good people and all that, but occupying as it does a position so far from the center of gravity, it would inconvenience too many citizens to locate it there."

And in a front-page *Pioneer* news item the following week (October 19), readers were told, "No one ever seriously felt that Culver as a site for County Seat deserved much consideration. The sieve-like walls and roof of the county courthouse there evidence that Culver itself regards her tenure as short-lived." The *Pioneer* sneered in passing at Metolius's county-seat aspirations, referring to the town's "hopeless race" for the prize, and noting that, back in 1914, the town "didn't even fight for county division, whereas Madras and Culver did." But the main focus was on Culver, of course, and in its final preelection issue of November 2 the *Pioneer* somehow procured and ran a clever page 1 cartoon, showing two dapper gentlemen (one of them labeled "Public Opinion") in a horse-drawn buggy loaded with ledgers, with unprosperous-looking settlements captioned "Metolius" and "Culver" behind them and a thriving town labeled "Madras" in front of them as their destination. As cartoon prophecies go, however unfair, this wasn't far off the mark, except that, as we'll see, the real court-removal wasn't nearly as orderly or respectable!

Above the cartoon, the *Pioneer* (now calling itself "Jefferson County's Official Newspaper") ran a preelection banner: MADRAS FOR COUNTY SEAT! VOTE 322 X YES AND 325 X NO." The numbers corresponded to how voters found the county-seat measures identified on their ballots a few days later—"Madras 322" and "Metolius 325." As everybody knew by then,

FISHERMAN'S LUCK

Cartoon in Madras *Pioneer* of removal of county government to Madras, 1916

Culver had long since opted out, without public explanation, and was not listed on the ballot.

The outcome of the election probably surprised nobody in the county. Madras-aligned candidates for county office swept the field, led by Alonzo Boyce (who defeated William Boegli) and Roscoe Gard, reelected as a commissioner. On the "Madras for County Seat" part of the ballot, the vote was "yes," 839, and "no," 514. For Metolius, it was "yes," 448, and "no," 1028. The Madras "yes" votes amounted to 61 percent of the total votes on that measure; the "yes" votes for Metolius came to 44 percent—so, according to the county-seat-removal statute requiring an affirmative vote of three-fifths (60 percent), Madras was narrowly the winner (see *Pioneer*, January 4, 1917). In the various injunctions and appeals filed by Culver following the election, these numbers and the "Madras Wins" conclusion were never challenged in themselves. But at a distance of one hundred years, it's fair game to speculate about what might have happened to this outcome if Culver had gotten itself on the ballot, along with Madras and Metolius.

If the Culver leaders had taken steps to add their town to the county-seat part of the 1916 ballot, either by petition or by following up the implications of Attorney General Brown's opinion on that subject and getting on the ballot some other way, would Jefferson County voting have been significantly altered? The assumption in 1916 was that, with the ballot as presented, Culver supporters would vote "no" on both Measure 322 Madras and Measure 325 Metolius. If this is what happened, it clearly wasn't enough—but if Culver *had* been a voting option, could it have drawn enough "yes" votes (and "no" votes for Madras) to reduce the narrow Madras victory margin to less than 60 percent of the vote? This would have resulted in a "no-contest" outcome according to the statutes—and what such an outcome would have led to is that Culver by law would continue on as temporary county seat for four more years, until the 1920 general election. By then, possibly, county voters might have decided that Culver had been doing a decent job with the county seat for six years, and might as well carry on—permanently. (On the other hand, it is unlikely to the vanishing point of possibility that Madras would not have fiercely challenged such an outcome!)

If nothing else, such speculation after a century serves to underline some hard questions about Culver's tactics and strategies for retaining the county seat. Did town leaders like Bill Barber, J. C. Cockerham, Ira Black, and W. P. Meyers really convince themselves that their cause would prevail in 1916 without being on the official ballot? Or did they reason that their town would lose out in the vote anyway, and that their best chance would be to challenge the validity of the vote in the courts?

As it happened, this is what they did, very soon after the November 7 election—first in obtaining an injunction (through the Crook County Court), which created a "temporary restraining order" blocking the official canvassing of the county-seat balloting by County Clerk W. E. Johnson (a Madras resident), and ultimately, when the injunction was reviewed on the circuit court level and dismissed by Judge T. E. J. Duffy, in an appeal to the Oregon Supreme Court—which dismissed the appeal in March 1917, after the county government had been "removed" to Madras. (The supreme court decision was *William A. Barber, Appellant, vs. W.E. Johnson, County Clerk of Jefferson County, Oregon, Respondent*—Oregon Supreme Court Official Case Report, March Term, 1917, in Jefferson County Historical Society Archives).

The Culver argument before both courts sought to invalidate the 1916 vote on two main points: (1) that the official notice to voters of the county-seat-removal ballot was improper and insufficient, and (2) that use of the initiative-by-petition process for the purpose of relocating a county seat was in itself inappropriate and in fact illegal. In hindsight, it has to be said that both this line of approach and (especially) its timing were ill-considered and ill-advised. Both Judge Duffy and (arguing for Madras before the supreme court) William U'Ren made short work of the first point, noting how fully the county seat issue had been publicized throughout the county in the run-up to the general election, and dismissing out of hand some minor complaints about the quality of the paper of the petition form on which the signatures had been gathered.

About the second argument, the use of the initiative process, the Culver injunction had asserted that "the initiative and referendum provision of the [Oregon] constitution and general laws do not authorize the removal and establishment of a county seat by the action and vote of the people." To this charge Judge Duffy and later, tacitly, the supreme court responded by noting that the initiative process had in fact been used repeatedly since 1907 to place local (i.e., county and city) measures on ballots (including, of course the bill creating Jefferson County), without successful legal challenge; indeed, as William U'Ren observed in his brief before the supreme court, local measures had been proposed by initiative in six different Oregon counties in the general election of 1912.

The suggestion in the Culver suit that earlier statutes restricting the initiative process were somehow still in force and should invalidate the 1916 vote was dismissed by both courts on the grounds that the initiative process laws now on the books had repealed all these restrictions (requiring, for example, a petition to gain signatures of three-fifths of the voters, and requiring it to go to the county court). William U'Ren drily summed up this argument before the supreme court: "The Court is now asked to nullify the popular vote on this measure because the people followed the latest provisions of the Constitution and general laws . . . instead of following an obsolete statute."

But Culver's postelection appeals received an even sterner rebuke from the judiciary. Having rejected the objections against the use of the initiative process, Judge Duffy took notice of the fact that the Culver appellants had waited until *after* the November 7 voting to file their injunction, and he went on to declare that their claims were fundamentally invalid because they were in effect guilty of laches, meaning "a culpable delay in asserting a legal right or claim." Noting that an injunction or appeal could and should have been filed as soon as possible after the April 25 delivery of the Measures 322 and 325 signed petitions to the county clerk, and certainly well before the November 7 election, Duffy declared that "Plaintiff has not shown such good faith as would entitle him to the aid of a court of equity."

Duffy's reproof goes further on the score of "good faith" and motives. He wrote, "[Plaintiff] has sat by and permitted the people of Jefferson County to vote upon the measure knowing as stated in his complaint, that the proceedings were invalid, and further, thinking that if the measure was defeated no harm to him would result, but if the measure carried, then he could institute these proceedings to set the election aside."

The legal doctrine of laches (from the Latin word for "lax") goes back to Roman law, and is relatively unfamiliar now mainly because legal actions such as injunctions, restraining orders, and appeals are expected to be timely, not delayed. It's frankly hard not to agree with Judge Duffy's analysis of the thinking behind the Culver action—but in any event, and by any standard, the timing of it was a major blunder. Whether it was based on desperation, or legal ignorance and bad counsel, or both, we're not likely to know. If county District Attorney W. P. Meyers was the source of this and other missteps, it looks like they were compounded by a headstrong attitude on the part of his colleagues, believing what they wanted to believe.

Writing years later, William Boegli's son Willis remembered Meyers as "a red-headed attorney who was smart and vigorous, and he looked through everything he could find in the law and everywhere else, to find a way for Culver to be the permanent county seat. But he couldn't quite hack it" (Boegli, unpublished ms, p. 13).

But to finish our story, we need to back up to the weeks in November and December 1916 after the restraining order blocking canvassing and validating the county-seat vote had been filed. Tensions must have been fiddle-tight in both Madras and Culver as Judge Duffy's verdict was awaited. Did newly elected county Judge Alonzo Boyce and the other new county officials informally contact their counterparts in Culver, suggesting that, according to law, an orderly transfer of county records and materials would be in order? Given the circumstances and feeling involved, it's hard to imagine that they would do so—and even harder to imagine anything like a civil response from the embattled other side, if they had! But the strict terms of Measure 322 were not left to anyone's imagination: "On or after said first day of January [1917], the County Court shall remove all the county records, books, office equipment and other county property from Culver to Madras."

On Saturday, December 30, 1916, Judge Duffy announced his decision, dismissing Culver's injunction. That evening, William U'Ren telephoned the news to Orin Pearce in Madras, and through him advised the Madras contingent that they were now free to legally remove the county court to Madras. U'Ren came up on the train from Portland on Sunday and met with the Madrasites, advising them to make their move Monday morning, New Year's Day, 1917. According to reports at the time, a prime reason for acting so quickly was to forestall further attempts at injunctions and delays by Culver: the county's business had been interrupted long enough. As it happened, snow fell Sunday evening, and continued to fall the next morning, making the roads slippery. Undaunted, the Madras bunch set out very early January 1 in a raggle-taggle caravan of wagons, buggies, Model Ts, and trucks, even a sleigh or two.

Whether the Culver officials had heard about Judge Duffy's decision is not clear. Probably they had; certainly they had been expecting it for some time. At this date, it's also impossible to know whether the courthouse was supposed to be unlocked and open for business that morning—it was, after all, New Year's Day. Meaning that the night before was New Year's Eve, and

The "courthouse raid" in Culver, January 1, 1917

part of the folklore of the "courthouse raid" is that some Culverites were "sleeping it off" the next morning, while some if not most of the Madras invaders had spent the night "fortifying" themselves for the exploits to come. If so, both sides were in violation of Oregon's new prohibition law, on the books since New Year's Day 1916.

In Howard Turner's recollection forty years later, "very few of the Culver people appeared while the work was going on—many of them remained up until midnight thinking that we would come after midnight, so they were slow in appearing on Monday morning" (pp. 136–138). In Turner's memory, at least, the removal was well organized and orderly, with "cars to carry the books and things from the Clerk's office, heavier wagons and sleighs to load the furniture, safes, and so on." Judge William Boegli later complained that his personal typewriter was carried off to Madras; School Superintendent Lillian Watts had already requested that her office be left alone—she would do her own moving later, and (characteristically) she did.

Quite remarkably, there was no violence, and the only threat of it came when Sheriff Ira Black appeared early on, armed, and perched himself on a big safe containing county tax payments and records, and announced that (in spite of the November election) he was still a bonded county official and would not surrender the safe to anybody! (Boegli, p. 13). Only much later was the safe hauled away—but in the confusion that morning someone did manage to steal the "County Sheriff" sign from his office door. As soon as he could climb off the safe, Sheriff Black fired off a telegram to Governor George Withycombe in Salem: "A mob of about 100 came to Culver today and forcibly removed County office equipment and records without an order from the County Court or any court. I could not prevent it without great danger of life." Black's message ended with a request that the state militia be sent up immediately (Culver *Tribune*, January 14, 1917).

As the mass carry-out got under way, erstwhile District Attorney W. P. Meyers showed up with his wife. As Mrs. Meyers pointedly began to write down names of the invaders on a list, her embattled husband told them that if they didn't cease and desist, he would "have them all in the penitentiary in 24 hours." To which his legal opposite number, William U'Ren, replied from the stairway door, "Go to it, boys, I'll defend you" (Turner, p. 138). It's an exchange that could serve as an emblem of the whole story.

So it went that snowy morning, with the cars and trucks running ahead to Madras, unloading, and then returning to Culver for another load before the heavy wagons and sleighs were ready to leave. On their second run, midway to Madras, the car-drivers for some reason convinced themselves that, after their departure, a gang of Culverites had gathered at the courthouse, perhaps overpowering the remaining Madrasites, and were reclaiming the court items. So they turned around and sped back—only to meet the horse-drawn vehicles, lumbering toward Madras unhindered.

As the new Madras City Hall-cum-courthouse on C Street wasn't ready for occupancy, the official baggage of Jefferson County was temporarily housed all over town—perhaps there was also an element of security against a possible counter-raid in this dispersal? The county clerk's office, records and all, were stowed in a building owned by "Doc" Haile; the sheriff's department went into a building that had formerly been the White Elephant Saloon, and other county operations were lodged in the private dwellings of the elected officials involved (Turner, p. 138).

News of the New Year's Day courthouse event made minor headlines in the Portland newspapers; back home in Jefferson County the coverage was predictably partisan. The Culver *Tribune*'s headlines for January 4, 1917, ran, "Records of County Are Taken by Mob" and "Lawbreakers Enter County Seat and Loot Court House." The *Pioneer's* front-page banner for January 3 rose to and perhaps slightly above the great occasion: "DELEGATION OF DETERMINED NORTHERN JEFFERSON COUNTY AND MADRAS CITIZENS DESCEND ON TEMPORARY COUNTY SEAT AT CULVER AND TAKE COUNTY RECORDS TO MADRAS, THE PERMANENT COUNTY SEAT, EXECUTING THE WILL OF THE PEOPLE" (*Pioneer,* January 4, 1917). Elsewhere in that issue, the *Pioneer* quoted a Madras businessman named S. J. Celles, who had been a participant in the mission: "Yes, it was just about the biggest New Year's lark we ever had in our part of the country!"

Now jump ahead one hundred years, and let's suppose that these public-spirited but conflicted people could somehow ask their Jefferson County inheritors for their opinions on the doings back then, and how things have turned out since. What would today's citizens say? Looking at the historical record (as sketched here), they might note how swiftly the "the great courthouse raid" and "the theft of the county seat" became the stuff of legend, transforming and simplifying into a rousing story the actual historical circumstances as they were. Both the Culver and Madras versions of the legend are, of course, heroic and self-righteous, and highly selective, as such legends always are. The Culver version maximizes the outrageousness of it all, the unfair assault on Culver's hopes and prospects, and conversely suppresses the fundamental strategic and legal errors on their part, and likewise what seems to have been a certain collective bullheadedness that did not help their cause at all. In the Madras version, along with emphasis on the legality and righteousness of the removal, there is much minimizing of how persistently overbearing, condescending, and insulting their spokesmen were all along, making the economic and demographic differences between the two towns much sharper and more injurious than they needed to be— the expression "sore *winner*" comes to mind.

After a century (and what a century!), perhaps the "county seat" and "Madras versus Culver" legends no longer serve, as they once did, to perpetuate real conflicts and animosities in the county, but instead exist, entertainingly, as vivid elements of a collective folklore, reminding modern county residents, as folklore often does, of where they've come from and where they live—not in Crook or Deschutes Counties, and for sure not in Multnomah. But after more than a century (in 2014, the county centennial was peacefully celebrated in both Madras and Culver), what's *not* legend is the rich and eventful, and in the main progressive, story of all that's happened in these parts since those heady days of separation, removal, and agitation. In the shaking and moving of the early activists like Bill Barber, Turk Irving, O. C. Young, Howard Turner, William Boegli, A. D. "Dick" Anderson, John King, Roscoe Gard, W. P. Meyers, William U'Ren, and many others, a county got itself born, and managed to get past its early conflicts and traumas, and in doing so learned how to get along in pursuit of the common good, most of the time.

Looking back over the county's history, it's clear that from the beginning its residents have been in the main lucky in their choice of civic ancestors, so to speak; and if the future of Jefferson County looks mostly bright today, that's true in good part because our forebears thought so, too, in their time, and took bold steps forward on behalf of posterity.

Seven
Local History on Stage: Five Skits

The impulse to celebrate local history and lore runs deep in both small-town and urban America, expressing itself in centennials, sesquicentennials, and so on, and for that matter in yearly celebrations of local pride like (here in Oregon) Verboort's Sausage and Sauerkraut Festival, Powell Butte's Lord's Acre, and Culver's Crawdad Festival.

On occasion, this impulse inspires the mounting of theatrical reenactments of history. In this vein, for a series of town and county centennials in Jefferson County between 2010 and 2014, I wrote a number of short skits, each attempting to stage a significant episode from local history. They were influenced by conversations I had years ago with the Canadian writer Michael Ondaatje, who had worked in the 1970s with the experimental theater group Theatre Passe Muraille. Ondaatje and his troupe visited small western Ontario farm towns, collecting stories about their history, then writing and performing short plays based on their field work, for local audiences. By all accounts, the locals greatly enjoyed the shows (see Ondaatje's 1974 documentary film, *The Clinton Special: The Farm Show*).

Informal research replaced actual fieldwork in our project, but like Ondaatje's group we had the goal of bringing pivotal or revealing moments of local history to life on stage and, in general, of creating a sort of dramatic mirror to engage and reflect issues that have persisted in our communities over many years. So we put on skits with a comedic (but not farcical) tendency on local "moonshining" during the Prohibition Era ("The Singing Moonshiner of Camp Sherman"), on the emergence of women as local political leaders after they got the vote ("The Women's Revolt in Madras, 1922"), on the once-contentious question of where the Jefferson County seat should be located ("The Great Courthouse Raid"), on the ambivalence of small towns toward visits by VIPs ("How Jim Hill Stopped in Madras," "The First Lady Passes Through Town"), and so on.

Our Centennial Players performed the skits with capable gusto all over Jefferson County, in indoor and outdoor settings, with minimal sets and props; and our audiences were very appreciative. Whether lighthearted theatricals like the following can really contribute to a community's historical sense of itself is something readers will have to decide for themselves— but the skits *were* great fun to work up and put on, in the name of history. If they can serve as models for similar stagings of local lore elsewhere, so much the better.

How Jim Hill Stopped In Madras

Cast

BEANIE SELLARS, *a saloonkeeper*
JIGGS MCLAUGHLIN *and* ALF PARKEY, *"good ol' boys" about town*
CHARLIE CHURCHMAN, *Oregon Trunk stationmaster in Madras*
JAMES J. HILL, *president of Great Northern Railroad Corporation (includes Oregon Trunk). Hill is elderly but bearlike, with a shaggy beard and a fierce expression.*

Settings

SCENE 1: Beanie Sellars' saloon in Madras, October 5, 1911, afternoon.
SCENE 2: Night, a short distance up the tracks from the Madras Depot. JIGGS, ALF, BEANIE along the tracks; ALF holding a red railroad emergency lantern. For Hill's personal railroad car: a dark wall, with a door—preferably a sliding door—with space for Hill behind it, backlit. A CD player with suitable railroad sound effects.

Scene 1

[*Beanie in his saloon, wearing a white apron, wiping a table. Enter* ALF PARKEY *and* JIGGS MCLAUGHLIN.]

BEANIE: Howdy, Alf, howdy, Jiggs! You boys look like you could use a stiff straight shot of something. I've just got some jugs of Missouri Mule made by my friends up on Grizzly, guaranteed to be at least two weeks old! Shall I set you up?

ALF: OK by me, Beanie. And pour one for Jiggs too, on me.

[BEANIE *pours two glasses out of a jug, and sits down with the two.*]

JIGGS: Like I was saying, Alf, it just don't seem right. Here the town of Madras practically made the Oregon Trunk Railroad line possible—put up with all that construction riffraff while they was building the line in these parts, threw that big Railroad Day celebration two years ago last February when they arrived—and Jim Hill didn't even come out for it! And then he did come out to Bend that October for *their* celebration, driving a dadgum golden spike and all—and he came right through Madras on his way back that time without stopping. And now he's back in Bend for some other railroad powwow, and they say he'll just breeze through here tonight again without stopping, dadgum it!

ALF: Now Jiggs, he *is* an old man, you know . . .

JIGGS: I don't care if he's as old as Methuselah! I just think he owes *us* something, just a short stop here, a few words of recognition!

BEANIE: Well, here's somebody you can tell your grievances to! Our very own Oregon Trunk Station Master, Charlie Churchman!

[*Enter* CHARLIE CHURCHMAN, *still wearing his Oregon Trunk Railroad cap. Sits down with the others;* BEANIE *pours him a glass without being asked to.*]

ALF: Charlie, Jiggs here is all riled up because your man Jim Hill isn't stopping in Madras on his visit to Central Oregon.

CHARLIE: Well, he may be my boss, but he's not my man, and I agree with Jiggs. [CHARLIE *warms to the topic.*] I think it's a disgrace that he's ignoring the town his own promoters called "The Gateway to Central Oregon"! Hell, if Madras is the gateway, that must make Bend the back door! [*takes another drink*] I tell you, as stationmaster here, I'm *professionally* embarrassed!

BEANIE: Lotta folks feel the same way about it, Charlie.

ALF: Yeah, somebody ought to do something . . .

[*Long reflective pause, broken by*]

CHARLIE [*conspiratorially*]: Okay, here's what you can do, if you've got the nerve. Stop the train tonight! I know for a fact that it's due through here at 9:25.

JIGGS: But how can we do that?!

CHARLIE: Simple . . . that line between here and Bend was so hastily built, they're still walking the tracks every day, and stopping the trains for all sorts of problems. I can get you some flares and torpedoes, and I guarantee you they'll stop!

BEANIE: But Charlie—you could lose your job!

CHARLIE: I didn't say I was going to be there, and you boys are going to keep this a secret, okay? But if they do find out and fire me, I'll just go to work for the Harriman outfit. They've already approached me . . .

JIGGS: Charlie, you're a crackerjack! Give us those flares and torpedoes, and we'll do the rest!

[*All get up excitedly and follow Charlie out.*]

Scene 2

Night, a short distance up the tracks from the Madras Depot. JIGGS, ALF, BEANIE *along a wall;* ALF *holding a red railroad emergency lantern.*

ALF: I can hear it coming, boys! [*sound effects of approaching train*] I sure hope we got those flares lit OK!

[*Sound of train slowing down, and stopping. The three walk rapidly along wall to door, on which is emphatically written*

OREGON TRUNK RAILROAD
PRIVATE CAR OF JAMES J. HILL
DO NOT DISTURB!]

BEANIE: Jiggs, you're the one to rouse the old guy!

JIGGS [*very nervous*]: I am?

BEANIE and ALF: We'll back you up!

[JIGGS *reluctantly approaches door, knocks timidly with one hand*]

ALF and BEANIE: Harder, man!

[*Jiggs pounds on the door with both fists, and all three shout*]

ALF, BEANIE, JIGGS: We want Mr. Hill! [*repeat*]

[*Indistinct noises behind door, and then it suddenly slides open, revealing* JAMES J. HILL *in his nightshirt and night cap. Hill glares down at the men at length, in silence, and then says*]

Hill [*very gruffly*]: I don't know how you rubes got this train stopped, but I can guess. Do you know there are criminal laws against interfering with trains? [*pause, still glaring*] Well, now that we're stopped, what do you want?

ALF, BEANIE, JIGGS [*all talk at once, and then* ALF *takes the lead, very apologetic*]

ALF: Mr. Hill, we're very sorry to disturb you, sir, but the people of Madras wanted you to stop here before you left the territory. Now that you're—uh—stopped, could you say a few words?

HILL: Well, I'll be a hornswoggled son of a gandy-dancer! [*grins in spite of himself, and relents a little*] I'd have thought that building 110 miles of track up the Deschutes River would be enough statement from me! But all right: you tell your people that I like their spunk! Reminds me of the little backcountry town I grew up in, in Ontario, Canada—good people, salt of the earth, proud of their town! Well, we've spent nearly fifteen million dollars on this railroad because we believe in the future of towns like Madras, Metolius, and Culver; and a hundred years from now, because of our hard work and yours, this will be a great piece of America, or my name isn't Jim Hill! [*he pauses, grins*] Now boys, if you'll let an old man get back to his bed, good night! [*Hill turns around, and the door closes. Sounds of train starting up and departing.*]

ALF, BEANIE, JIGGS [*look at one another, dazzled, and break into song*]: For he's a jolly good fellow, for he's a jolly good fellow, for he's a jolly good fellow . . .

The Great Courthouse Raid

Cast

TIFFANY SCHRUM, *roving reporter for KGB-TV, Portland—loud, brash, very aware of her TV identity, given to trying to "direct" the scenes she's in*

MITCH, *Tiffany's TV cameraman, with a big old-style VHS camera labeled "KGB-TV" and battery-pack*

SHERIFF IRA BLACK, *big, bristling, loud voice (in fact a new county sheriff has been elected in November 1916, but Black thinks he is still on duty)*

W. P. MEYERS, *acting as county district attorney, but in same situation as sheriff; intense, self-confident*

Mrs. Meyers, *feisty*

William U'Ren, *distinguished, formal, "lawyerly," from Portland—"older"*
   (last name pronounced u-REN)

C. P. "Charlie" U'Ren, *William's younger brother, mayor of Madras, a*
   good ol' boy.

Howard Turner, *Madras town leader, dapper, businesslike (not a good*
   ol' boy).

Two or three fellow travelers from Madras, *to do the moving.*

Setting

Culver, Oregon—January 1, 1917—snowy, cold.

   Temporary Jefferson County Courthouse, front door center stage back. Large sign, Jefferson County Court House, over door. Props (if outside): door (maybe in a light wood/canvas wall 12' by 8'); "Court House" sign; mock-up of big black safe, dials, etc.—strong enough for Sheriff Black to sit on; boxes, ledgers, etc. If available, two or more Model Ts, parked behind audience? Old-style VHS shoulder-mount TV camera, with battery pack.

   [*Enter Tiffany and Mitch from front, approach courthouse door and stop, Tiffany on one side, Mitch on other.*]

Tiffany: OK, Mitch, we'll set it up out here. I'll do the lead-in, and by then there should be some action. Roll it . . . [*assumes her on-camera manner, very arch*] Hi! I'm Tiffany Schrum, your roving reporter from KGB-TV in Portland, and I'm up here in the little town of Culver to cover what seems to be breaking news, on a very cold and snowy New Year's Day, back in 1917. In front of me is the front door of the temporary Jefferson County Courthouse here in Culver. In case you haven't heard, when Jefferson County was created out of Crook County in 1914, Culver got to be the temporary county seat, but in the election last November the voters apparently gave the county seat to Madras—another little burg back over there [*gestures vaguely in an eastern direction*]. So Culver didn't like that outcome, and challenged the election in the courts on the grounds that our famous "Oregon System" of initiative and referendum can't be used on the local level [*pause*]. Beats me, folks, but just yesterday the circuit court judge on the case dismissed it, and that's all it took for the eager-beavers in Madras to get together this morning and come up here to try to carry the county seat back to Madras bare-handed, so to speak. At least that's what we've been told by "unnamed sources." As you can see, nobody here yet—maybe both sides are sleeping it off this morning after a big New Year's Eve! I don't suppose the new state Prohibition law counts for much up here in the boonies! [*laughs at her own joke, but runs out of "filler" and says to* MITCH] Cut—no use wasting batteries [*pause, she looks around, and then says as if to herself*] Honestly, I don't understand why we've been sent back to this godforsaken place, on New Year's Day 1917, in the snow. Is this supposed to be history in the making, or what?

> [*Enter stage right Madras group:* HOWARD TURNER, WM. U'REN, CHARLIE U'REN, EXTRAS—*one trundling a furniture-moving dolly. They head for the courthouse door—*TIFFANY *signals to* MITCH *and they move to intercept them.* HOWARD TURNER, *in the lead, tries the door, opens it, holds it open for the others to go through, and is about to go in himself, but* TIFFANY *hails him*]

TIFFANY: Sir, good morning! I'm Tiffany Schrum, roving reporter for KGB-TV in Portland, and we're up here to cover what we hear is going to be a big courthouse raid from Madras this morning! May I ask you your name? Is there going to be trouble?

HOWARD TURNER [*impatiently*]: Howard Turner. Well, I wouldn't call it a "raid," and no, we're not expecting any trouble.

TIFFANY: But Mr. Turner, can you explain to our viewers what right you have to come up here to Culver and remove the county seat to Madras?"

HOWARD TURNER: Culver got the county seat temporarily in 1914, just until the next election. We had that election last November, and the people of Jefferson County voted to make Madras the official county seat as of January 1, 1917. That's today, young lady, and now if you'll excuse me, we have a job to do—carrying out the will of the people! [*He goes through the door.*]

[*Muffled voices from behind the door, some angry*]: "You have no right!" "We're acting on Judge Duffy's decision!" "You can't take that!" "You're breaking the law!" "Get out of our way!" etc.

> [*Door flies open and Madras crew come out loaded with boxes and so on, carry them out to Model Ts, and return for more. A large*

black SAFE *comes out on the dolly, but once it's outside everything*
stops with arrival, through door, of SHERIFF BLACK]

SHERIFF IRA BLACK [*bursts out of the door, wearing a big hat and a large*
star, with a large revolver in a holster. Comes up to safe, puts one hand
on it, and proclaims]: I'm Ira Black, and I'm still sheriff of this county!
That means that I'm the collector of taxes, and a bonded official! I'm
here to see to it that no bunch of renegades is going to get off with this
safe, with the taxpayers' money inside!" [*He emphatically sits down*
on the safe.] Now you boys might as well go on home to Madras—I've
telegraphed the governor in Salem and told him that Culver has been
invaded by a mob, and I've asked him to send up the state militia by
the next train!

[*This declaration temporarily stops the Madras crew in their*
tracks. They look at one another uncertainly.]

HOWARD TURNER (*to* U'REN): Well, Mr. U'Ren, what do we do now?

WILLIAM U'REN [*calmly, patiently*]: Howard, since the election he's no
longer sheriff. But he's got a gun there, so let's just let him perch on
the safe, and work around him.

[TURNER *and others go back through door for another load of*
stuff.]

TIFFANY [*advancing to* U'REN]: Sir, I'm Tiffany Schrum, roving reporter
for KGB-TV in Portland! Are you William U'Ren, the father of the
famous initiative and referendum system? We heard you might be up
here this morning. Can you tell our viewers what's going on?

WILLIAM U'REN: Always glad to see journalists doing their job—even
your kind. I'm here because the City of Madras asked me to serve as
their legal counsel—and my brother Charlie is mayor, so how could
I decline? [*Charlie waves to the camera, sheepishly.*] Now [*sternly*],
if Culver hadn't made their groundless judicial challenge to the
election, this legal transfer of the county seat to Madras could have
been carried out peacefully a month ago, and we wouldn't be up here
this morning trying to get the county government back on track!
But I will tell you and your viewers this—what's happening here is
another vindication of our initiative system of direct legislation by
the voters—which, I remind you, was how the people of Madras and
Culver and Metolius and so on created Jefferson County back in 1914,
working together!

SHERIFF IRA BLACK [*from his perch on the safe*]: Hogwash! If the governor and the state militia don't stop you bureaucratic bandits, the supreme court *will*, mark my words!

> [TIFFANY *and* MITCH *move over to* SHERIFF BLACK, *as if to interview him, but again, everything stops with the arrival stage left of ex–county District Attorney W. P.* MEYERS *and his wife. As* MEYERS *confers inaudibly with* SHERIFF BLACK, MRS. MEYERS *walks around, pointedly writing names of the Madras group down on her clipboard. She bustles up to* WILLIAM U'REN]

MRS. MEYERS [*boldly*]: I believe you're the famous attorney William U'Ren [*she archly mispronounces it as "urine"*] . . . How do you spell your name?

U'REN [*good-humoredly*]: Any way you like, young lady—but for the record it's pronounced "u-REN"!

> [W. P. MEYERS *ends his conversation with* SHERIFF BLACK, *comes to stage-center with resolutely folded arms, and proclaims for all to hear*]

W. P. MEYERS: I am W. P. Meyers, district attorney of Jefferson County, and I'm here [*glares at* U'REN] in the name of *the law*! [*Pause as he looks around at the Madrasites*] If you don't cease and desist immediately, I will have each and every one of you in the state penitentiary within twenty-four hours!

> [*The Madras group all look for assurance to* WILLIAM U'REN]

WILLIAM U'REN [*evenly*]: Go to it, boys—I'll defend you!

> [*Reassured by this, Madras group pick up their boxes etc. and exit to the Model T's, leaving* SHERIFF BLACK *on his safe, and* MR. AND MRS. MEYERS *standing on either side of him, and* TIFFANY *and* MITCH *in front and to one side, recording all this,* TIFFANY *scribbling notes.*]

W. P. MEYERS [*to* SHERIFF BLACK]: Well, Ira, I guess we've done about all we could, without more troops. Speaking of troops, you don't really think the governor is going to send up the state militia, do you? It was a brave stand, but you might as well climb off that safe.

SHERIFF BLACK [*explodes*]: *"Hell no!* Those SOBs could come back any minute, and I mean to sit on this thing until hell freezes over! [*pause*] But you might bring me a blanket, and some coffee.

W. P. Meyers: Suit yourself, Ira—you're a real man of principle! Wife, we've got chores to do at home. . . . [*reflective pause*] Well, life will go on, I reckon, the way it usually goes—gains and losses, losses and gains. . . . But you know, I'm thinking that if we could look forward one hundred years from this morning, we'd see that Culver has more to make of itself than just be the county seat once upon a time—lots more! And I'll tell you something else: whatever happens to the safe here, and Ira, we're going to take this sign off the door for safekeeping, and maybe hang it up in the Culver City Hall, when we get around to building one! [*Takes* Jefferson County Courthouse *sign from above door and puts it under his arm*] So long, Ira—we'll be back with a blanket and a thermos of hot coffee! (Mr. and Mrs. Meyers *exit stage right*)

Tiffany [*to* Mitch]: Wow—hot stuff, even if there was no bloodshed! If we can get this back to Portland in time, Mitch, it'll make Prime Time News for sure! Maybe even go national! Maybe . . . even go viral, on the Internet!"

[*Exit* Tiffany *and* Mitch *center stage and out*]

The Singing Moonshiner of Camp Sherman

Cast

Jefferson County Sheriff, *in rough work clothes, wears a star-badge*
Bill *and* Sam, *two deputies, in rough work clothes*
Henry, the Federal Agent *("revenuer"), wears some sort of uniform, and a badge*
The Singing Moonshiner, *younger man, bristly moustache, unkempt, "wild," wearing ragged bib overalls*

Setting

About 1924, in the middle of the Prohibition era. A clearing in the woods somewhere west of Camp Sherman. Maybe a few cut pine or fir trees. Center stage/back, the front of a rough lean-to cabin, with a door—maybe just painted canvas over a light frame, but the door is real, with Private!

Keep Out! crudely painted on it. On one side of door, the rudiments of a moonshiner's still apparatus—boiler (old cream can?) on a rickety black stove, with a section of coiled copper tubing, leading from boiler to a glass gallon jug marked "XXX"; other jugs nearby. A tub or barrel labeled "Mash." Maybe a folding camp chair or stool.

[*ENTER, on one side,* Sheriff—*warily, furtively, trying to remain concealed, maybe behind one of the trees. Looks the scene over, then looks back offstage, says in a loud stage-whisper*]

Sheriff: OK, come on—but keep quiet!

(*ENTER, as if just behind* Sheriff, *the deputies* Bill *and* Sam, *and the* Agent. *All are armed, either with sidearms or shotguns. What follows should be in stage whispers if possible, except as noted*)

Sheriff: OK boys, it looks like we've come to the right place all right. No mistaking the smell of rot-gut moonshine mash, eh, Henry?

Agent: Yeah, *phew*! It's rank enough to give you a hangover!

Sam: Well, I don't know—it's making me thirsty just smelling it.

Bill: Keep talking like that, Sam, and we'll have to turn you over to the Ladies Christian Temperance Union for retraining when this raid is over!

Sam [*doubtfully*]: I know we've got a job to do, but it just seems to me like a waste of time. [*As Sam warms to his speech, he becomes louder and louder.*] OK, we bust up this still, and pour the hooch in the bushes, and maybe arrest the moonshiners—but we know from the start that there's not a jury in Jefferson County that will convict them, because they're all customers, probably, so the moonshiners just go scot-free and start up business in some other neck of the woods, and—

Sheriff and Agent [*together*]: *Hush*!

Agent: Keep your shirt on, son! This may be just the raid where I can finally build a *federal* case. [*Official tone, and growing louder*] I remind all of you—we're dealing here with enforcing the Eighteenth Amendment to the federal Constitution of the United States of America—and if federal law isn't enforced out here in the Oregon puckerbrush, by God, our nation will be in deep trouble in jig-time!

Sheriff: Pipe down, both of you, or we'll wake up the gang! But he's right, boys, we have our work to do, whatever three-ring circus those shyster defense attorneys in Madras make of it! Now in just a little bit, it'll be light enough for us to move in and—

> [ALL *freeze, as the* MOONSHINER *steps out of the door. He yawns and stretches, maybe pulls his other shoulder-strap on, then "focuses" and looks all around the clearing—then goes to the still, opens the stove door, pokes around, adds wood, putters with the coils, smells the outlet, maybe wets his finger with the hooch dripping out and tastes it appreciatively, looks around again, and then goes back inside.* ALL *unfreeze*]

SHERIFF [*still in stage whisper*]: Well boys, it looks like this is another one of those one-man operation after all. Should be easy to settle his hash. Bill, you go around on one side of the shack to be sure he doesn't sneak out the back; and Sam, you stay back out here to cover Henry and me as we go in.

> [ALL *pull or level their guns, but suddenly freeze in their tracks, as weird sounds are heard coming out of the shack—snatches of popular songs, maybe a hymn or two, some in falsetto, some in bass, maybe some speech thrown in (opening of Gettysburg Address?), all in rapid succession, from low to high and very loud to soft as each song starts. If possible, the singer should be moving around the cabin and maybe turning around, as he sings, heightening the effect of several "singers." The performance should go on for a minute or so, and then stop abruptly.* ALL *unfreeze, and the men look at one another with alarm.*]

SHERIFF [*daunted*]: Sounds to me like there's a whole gang of them in there!

SAM [*excitedly*]: Yeah, I know I heard at least four or five voices—really weird!

BILL: And it sure sounded like there are *women* in there with them!

SHERIFF [*to* AGENT]: Henry, what do you say we back off and go after reinforcements? It could be a mean bunch in there, not just ornery but maybe crazy, or at least crazy-drunk on their own hooch! You know what drinking that stuff can do to your brain!

AGENT [*resolute*]: No—whatever they are, we've got 'em dead to rights, a whole gang, including their molls, maybe with big-time connections in Portland or Seattle. It's the case I've been waiting for! Hold on—

[*Breaks off, as* MOONSHINER *emerges again—stands by the door, looks around, maybe blows his nose—and then resumes his multi-voiced "performance," perhaps adding to it, and if possible making goofy faces, and maybe dancing a little.* POSSE *listens and watches, spellbound, until he stops, and* SHERIFF *blurts out*]

SHERIFF: Well, I'll be a cross-eyed, knock-kneed son of a monkey's uncle if I ever heard anything like this! Boys, it looks like we've got us a one-man band, after all—let's take him!

[*They rush the* MOONSHINER, *surround him, handcuff him. He surrenders meekly.*]

SHERIFF ["*officially*"]: You're under arrest, young man, for violating the statutes prohibiting the manufacture of alcoholic spirits under the laws of the State of Oregon. We're taking you to the Jefferson County Jail in Madras, where you may face additional federal charges under the Eighteenth Amendment. Do you have any questions? [MOONSHINER *is blank-eyed.*] If not, I guess I have one for you. What was all that caterwauling about just now?

MOONSHINER [*sheepishly*]: Well sir, I just get awful lonesome up here in the woods by myself, tending that still day after day, and so I've just gotten in the habit of talking and singing to myself. [*Pause, and then apologetically*] I didn't think nobody was listening!

AGENT [*sourly*]: Maybe if I can get a federal case on you, we can find you a nice place to perform in Sing Sing Prison!

MOONSHINER: No kidding?

SHERIFF: OK, let's get the wheels of justice moving. Henry and I will take the prisoner back to Madras. Bill and Sam, you close down the operation, and collect the evidence. We'll see you back at the courthouse.

[SHERIFF, AGENT, *and* MOONSHINER *EXIT.* BILL *and* SAM *remain, looking at the still.*]

BILL: Sam, I'm wondering if "collecting evidence" includes maybe tasting it? [*Pause, then* BILL *picks up the jug at the end of the coiled pipe, and takes a lusty swig out of it; recoils and smacks his lips*] One hundred proof, at least! [BILL *hands the jug to* SAM.]

SAM [*takes a swig, and, enthusiastically*]: I agree! Put me on the witness stand, and I'll testify to anything! What say we take one jug as evidence, and reserve this other one for—uh—"medicinal purposes?"

During "The Singing Moonshiner of Camp Sherman" skit, Camp Sherman, June 2014, two deputies celebrate the raid

[BILL *and* SAM *shake hands, then unceremoniously tip over the still, the mash barrel, and the extra jugs, and* EXIT, *each carrying a jug. Both are grinning.*]

The 1922 Women's Revolt in Madras

Cast

HOWARD TURNER, *narrator (and mayor), middle-aged, always wears a business hat and glasses*

GRACE SHUGART, *forties, feisty*

ESTELLE SNOOK, *thirties, wife of the town doctor, independent*

HAZEL ARNEY, *thirties, friend and neighbor of the first two, enthusiastic*

UNIDENTIFIED MAN *who nominates Lambert (somebody in the audience?)*

Settings

OPENING: TURNER talking to the audience casually, informally
SCENE 1: Kitchen of the Shugart house, table with a tub and a small wash-
board; copy of *Pioneer*; ESTELLE and HAZEL bring in two buckets
SCENE 2: In the midst of the audience, a town meeting—the women have
a banner

HOWARD TURNER: Howdy, I think we've met—my name is Howard
    Turner, and in 1922, I was still mayor of Madras. But I wanted to step
    down. . . . Time for new blood in city hall! So in October I called a
    special "town meeting"—I think you'd call it a "caucus"—to see if we
    could stir up some interest in city government. Well, we did—but not
    quite what us old boys were expecting!

Scene 1

> [GRACE SHUGART *in housedress and apron, is washing clothes
> with a washboard in a tub. She is making hard work of it, and is
> scowling. A knock on the door.*]

GRACE: Come on in, whoever you are!

> [*Enter* HAZEL ARNEY *and* ESTELLE SNOOK, *both a little younger
> than Grace, dressed similarly, and each carrying a bucket.*]

HAZEL and ESTELLE: Morning, Grace!

GRACE: Morning, girls, what's up?

HAZEL: Well, here it is washday, but neither one of us has running water
    again this morning, and we thought maybe your faucets were still
    running, and we could borrow a little?

GRACE: Not a drop here for two days—so much for using my new Maytag
    washer. Here I am scrubbing like the Irish washerwoman! All the
    water I've got is in this little tub, which I stole out of Art's bath last
    night before he climbed in! Sorry. [*She pulls her hands out of the
    tub, dries them on her apron, and glares at her friends.*] I say this is
    outrageous—all summer long, our tap water goes off, comes back
    on, goes off, comes on, and all because they can't hook up the new
    city well to the mains. It's probably unsanitary—so they tell us to boil
    our water! And just last week the council announced they were going
    to raise our rates from ten cents a gallon to twenty cents! [*getting*

steamed up] It's . . . it's an insult to the women of Madras! Why are we
putting up with it, I ask you?

> [ESTELLE *and* HAZEL *nod in agreement, but don't know what to*
> *say.*]

HAZEL: Well, the blame lies with city hall—my husband says most of that
bunch don't have enough gumption to set a mouse trap, let along fix a
water system!

ESTELLE: Yes, and that's the reason it's a waste of time just to protest. We
need to *act*! [*sees a copy of the* PIONEER, *picks it up, scans the front
page*] Hmmm . . . maybe I've got an idea. It says here that Howard
Turner, our illustrious mayor, has called a special town meeting
next week, so that [*she reads*] "the citizens of Madras can assemble,
to nominate their own candidates for city office in the November
elections. [*reflective pause*] Girls, are you thinking what I'm thinking?

HAZEL: Well, if you mean would I nominate my husband or any of his pals
for city hall—forget it! Oh, they talk big about politics, but would they
do anything that mattered—like get the water system fixed? Bunch
of lollygaggers! [*pause*] No offense, ladies, I'm not talking about *your*
husbands, necessarily . . .

ESTELLE: And I'm not talking about nominating anybody's husband,
Hazel! [*becomes a little conspiratorial*] Think about what happened
two years ago with the Nineteenth Amendment, and before that, with
Oregon's women's suffrage in 1912. Women finally get the vote—big
deal, but how many women have we elected to office since then? If
we're voters now, it doesn't just have to be for men!

GRACE: Estelle Snook, are you suggesting that we actually go to the town
meeting next week and nominate women?

ESTELLE: That's exactly what I'm suggesting—a slate of women! And it
starts right here in Grace's kitchen, on washday: Grace Shugart, I'm
nominating you for Mayor of Madras!

GRACE [*in wonder*]: You are?

ESTELLE: You bet I am—and who do we nominate for city council?

HAZEL [*getting into the spirit of it*]: I nominate Estelle for
councilman—er—woman!

GRACE [*also catching the spirit*]: And I nominate Hazel for councilwoman!
> [*They grin at one another in mutual amazement.*]

ESTELLE: Now, not a word of this to our husbands. There'll be plenty
of time to organize our campaign after we're nominated. But I'm
thinking of a campaign slogan that will convince every woman in
Madras to vote for us: MORE WATER FOR WASH DAY!

[GRACE *strips off her apron and waves it like banner, as they* EXIT]

Scene 2

The town meeting the following week. HOWARD TURNER *arrives at the
meeting, a little officiously.*

HOWARD: It's good to see such a fine turnout for this special town
meeting! Democracy in action, as they say! Now then, I now declare
that nominations are in order for mayor.

UNIDENTIFIED MAN: I nominate Louie Lambert! [*and, in a stage whisper*]
He's a shoo-in!

HOWARD: Now, no campaigning yet, boys! Any more nominations?

ESTELLE [*jumps up, loudly*]: I nominate . . . *Grace Shugart for mayor of
Madras*!

[*General shock and amazement—people look at each other in
disbelief.*]

HOWARD [*poker-faced*]: Thank you, Mrs. Snook. Uh, any further
nominations? [*pause*] There being none, I declare that Louie Lambert
and—uh—Grace Shugart have been nominated for the office of
mayor. Now let's have nominations for city council—there are two
positions open.

[HAZEL *and* GRACE *jump up in rapid succession.*]

HAZEL: I nominate Estelle Snook for city councilwoman!

GRACE: And I nominate Hazel Arney for city councilwoman!

[*By now the audience is totally agog—what's happening?*]

ESTELLE: I move that nominations be closed.

HAZEL: I second the motion.

HOWARD [*a little flustered*]: Now wait a minute, ladies; we can't rush
things here—this is important business! Any further nominations for
city councilman [*pause*] or—woman?

HOWARD [*shifts back to his role as* NARRATOR]: Well, they finally did get
two men nominated for city council, but I tell you, those women were
organized, and they went right on and nominated women for every
city job except for town marshal and dogcatcher! The Madras *Pioneer*

predicted that, come November [*reads*] "Grace Shugart will probably
head a women's administration of the affairs of the City of Madras for
the next four years."

> [*As he speaks,* GRACE, ESTELLE, *and* HAZEL *unfurl their banner—*
> MORE WATER FOR WASH DAY—ELECT GRACE SHUGART MAYOR
> OF MADRAS!—*parade with it around the stage, chanting their
> slogan, and* EXIT.]

HOWARD [*continuing as* NARRATOR]: Well, as soon the meeting ended,
it was the talk of the town—biggest thing since Armistice Day, up
and down Main Street, there were old boys haranguing one another:
"Women! They got the vote, and they got Prohibition—and now they
want to run things!" Myself, knowing the politics of Madras, I was
thinking that it might not be such a bad thing for a change—but of
course I kept still.

Well, the ladies did do some campaigning, but very "ladylike"—and
behind the scenes, the good ol' boys of the town got busy organizing
their opposition. The men who could control their wives did so, I
reckon, and there was a lot of small-town "horse-trading" in the
votes department—and come November, not one of those women
candidates was elected, not even feisty Grace Shugart! The good ol'
boys of Madras had their way, after all. But, you know, looking back
on it, some things *did* change around here even though the women
lost. For one thing, the water system got fixed right away, and before
the election, every washday morning you could hear the Maytags
running all over town.

And in a few years, a friend of Grace and those other women, Millie
Morrow, was elected to city council, and did a fine job; and so the
way was cleared for a long line of strong, capable women to step up
into public service in the city and the county—Lillian Watts, Louise
Irving, Nellie Watts, Elva Townsend, Mary Norton, Elaine Henderson,
and many others—and I hear that in this centennial year you're
celebrating, you've got a young lady mayor, Melanie Widmer! Well, let
me tell you, Grace Shugart and her uppity friends would be proud of
her!

> [*EXIT*]

The First Lady Passes Through Town in 1934

Cast

SID *(Percival), city manager*
TURK *(Lewis H. Irving), lawyer, bon vivant, originally from Virginia*
MAY B. *(Johnson), longtime editor of the Madras PIONEER*

Setting

August 1934. Madras, Oregon (pop. about 400 and dwindling). Main Street (5th), east side, near intersection with D St. Action takes place on the sidewalk; the "crowd" that gathers is the audience. Props: A concealed tape player containing a recording of the sound of Eleanor's car as it approaches at speed, growing louder; slows down with shifting of gears close up, and then accelerates and shifts up, and fades away in the distance. Maybe it could be concealed in a bag or satchel carried in by one of the characters.

ENTER SID. *Takes his stand as if on a sidewalk; looks intently to his left as if up the street, shades his eyes with his hands to see better; checks his watch, resumes looking.*
ENTER TURK. [*Takes in* SID's *appearance, then says, jestingly*]
TURK: Well, Sid, are you waiting for the bus to carry you out of this one-horse town to the bright lights and fleshpots of Maupin, or The Dalles? That bus left last night.
SID [*continues looking up the street, not at* TURK]: Never mind, Turk, she's coming through here—any time now!
TURK: *Who's* coming through? Mae West and the Daughters of the Nile? Or it is Bonnie, with Clyde?
        [*ENTER MAY B., who stands eyeing the two men.*]
SID: No, no, you dope—it's the First Lady! I just heard about it on my radio—she left Bend about an hour ago, traveling this way on The Dalles-California Highway! She's probably passing through Culver right about now!
TURK: I don't know who you mean. The only "first lady" I know is my wife, and I only call her that when she's on my case.

MAY B.: C'mon, Turk, don't play thick-headed; you know who he's talking
about. It's Eleanor Roosevelt [*she and the others pronounce it "ROOS-
evelt"*], FDR's wife! It's all over town—look at all these folks coming
out to catch a glimpse of her.

TURK [*feigning surprise*]: So it's Eleanor Herself—imagine that: her
coming into this nest of Republicans! [*pauses to look around and
check out the gathering crowd*] I've not seen so many people on Main
Street since the repeal of Prohibition! Is she traveling with an armed
guard?

MAY B.: No, silly—the man on the radio said it was just her and a lady
companion, traveling by themselves in a Ford convertible. Now I call
that being bold and independent, for our First Lady!

TURK: Well, let's hope that one of them knows how to change a tire.

SID: I guess they've driving up from San Francisco on their way to meet up
with FDR in Portland. They spent last night at the Pilot Butte Inn in
Bend, and Eleanor gave a little speech after breakfast. Do you suppose
they might stop here? Now that would give Madras a lift, wouldn't it!

TURK: Well, now, let's figure—they've just driven down from Bend, so
they won't need gas, or a rest stop, and I somehow doubt that Eleanor
will need to powder her nose . . . so no, unless we scatter some
roofing nails on the street for them to run over, I doubt that they'll be
stopping here.

MAY B.: Oh Turk, you're impossible. By rights they *should* stop here!
We're just as important as anybody else on her route—even if most of
us didn't vote for her husband. I could run a photo of her in the paper,
posing with you two renegades as leading citizens, and I could do an
interview.

TURK: Yes, and by all means ask her what the New Deal is going to mean
for Madras and Jefferson County. Are they really going to turn the
whole county into an experimental grazing project, like we've heard?

SID [*wistful*]: Well, it'd be a shame if she doesn't stop, at least for a bit.
Look at all these school kids, with their little flags! You'd think they
would have given us some notice that she was coming—we could
have hung a "Welcome to Madras" banner over the street, and maybe
brought the high school band to play, and given her the key to the
city!

TURK: Key to the city?! If there is one, I doubt that His Honor the mayor
would give it up. Listen, you two—let's not get carried away . . . next
thing, you'll be wanting her to throw New Deal candy at us innocent
bystanders! Tell you what: let's take a vote, and see what people
expect. [*Raises his voice, as if to the crowd*] Hey folks, is the First Lady
going to stop in Madras, or isn't she? Everybody who thinks she *will*,
raise your hand? [*Pause*] Now, everybody who thinks she *won't* stop,
raise your hand. [*Pause*]

[*If a clear majority votes Yes,* TURK *shrugs and says*]: Clearly there are
fewer sensible people in Madras than I'd thought!

[*If a clear majority votes No,* TURK *says*]: Like I always say, Madras is a
very sensible town! This reminds me of when I was a boy in Virginia—

SID and MAY B.: Shush—listen! [*They lean left, and cup their ears
attentively.*]

SID [*excitedly*]: I hear a car coming—sounds like a Ford V-8!

> [*Recorded sound plays: at first very faint, then louder as if the car
> is approaching, then very loud but audibly slowing and shifting
> down—keeps a slow steady pace for maybe thirty seconds, while*
> SID, MAY B., *and* TURK *hail the occupants*]

SID, MAY B., and TURK: Welcome to Madras, Mrs. Roosevelt!

God bless the president!

Come back when you can visit, and drive safely!

> [*Meanwhile, the noise of the car speeds up, shifts into higher gears,
> and the volume rapidly fades as if into the distance. A silence
> ensues, for maybe fifteen seconds*]

SID: Well, OK, she didn't stop—but did you see you see how she waved to
us, real friendly?

MAY B.: I recognized her right away by her smile. She sure isn't pretty, but
she has a kind look.

TURK: And I've already got the lead for your story in the paper, May
B.—"When First Lady Eleanor Roosevelt reached Madras about
11 a.m. last Friday, she didn't stop, but her auto was seen to slow
perceptibly. [*takes arms of both* SID *and* MAY B.] Come on, you two
disappointed dreamers, I'll treat you to lunch—the special today at
Doty's Café is meatloaf!"

> [*EXIT*]

Eight
The Mystery Homesteaders

The beginning of the end of this story came in the early 1970s, when a young man named Rick Donahoe was tearing down an old outbuilding on his farm north of Redmond, Oregon. In one of the walls, he found a tattered ledger-book, its pages filled with daily entries in pencil, dating from January 1912 to September 1917, beginning in central Michigan (Saginaw County) and abruptly breaking off somewhere east of Madras, Jefferson County, Oregon.

It didn't seem to be a proper diary—more, he thought, a kind of "day book" or journal, keeping careful track of work, visits, income, and expenses for a family, with very little of a personal nature registered. It was definitely not a self-conscious literary record. But who kept it? There was no name, but clearly the writer was part of a farming family, first in Michigan, and then, after the move to Oregon, they were homesteaders, struggling to prove up on and gain title to the 160 acres they'd claimed. But where? Was the writer a man or a woman? (How the book ended up in a shed many miles from its place of origin was, and remains, part of its mystery.)

Rick Donahoe was fascinated by the ledger-book and the story it might tell, if he could identify the writer and locate the homestead. He carefully transcribed it in typescript, and even drew up an alphabetized index of names of people mentioned in the entries. Eventually he and his wife Mary sold their farm and resettled in Ohio, and in 2010 he contacted me, wondering if the Jefferson County Historical Society would give the "mystery ledger" a home in our archives—and if I personally would like to take a crack at solving its puzzles.

It's pleasant to share an obsessive interest in something that seems important, and inscrutable. So it's been great fun sharing the ledger and its challenges with Rick Donahoe—and the information that has come to light about its historical significance and the identity of its author and her family over several years of research owes a great deal to him. He was the finder of it, after all, and more crucially, its first keeper: it was his shrewd recognition of its potential value as a document that led him to save and transcribe it. It's a cautionary exercise to reflect on how many similar tattered records of our Central Oregon past have been accidentally found, idly leafed through—and thrown away. This one, at least, has found an archival home, for future readers to study.

When I received the journal from Rick Donahoe, along with his typed transcript of it and the index of names mentioned in the second, "Oregon," half of the record, I immediately looked over the index, thinking that some of the names would likely be those of neighbors of the homesteaders, wherever they located. Sure enough, there seemed to be a pattern of references to early-day settlers known to be out in the country east of Hay Creek Ranch, between there and Blizzard Ridge—the Lippes, the Kibbees, Tom Power, Bruce Shawe, Ed Allen, and others. Other names tallied with people known to be living in and around Madras between 1913 and 1917.

One of these, frequently mentioned at the beginning, was just named "Ben." By this time I had noticed, on a short list at the back of the journal, the names Gay Larkin and Ethel Larkin. Could Ben, I wondered, be Ben Larkin, a pioneer Madras harness and saddle dealer, and if so, were Gay and Ethel Larkin our mystery homesteaders, perhaps drawn out to Central Oregon by their relative's presence as a local businessman? So, juggling hunches, I turned to the Internet, specifically to Ancestry.com, and entered "Larkin, Gay" for the 1910 census in Saginaw County, Michigan.

Bingo: Gay (born in 1877) and Ethel (born in 1888) Larkin, husband and wife, were living then in the township of Albee, and had a daughter, Mildred. Next I accessed the 1920 census for Jefferson County, Oregon—bingo again: the Larkins were now living on a farm near Hay Creek Ranch, and by now had five children. Knowing that Ben Larkin had come to Madras about 1906, I next checked him out in the 1910 census for Oregon, and confirmed my hunch that he was Gay's brother, two years his senior.

Now it remained to identify the keeper of the journal, and to locate the Larkin homestead. The entries made it clear that Gay came out from Michigan in September 1913, presumably to look for a homestead site and file a claim on it; and that Ethel and Mildred and their children came out (by train) in midwinter of 1914. From this, it was an easy step to deduce that Ethel was in fact the keeper of the family record—in Michigan, she

Gay and Ethel Larkin's
wedding photo

records Gay's departure for Oregon, covers the family's doings for the next
five months (including a farm and household sale and farewell visits with
their family and friends), and then in her characteristically dry language
apologizes for writing no entries for a month—"Lost all time having sale
and visiting, and moving on a tedious journey. Arrived in Madras Feb. 1,
at 6 am."

Entries in March 1914 mentioning that the Larkins were "going out
to the ranch" (evidently they were staying in Madras, perhaps with Ben)
indicate that Gay had in fact filed on a homestead after he arrived the previous September. So the next step toward locating the place was to consult
Madras Land Office records (in the Jefferson County Historical Society
Archives) for homestead filings in the last months of 1913. Sure enough: on
September 16, 1913, Gay C. Larkin filed on 160 acres legally described as
"the East 1/2 of the NE 1/4 and the North 1/2 of the SE 1/2 of Section 17,
Township 11 South." By transferring these coordinates to a sectional map
of Jefferson County (then part of Crook), it was easy to identify where the
Larkins had "located": about seventeen miles east of Madras, off the road to

Ashwood (then still under construction) and up Little Willow Creek south
and east and about a half mile up the draw of one its tributaries, known
locally as Jim Creek, in honor of three bachelor settlers there named Jim.
Later, in 1914, the Larkins filed what was known as an "additional" claim of
forty acres, on the southeast side of the property.

Looked at today, a century later, the place (now part of Hay Creek
Ranch) reveals virtually no signs of the Larkins' industrious occupation—
no buildings or corrals, no domestic trees, very little in the way of scrap
wood and metal, only a few faint traces of roads. But as homesteading sites
go in this upland range country, it has its merits. There is a spring (with
remnants of a spring box and a pipe) above the little knoll at the bottom
of the draw where the house was apparently located, with open ground on
either side of the draw for small fields and pasture. The main acreage for
crops lies along the top of the ridge above and south of the draw, paralleling
it—"up on the hill," as Ethel called it. The impression is of a rather sheltered
farmstead, without being unduly confined or closed in.

It also seems now like a very lonesome place—but of course at the
time the Larkins took it up, at the very peak of the local homesteading
boom, they would have had neighbors on every side, most of them no more
than a mile or two away, though they would not have been able to see each
other's kerosene lamps at night, given the terrain. Such were the rigors of

Ben Larkin's harness shop in Madras, ca. 1913

homesteading out here, especially during the years of the Great Drought, that "the neighborhood" was nearly empty by 1930.

So far we've gotten Gay and Ethel Larkin identified and landed on their claim—but of course these answers, though important, lead us on to further questions equally important for understanding them as Central Oregon homesteaders and Ethel's journal as a unique source document. How did they live in Michigan, and why did they leave there in 1913–1914 and attempt to take up free land in Oregon? What was the "economy" of their lives in both places, and what continuities and discontinuities were there between the one and the other? And two overarching questions, in equal measure difficult to answer, and impossible to ignore: who were they, these intrepid young people? And, in their lives and doings in Oregon, were they in historically useful ways representative Central Oregon settlers of their time?

The farm they left behind in Michigan was located southwest of Saginaw. Gay's father, Almon Wakefield Larkin, had settled in the area in the previous generation, and it's unknown whether Gay owned his own farm or rented it. In Ethel's daily record, we learn that they raised corn, oats, potatoes, beans, and hay, marketing the last two crops when they had a surplus. Their land apparently had some hardwood timber on it, maple and hickory, and they regularly cut and sold "hub poles" (apparently blanks for making wagon-wheel hubs), "hickory butts" (?), "traverse poles" (?), and "bolts and spiles" (?). In early spring they tapped maple trees for syrup.

And they kept livestock: milk cows, chickens, pigs, and what seems to have been a sizeable string of workhorses, enabling them to work their own land and do extensive "custom" farming for neighbors. In addition to all this, they both worked intermittently as farriers, shoeing horses, "floating" (filing) their teeth, and so on; and also at need they repaired watches and clocks. The impression is that they were both very industrious—but Ethel's Michigan entries make it clear that they were not thriving financially, in fact struggling to keep up with various loans and "notes" they'd taken on to keep operating.

Underlying their struggles in Michigan, and almost certainly prompting their departure, was the unfavorable situation of their farm—in a low, marshy region, where several rivers and creeks converge and flow into the Flint River, which runs into Lake Michigan. Chief of these streams is the Shiawassee River. Whether their farmstead adjoined it or one of the others,

Ethel's journal graphically records no less than six flood episodes between March 1912 and March 1913—twice flooding the first floor of their house, immersing a cow in the barn, and drowning a pig. She wryly notes that in the flood of May 1912, "we caught 4 fish in our field." Whether they actually lost crops to the overflowing water is not clear—certainly so much moisture on their lands couldn't have been beneficial. But one frequent item on her record of household expenses, quinine, suggests that living in such a damp, flood-plagued locale was downright unhealthy. Quinine in those days was the universal medicine for malaria, or "fever and ague," and people in mosquito-infested lowlands often took it as a preventive agent. The journal doesn't mention malaria, but the risk of catching it must have been a worry.

It's typical of Ethel's way of recording their daily lives that she offers no commentary on what must have been their growing dissatisfaction with trying to farm in Albee Township, and likewise no reflections on their momentous decision sometime in 1913 to pick up stakes and move to Oregon, no doubt with the encouragement of Gay's brother Ben in Madras. At the very least, he could have assured them that their homestead out there would not be subject to endless flooding!

Although the Larkins were ready to leave Michigan for a new life in the West, Ethel dutifully spent much of her final weeks visiting relatives on both sides of their marriage, saying goodbye to people she would very likely never see again: Gay's parents, hers (the Newmans), her grandparents, favorite cousins, and so on, in what seems to have been a close extended family. When she finally boarded the train (probably in Saginaw), she was traveling with son John (age three); infant daughter Lilia; and stepdaughter Mildred (age ten), Gay's daughter by his first wife Lillie Eisenhauer; that marriage had ended in divorce in 1906, and Lillie had died later that year. Gay and Ethel's first-born, Wilfred, had died in infancy in 1908.

She may have had another traveling companion besides the children. In early summer 1912 she indicates that someone named "Jim" was working for them regularly, and within a few days after her arrival in Madras, she notes that Jim and Gay were helping Ben Larkin in his shop. When they took up their homestead below Blizzard Ridge, he was clearly a crucial member of their team. But who was he? The identity of Jim remains one of the journal's mysteries—but a plausible guess is that he was James Kentner, a young neighbor in Albee Township, mentioned in the journal as a visitor, and then, soon after the visit, the regular presence of "Jim" begins. He seems not to have been a relative. Between the adult Larkins in age (he would have been about twenty-nine in 1914), Kentner was married to a woman named Mildred, confusingly the same name as Gay's daughter. Whether Mildred Kentner came out on the train with the others is unknown, as is their place of residence in Oregon, whether with the Larkins at their farm-stead or elsewhere. Most of the journal's references to "Mildred" are clearly to young Mildred Larkin, but some appear to point to an adult—that is, to Jim Kentner's wife.

Twice, later in the journal, Ethel takes Jim on a homestead-finding tour, looking for a place of his own. There are frequent references to his being sick, and if "Jim" really was James Kentner, our last possible glimpse of him beyond the journal is sad—the 1920 census locates "Kentner, James" as a patient in the State Hospital in Pendleton, which in those days housed tuberculosis patients—and the insane.

Whoever he was, and whatever his end, Jim figures in the journal as an essential participant in the day-by-day work of the Larkins' homesteading operation, even to the point of helping Ethel on occasion with the washing. There is one reference to "Jim's wages," but it's not clear that he was on a regular salary: my guess is that he was in some sense a kind of working part-ner in the Larkins' venture, sharing in the work (including outside jobs they took on) and in the profits (when there were any), and looking meanwhile to find a homestead of his own. Such arrangements, as loose and casual as they may seem, were not uncommon in homesteading days. Very few "entrymen" could afford a regular hired man per se—but a cousin or younger brother or brother-in-law might help out at the outset of "proving up." What's unusual about Jim is that he does not appear to have been a relative.

After writing on March 18, 1914, "Got the tent," a few days later Ethel reports that "Gay and I went out there and stayed out there all night." Soon they were plowing and seeding barley, oats, and wheat on the new land. On May 29, she reports the following: "Stayed home and took care of me all day. The baby was born in the evening." (This baby was Gladys.) But within a few days, she was back at work, fixing up a well for Mrs. Percival in Madras and helping in Ben's shop. It was the same with her next baby, William, born July 23, 1916, which happened to be a Sunday. "Sat around and slept all day. A baby boy came at 1 minute after 12 a.m." Soon she was back at work.

And so it went day by day on the Larkin farm—Gay, Ethel, Jim, all working, whether on the farmstead or "for hire" to their neighbors, or in Ben's shop—apparently Ethel was able to manage their teams of horses and mules as well as the menfolk and did so at need, with stepdaughter Mildred minding the household and the children, John, Lilia, and baby Gladys. Looking at the details of the Larkins' work overall, two clear impressions emerge. First, they worked even harder on their Oregon homestead than they did in Michigan, taking only Sundays off (but not, apparently, for church). And second, they were attempting to maintain a very strenuous balance between laboring on their own place on the one hand, with an anxious eye on making it begin to pay as soon as possible, and "proving up" on it to gain title, and on the other hand "working out" for hire, whether with their teams on other farms or doing various physical jobs. The outside work carried the advantage of immediate payment, which in their early years at least was essential for paying the bills and supporting the ongoing homesteading project.

A rough tally of days spent by the three of them working on the home place as against working out totals 513 days working at home compared with 323 working for hire. That seems about right, for homesteaders with their limited resources. Other settlers didn't have to work out; some in fact had "day jobs" in Madras and relied on strivers like the Larkins to do most of their farm work for them. The point is that, at least in this time and place, there was plenty of work to be done, and impecunious and industrious settlers like Gay, Ethel, and Jim were willing and able to do it—as long as it didn't undercut their own homesteading—and as long as they could stand up to it physically. Given the work record in the journal, it's a wonder that they did.

By late June 1914, with barley, wheat, oats, corn, and potatoes planted and a vegetable garden started, they were ready to establish themselves permanently on the place and build their house. The sequence of Ethel's entries at this time is worth following in full:

June 27: Moved out to our own ranch.

June 28 (Sunday): Tipped [?] our furniture all down the hill and sat around.

June 29: Made up our minds where we wanted the house and went for lumber in the afternoon [probably to Grizzly].

July 1: Layed the foundations to the house and lower floor.

July 2: Went to the mill and got another load of lumber.

July 3: Put up the sides and got the pigs home from Lippes.

July 4: Put up the ends and worked on the siding.

July 6 was a Sunday ("Sat around all day," no doubt impatiently!), and then they resumed working out for a few days, before returning to the house-in-progress on July 10: "Went for another load of lumber at the mill. Owe them $10.58." From here on the house occupied them full time until July 20: "Worked on the house and moved into it." No use wishing that Ethel had verbalized what they must have felt about their achievement—out of the tent and into their own house, in less than a month!—but it is easy to imagine what her bare words imply.

From here, the Larkins and Jim resumed their alternation of home work and hiring out—harvesting their first crop of wheat ("1785 lbs."), hauling rocks off their fields, preparing for the next year's crops—and going forth with the teams to plow, disk, and harrow ground for neighbors, including at length "Mr. Cook" (probably Riley Cook, principal of the Madras School, who had taken up a homestead). And Gay and Ethel also on occasion carried on with the odd jobs they took on back in Michigan—doing

The Larkins' homestead house site on Jim Creek, today

farrier work, fixing timepieces, cutting and selling wood for fence posts and firewood. Gay also seems to have been a horse-trader of sorts, buying and selling when he could. And now and then they rented out pasture for neighbors' livestock.

Frequently, in fact weekly during the summers, they hauled water for themselves and (for pay) for neighbors. Given the spring on their place, this seems odd, but probably their growing collection of livestock consumed more water, at least in the hot months, than the spring provided. In addition, they both undertook to hire on as "locaters" for homestead seekers. This was an officially important and also a notorious job—all too often, unscrupulous locaters would take unwary would-be settlers in hand, show them properties already filed on or otherwise unavailable, pocket the nine-dollar fee, and leave them to discover at the nearest Land Office that the place of their dreams was not to be had. As noted above, Ethel, in fact, twice took Jim on locating excursions, but only charged him $4.50 for each search. Apparently, he didn't find what he was looking for.

With the outbreak of war in Europe in August 1914, there was a nation-wide campaign to obtain horses for the Allied forces and also for the US Army. So Gay tried (unsuccessfully) to deal several of their older work-horses to "the Artillery" as Ethel calls it; and later, in 1916–1917, he actively scoured the countryside for scrap metal to sell to the government for the war effort. His most ambitious outside job during the period of the journal seems to have been a month of work, in July 1917, presumably with a team pulling some sort of "fresno" style excavator, on what became the Brewer Reservoir south of Hay Creek Ranch headquarters. The reservoir impounded water for irrigation of fields around the ranch, and it is still in use today, along with the Little Willow Creek Reservoir (built during World War II), just off the Ashwood Road and only a mile or so northwest of the Larkins' place. Gay's absence from the farm during the very busy month of July must have caused problems. Ethel notes more than once that Gay was "still not back home," and finally, when Jim had one of his sick episodes, she went after him.

In large part because of their outside work, the Larkins were "on the road" a lot (or what passed for roads back then), including frequent trips to Madras, Culver, Ashwood, Grizzly, and so on. Roundtrip to Madras would have been about thirty-four miles, but they went often, usually for half a day, including business there. How were they able to cover the ground so quickly? There is no evidence in the journal that they owned a car, and there is no mention even of a buggy—so perhaps they had good fast horses, and of course in those days before extensive fencing they could probably go by the shortest routes, cross-country. Still, their speedy travel seems remarkable.

The farm-work vocabulary that the Larkins brought with them from Michigan is amusingly different from its Oregon equivalent. "Floating" horses' teeth meant filing them down when they were growing too long; "tapping" horses meant horseshoeing. "Dragging" a field (they did a lot of it) apparently meant harrowing it to break up clods, which on the Larkins' black, "dobey" upland soil could become massive, and an obstacle to cultivation. "Rolling" and "pulverizing" probably meant the same, only using some sort of rolling device. They "drawed hay all day," apparently hauling it and stacking it. When they went wood-cutting, they would get a "jag" of wood—what quantity this was is unknown. One wonders how often the Larkins, initially using such "foreign" terms, had problems doing the right job for their neighbors!

Fortunately for young Mildred Larkin (and later her younger siblings), a one-room school, Fairview, opened the year they arrived on the ranch, 1914. It was located only about a mile away, over two small draws and ridges, southeast of their place, on land donated by one of their near neighbors, Tom Power, who had found his way to Central Oregon in 1910 from Newfoundland by way of Nevada and Alaska, and would eventually serve as judge of Jefferson County through World War II and on into the 1950s. The teacher at Fairview was a young man, Bruce Shawe, who had his own homestead northeast of Hay Creek headquarters; he was a younger brother of another settler, Victor Shawe, also a homesteading teacher, who for a time served as superintendent of Crook County Schools and later became a popular writer of short stories in the *Saturday Evening Post*, many of them set in the range country between Grizzly Mountain and Ashwood. The Larkins worked frequently for both Tom Power and Bruce Shawe, "the teacher."

Fairview School regularly had up to twenty scholars, including children of families who were (judging from the journal) friendly neighbors of the Larkins—the Lippes, the Kibbees, the Garretts. The Lippes and the Kibbees had daughters about Mildred's age, and Ethel notes frequent visits to and from their places, including some sleepovers. She also mentions

Group photo of Fourth of July crowd at the Elkins place, 1915

attending "meetings at the school" and, at Christmas 1914, going to school "for the Christmas tree."

The outing at Christmas was rare for the Larkin family, it seems; about the only other serious social occasion mentioned is their going to "the rabbit drive" earlier that month (the mass killing of jackrabbits to control crop damage was a popular homesteading community event, usually followed by a potluck meal). On the Fourth of July, 1917, Mildred, now fourteen, "went to the picnic"—this was almost certainly that year's version of the famous Fourth of July celebrations at the Elkins place, a well-established ranch south of Hay Creek Ranch above Awbrey Creek, which usually ran for two days, included informal rodeos, a baseball tournament featuring local town teams, and ice cream, and usually drew over one hundred guests, many of whom camped out on the place. Evidently Mildred's parents were too busy to go, and no doubt they also missed a 1916 Fourth of July celebration promoted by another neighbor, by the name of Brewer, somehow staged on the summit of craggy Big Sheep Rock, visible on the skyline southeast of their place.

All in all, the Larkins were in the midst of a lively, sociable community of settlers; and even if they didn't gad about much socially and tended pretty strictly to business, they must have been sustained by the presence of such a neighborhood. As the years of her journal went by, Ethel recorded more and more frequent visits at their farm, sometimes even overnight, from the folks around. Once or twice they even played cards.

What about the folks back in Michigan, including their parents and siblings? On that topic the journal poses two minor mysteries. One involves the arrival of someone identified as "Pa," on October 18, 1916. Almost certainly this is Ethel's father, Charles Newman, whom she regularly calls "Pa" in the Michigan portion of the journal. His wife, Ethel's mother Emily, may or may not have been living at this time; if she had died, it wouldn't be surprising that he would come out for a visit. A complicating detail, however, is a January 1915 reference to Gay and Ethel going over to Hay Creek to "fix up Pa's guardian letter." This might suggest that he was somehow incapacitated mentally or physically—but after his arrival in Oregon he was clearly able to busy himself usefully at the homestead, making a churn dasher for Ethel and a chair for the baby, William; and later, in 1917, he moved into a place of his own, evidently somewhere nearby. There is no record of his filing an actual homestead claim or buying a "relinquishment," however, and whether he stayed on in Oregon past 1917, or moved back to Michigan, is unknown, with no clear 1920 census records or death records for him in either state.

The other mystery came on Sunday, May 13, 1917. Ethel's terse entry reads: "Ben came and got Gay toward night—going for Michigan." No reason given, and all we can tell about the brothers' sudden departure is that Gay did not return for nearly a month, reappearing on the night of June 8, when Ethel met him at Madras. One can only guess here, but the fact that both brothers made the trip may indicate some sort of Larkin family crisis, and the fact that their mother, Cora Goff Larkin, died on October 17 of that same year maybe suggests that her sons traveled all the way back to Albee Township because her death was thought to be imminent as early as May. Her death certificate indicates "paralysis," so perhaps she had suffered a major stroke back in May.

With her husband's return, Ethel's journal-keeping continues imperturbably, with the usual work detail: "June 11: Plowed all day and Pa fixed fence and Jim worked for Mr. Thomas"—with no further reference to the mysterious train trip. It must have seriously unbalanced their finances, but by the last entries in the journal, at the end of September 1917, with Gay out threshing wheat and Jim sowing rye and Ethel picking fruit somewhere ("for pay"), the impression is strong that they were back on track, forging ahead, doing reasonably well. That impression tallies with an auspicious entry for early that year, January 31 and February 1. January 31: "Went to The Dalles. Spent $4.50 for socks and rubbers and things that were needed. [She apparently means in Madras.] Then took the train to The Dalles. $7.20 fare. Feb. 1: Filed on our land. Cost $.55 for breakfast, $56 filing fees, $.75 for dinner, and $1 in trade on watches. $7.25 coming home, $.10 for candy." (The Dalles was where the US Land Office was located.)

Clearly, as indicated by the train fare, Ethel went on this crucial trip by herself. What it signifies is that their efforts at earning "free" land by homesteading were about to be officially rewarded. Under new regulations enacted in 1912, the year before Gay filed on the place, the minimum time required for "proving up" had been reduced from five years to three, and no doubt the Larkins worked even harder to be ready to file for "final proof" in 1917. Ethel's trip to The Dalles involved submitting an application with affidavits to the Federal Land Office there, leading to more paperwork, an on-site inspection, and five consecutive publications in a local newspaper of their filing to be granted "patent," or title to their acres. The Larkins' notice probably ran for five weeks in the Madras *Pioneer* or maybe one of the Prineville papers later in 1917. (During the local homesteading boom years, improbable newspapers like the Antelope *Herald*, the Ashwood *Prospector,* and the Mitchell *Monitor* and *Sentinel* sprang up and published for a few years, in part, it appears, to take advantage of fees from this "pub-lication" requirement.)

Presumably the Larkins finally received their homestead title, signed by President Woodrow Wilson, in later 1917 or early 1918, in the mail that came for them at Hay Creek. But by then Ethel's 1912 to 1917 journal had ended. What happened to them thereafter is all too briefly narrated (because of lack of records). One hopes that, having reached the major goal of attaining title to their land, they continued to do well on the place and at their jobs, despite the onset of the Great Central Oregon Drought after about 1920. Their family increased at regular intervals, with the addition of Lewis in 1917, Alta in 1921, Selma in 1925, and Minerva in 1929.

In 1923, they took a momentous step, one that seems consistent with their ambitions and not driven by desperation. They sold the homestead under Blizzard Ridge to Hay Creek Ranch "for $10 and other good and valuable considerations"—the full amount of the sale seems to be encoded in the standard phrase "other good and valuable considerations" as entered in the Hay Creek records; but it was assuredly enough to allow them to buy a ranch in Crook County north of Prineville, in what was becoming the Ochoco irrigated farming district along McKay Creek. And there, sadly, Gay Larkin died suddenly on October 19, 1932, age fifty-five.

Ethel tried to keep her large family together on the farm for a year or two, but then moved to Prineville to find work. On the occasion of her eighty-sixth birthday in 1974, the Prineville *Central Oregonian* described her as "sharp of mind and with a twinkle in her eye," and noted that she had raised five daughters and three sons, resulting in thirty-nine grandchildren and seventy-six great-grandchildren! She also noted with pride that when she and Gay first came out from Michigan, they landed in Crook County— but "we helped with our votes the next fall to divide the county in three parts—Jefferson, Deschutes, and Crook." (Actually Deschutes did not get itself separated, county-wise, until 1916.)

She died in 1977, and is buried with Gay in Prineville's Juniper Haven Cemetery. As far as I know, their children are all deceased, and the subsequent generations of Larkins appear to have left Central Oregon, a number of them settling in Grant County—but I have not been able to make contact with any of them about Gay and Ethel's homesteading legacy and the contents of her journal.

What can we make of that legacy, as uniquely documented in the journal? As it happens, the years around the Larkins' arrival in Central Oregon were the peak years in US homesteading history, with 59,363 claims granted nationally in 1913 and 53,308 in 1914. In the country where they settled, the boom ran from about 1909 to the end of World War I, encouraged by the arrival of the railroads in 1911 and by the sometimes overblown commercial appeals to would-be settlers made by the Oregon Trunk (Great Northern) and Des Chutes (Union Pacific) lines. In point of historical fact, the middle of Oregon from north to south was the last major homesteading area in the United States—two decades and more after Frederick Jackson Turner and other demographic historians had declared that the American frontier was closed—in effect no more free land, it was claimed. This is one reason, among others, why "the Larkin legacy" is so important—here's where, with people like them, a formative impulse in American history finally played out.

Here in the Oregon interior, as elsewhere along the march of home-steading in the West, our "entrymen" and "entrywomen" forebears have certainly not been forgotten. Much has been written on the subject, including numerous memoirs, mainly by the children and grandchildren of the settlers, much less commonly by the settlers themselves, and almost never on a day-by-day journal or diary basis. Inevitably, colored by family pride, nostalgia, and highly selective hindsight, many of these accounts tend to romanticize the homesteading experience, emphasizing the industrious and resourceful virtues of the families involved and the heroic mix of privations and elemental satisfactions and freedoms that they took equally in stride. "O Pioneers"—it is a collective regional narrative that parallels and in some respects completes the Oregon Trail story, as part of our Western American mythos.

There is also, however, another very different perspective on home-steaders and their lives, here in Oregon and elsewhere. It has been promoted by recent "revisionist" historians and, earlier, by writers of realistic fiction, notably by Oregon's only Pulitzer Prize–winning novelist, H. L. Davis. Davis grew up in and around The Dalles and, as a teenager, lived in Antelope and worked for the Antelope *Herald* as a typesetter. This was around 1907, and what he saw of loose caravans of would-be settlers straggling through Antelope and Shaniko into Central Oregon seems to have been the inspiration of a thoroughly negative, often contemptuous view of homesteaders in general. In his Pulitzer novel, *Honey in the Horn*, and in several of his essays, Davis depicts homesteaders as mostly improvident and feckless losers and tumbleweeds, incapable of making their hard work (when they did it) pay off in anything lasting. Denying the official premise of "proving up" by improving one's land—"A country didn't increase in value according to what you put into it," he once wrote—Davis more than once compared the homesteaders he encountered to the packrats that infested their abandoned shacks: "If there is a monument to busted home-steaders, the packrat deserves to be it. He is by nature one victim of the homesteaders' never-failing curse—a fury for beginning things and leaving them one-fourth done. It may have been from them that he learned his habits" ("Back to the Land," p. 299).

This facet of Davis's depiction of the interior Northwest he grew up in has mostly gone unchallenged, no doubt as a consequence of his stature as a writer, and it has had considerable influence. Probably, on this and other subjects, he was encouraged by his literary editor and mentor, the great iconoclast H. L. Mencken, to cultivate his own native cynical and pessimistic outlook. And maybe some of the would-be settlers he watched as a boy drifting through Wasco and Sherman counties *were* a shiftless, aimless bunch, or at least seemed so to a precocious youngster—more contemptible than pitiable, the Menckenian opposite of empire-builders. But others passing through then and there and later clearly did know where they were going and what had to be done to claim their lands, and did it, many of them, with lasting consequences; and of these the Larkins offer us a valuable example and a compelling basis for correcting H. L. Davis's ungenerous stereotypes.

Likewise (and on the other hand) the Larkins' record gives us a salient way to "adjust" the fond and often romanticized portraits of the Central Oregon homesteading experience given in many memoirs. Unmistakably, the Larkins, and their helper Jim, and no doubt later their children worked terribly hard, both on their own place and for others; and their lives as jotted down in Ethel's daily notes might seem unrelievedly bleak. Reading her spare account of what they did, physically, day by day, week after week, is daunting—a kind of vicarious ordeal in fact, for anyone familiar with old-time farm labor. How did they keep it up? Were they sometimes worn out, fed up, bored, hopeless, ready to quit? They must have had such dark moments, as well as intervals of satisfaction, even joy. But Ethel, judging from her journal-keeping style and the labors it records, seems to have been a remarkably focused individual, and likewise her partner, Gay; and if there are no frivolous, lighthearted entries or dejected asides or introspective digressions, occasionally one comes upon passages that, even in their flat language, hint at the emotional life, the downs and the ups, that they no doubt had in common with their neighbors out on the land. On Sunday, May 23, 1915, she wrote: "Sat around all day and listened to it rain." But earlier, on Sunday, June 27, 1914, she had written, "Moved out to our own ranch." And on July 20 of that year: "worked on the house and moved into it."

At such moments as these, we probably can't help wishing, as Ethel's unknown and accidental readers, that she had risen to the occasion a little, not just registering what had happened, but expressing in heightened language how she felt about it, what it meant to her. But that's a wish that's irrelevant to the document that she has left behind. In her very limited free time over six years, in Michigan and then in Oregon, she faithfully kept a daily record that basically says, on every page, "This is what we did."

Working on the Larkin journal, trying to *imagine* the living details it registers from a century ago, I have thought often of the homesteading tradition in my father's family (which by the way did not produce a diary or a journal). In important ways the Ramsey's experience as settlers here was very different from the Larkins'. They came out from northern Missouri, a decade earlier than the Larkins, in 1902 (by train to The Dalles, and then by wagons through Antelope to Madras); and, as avowed "dirt farmers," by coming early they were able to find better land, on the west side of Agency Plains, and more of it. They also came with more capital, and with the considerable advantage of being a large, extended family—grown and half-grown sons and married daughters, an uncle or two, even my grandfather Billy's elderly father John, who came out and stayed just long enough to prove up on his adjoining claim and then deed it to his son. They didn't hire out.

So, clearly, as settlers here the Ramseys were better set up from the start than the Larkins, and as they would say, they were able to "stick" to their original land and sometimes they even prospered over four generations. But at heart they were, I think, much like the Larkins: incorrigibly hard-working and frugal to a fault, stubborn as all get-out, ambitious in practical ways, neighborly, but abstinent when it came to the pursuit of pleasure. I doubt that they were acquainted with Gay and Ethel out below Blizzard Ridge (although the Ramseys were early customers of Gay's brother Ben, the Madras harness-dealer, and a 1920 "B. N. Larkin Harness and Saddles" calendar hung over my father's desk for many years); but I'd like to think that they would have understood and approved of each other, as dedicated homesteaders trying to make new homes in a hard land.

Nine
"Words Marked by a Place"
IN SEARCH OF A CENTRAL OREGON LINGO

When as children we begin to venture out beyond our family orbits, we inescapably learn by little shocks that the words we've acquired at home don't always mean the same to our playmates from other households, or don't even exist for them. When I was very small, I regularly put myself to sleep by running my thumb and forefinger along a seam of my britches, the lumpier the better, and making a monotonous little sleepy sound my family called "dudening." Until the first grade, I assumed that everybody dudened at need, and when I recommended it to my new friends at school, I was shocked that they had no idea what I was talking about.

A ruder surprise came when I discovered that the word I'd learned in my family for penis—"doojigger"—was in fact widely used, even by grown-ups, to identify all sorts of small implements and gadgets. My first reaction was acute embarrassment and indignation—to think that people would talk about private parts so casually! I think it was my older brother who explained to me that other folks didn't understand "doojigger" as I did, and in fact had other nicknames for the male part.

This early recognition that such words can arise and function in a kind of family dialect accounts, I suppose, for my lifelong fascination with the *local* dimensions of language—not just household usages like the above, but also regional vocabularies. Maybe the latter evolve over time out of the former? Both illustrate, I think, something important about the dynamics of language: the ways it can be shaped and colored by family speech and, more broadly, by all the circumstances—climate, terrain, ethnicity and race, economics, employment, and so on—that make a homeland distinctively itself. How could it be otherwise, given how intimately our words interact with how and where we actually live? As George R. Stewart says about American place-names in his classic study *Names on the Land: A Historical Account of Place-Naming in the United States,* local words and expressions seem to have "grown out of the life, and the life-blood," of the settlers of a region (p. 4).

The great American poet William Carlos Williams rejected the expatriate and internationalist agenda of his contemporaries T. S. Eliot and Ezra Pound, staying home in New Jersey and calling instead for a poetry grounded in American speech and alive to the lore of American places. Williams declared that "the local is the only thing that is universal. The classic is the local fully realized, words marked by a place" ("Kenneth Burke," p. 114). Williams is right, of course, about how the literary works we call "classics" are, for all their universality of meaning, usually firmly localized in their settings. Sophocles' last tragedy, *Oedipus at Colonus,* is set in his birthplace and hometown, just outside of Athens.

But it's Williams' notion of "words marked by a place" that especially interests me here. My home country, Central Oregon, isn't notable for the kind of distinctive accent and lingo that dialecticians and linguists celebrate in west Texas, say, or the Ozarks. Settlement here began only at the turn of the twentieth century, and the population remained sparse into the 1940s, so perhaps we're still relatively "green" in the growing of a local dialect. But as a native speaker and listener, I'm aware of words and turns of speech around here that do seem to be colorfully, expressively *local.* The fact that many of the locutions I know are associated with my own extended family may just be an accident of limited research on my part, something that a serious linguist would correct through fieldwork. If my hunch that regional dialects grow out of family usage is correct, maybe over the years our own Central Oregon dialect will be found to include local words and sayings like the ones I grew up with. What I want to stress is that, taken together, whether limited to our family or circulating over the region, they do seem to illustrate Williams' conception of "words marked by a place."

A bit of family history: My father's family came out here to homestead in 1902 from northern Missouri; farmers there for generations, they became dry-farming pioneers around Madras. The two homesteading branches of my mother's family, the McCoins and Mendenhalls, came out to Central Oregon from Kansas and eastern Tennessee, respectively, between the 1880s and 1900. The McCoins were horse-and-cattle people; the Mendenhalls (who first landed in Yamhill County) farmed, hunted, trapped, subsisted. It's probably rash to attempt to characterize whole families according to patterns of temperament, inclination, and shared ethos (although of course in small and for that matter large communities we do so all the time), but I'll risk this much. The Ramseys were *farmers* first and last—independent, ambitious, very hardworking, impatient, methodical, stubborn, and austere in outlook and manner. The McCoins, and especially the Mendenhalls, on the other hand, were generally easygoing, flexible, great lovers of hunting, fishing, and music, energetic but not notably ambitious socially or financially. What these families brought with them from their original homelands in terms of values, customs, and folkways, they largely continued in the "high desert" country of Central Oregon; but of course the realities of the new land they came to homestead challenged their old ways at every turn. And what I have inherited of their folk-speech indicates both continuity and adaptive change, the old modified but not displaced by the new, on a verbal level.

Now I'd like to open up my saddlebag of treasured words and sayings and briefly gloss some of them—if you will, one man's informal (and incomplete) contribution to some future Dictionary of Central Oregon Popular Speech. And perhaps it's simplest to begin with words, and then go on to sayings. In both categories, when I know or at least strongly suspect the family origin of a given entry, I'll say so.

We begin with words.

durgan (*noun*, Mendenhall). A severe tantrum: "When that little tyke didn't get what she wanted, she threw herself down on the floor and had a real durgan!" Generally used to indicate extremes of acting-out—rolling on the floor, screaming, holding the breath, and so on. Origins unknown; possibly derived from the Irish *dearg*, meaning red, flaming, bloody.

joober (*transitive verb, also noun*, McCoin and Mendenhall). A singing and dancing game for an adult to play with a toddler. The adult sits with spread knees and draws the child in, facing outward, then grasps the child beneath the knees and rapidly "runs" its legs up and down on the floor, while reciting variations on this song:

> Joober up and joober down,
> Joober all around the town;

Joober this and joober that,
Joober killed an alley-cat;
Joober up and Joober back,
Joober joober jumping-jack;
Joober here and joober there,
Joober joober everywhere!

Ad lib: With the last couplet, the adult might flip the child upside down with the exclamation, "Wheee!" or "Whoopee!" and then, if it wants more (usually the case), the game continues until the players have had enough.

Somehow, the practice of "joobering," which has persisted in my family for well over a century, has come down from a celebrated African American folk dance, the *juba*, which in turn seems to have originated in the cult of a West African deity by the same name. From the early nineteenth century on, mainly in the South, black performers (and later white blackface imitators) who could "pat juba" (accompanying their high-kneed dance moves by slapping themselves rhythmically) were very popular. When Charles Dickens visited New York in 1842, he saw and marveled at a famous pat-juba star named William Henry Lane, or Master Juba. How this important element of African American folk culture became a cherished children's game in an Anglo family in the far West is probably impossible to trace—but it typifies the often mysterious ways that folklore elements travel through space, time, and culture.

work-brittle (*adjective*, Ramsey). Descriptive of someone who is perceived as lazy, inclined to malingering, unwilling to "stay the course" in any job involving hard work. Part of an inventory of derogatory words used by the Ramseys and other farmers to label people who did not accept the proposition that hard work was an end in itself and a source of pride no matter how menial the job. (See also the following two entries.)

ribbon-clerk (*noun*, Ramsey). Someone, presumably male, whose job is to sell ribbons and other finery. Used with contempt to describe anyone seen as incapable by disposition or experience of "doing a man's job." Generally the usage carries with it a sexist insinuation that the subject is effeminate: "He had about as much gumption for farm work as a ribbon-clerk!" More generally, especially in modern times, used to disparage some badly designed, shoddily built tool or appliance: "Nowadays, most hand tools seem to have been designed and built by ribbon-clerks."

lollygag, **lollygagger**, **lollygagging** (*verb, noun, adjective*). A widely used expression, especially by farmers, but especially prominent in the Ramsey dialect, along with the above. A lollygagger is, in terms of the work at hand, a trifler, a slacker—distracted, nondependable, unwilling to "bow his neck" to the job (itself a favorite work term, derived from farming with harnessed mules and horses). Often, at least in my experience, associated with townspeople: "I tried to fill out my haying crew with kids from town, but they were all lollygaggers!" (See entry in *The Dictionary of American Slang*.)

heelstring nation (*noun*, Mendenhall). A homesteading-era label for a farming neighborhood seen as especially hard-pressed, impoverished, un-thriving. Among the Mendenhalls of Opal City, applied to an area to the southeast known as Trail Crossing (for a bridge nearby across Crooked River). Presumably referring to the idea that the folks there are so hard up, they're just holding on by their heelstrings. (For all I know, the citizens of Trail Crossing may have used the same label for the struggling farmers of Opal City.)

Jim Hill mustard (*noun*). When the Oregon Trunk and Des Chutes railroad crews were building their routes south from the Columbia River into Central Oregon between 1909 and 1911, one of the consequences of their presence was the appearance of a vigorous weed, apparently spread by the horses and mules used in the construction and possibly from imported hay and grain to feed them. Unchecked, the plant was capable of becoming a threat to local wheat fields, but local farmers took it in their stride and named it jokingly after James J. Hill, head of the Great Northern/Oregon Trunk. And it was soon discovered that the luxuriant sawtooth leaves of Jim Hill mustard, picked early, make delicious sharp-flavored greens, either boiled or eaten raw. Elsewhere, it was called "tumbling mustard" because, like other mustards and thistles, its leaves would dry up and curl into a ball (sometimes two feet across), and then in the winds of fall and winter, the plant would uproot itself and tumble overland for great distances, broadcasting its seeds as it rolled.

Chinese lettuce (*noun*, Ramsey). Another Central Oregon weed, *Lactuca serriola*, smaller than Jim Hill mustard and when green displaying juicy lettuce-like leaves—which are very bitter to the taste. Origins unknown; a guess would be that Chinese cooks on the early railroad construction crews in Central Oregon fancied it.

sweat-bee (*noun*, Ramsey). A small fly with oddly truncated wings—as if cut out with scissors; a serious nuisance in midsummer, especially in the range country east of the Deschutes Valley, because if allowed to land on your skin, it promptly nips out a small piece of hide and then settles down to drink the blood. Sweat-bees and horseflies can be, as the saying goes, a dynamite combination on a hot August day.

graydigger (*noun*, Ramsey and Mendenhall). Local descriptive name for the common California ground squirrel, *Spermophilus beecheyi*, which naturally nests in rimrocks but often takes up residency in barns and out-buildings and becomes a nuisance for chewing on leather and for digging up vegetable gardens.

silver thaw (*noun*, widespread). A winter-weather effect, caused by a pro-longed temperature inversion leading to dense fog, which freezes on trees, bushes, fences. A silver thaw is wonderful to see when it first appears, and especially if the fog lifts and the sun comes out to glisten in the crystalline ice (it may be that the "thaw" refers to this brief end-phase)—but if the inversion and the fog persist, day after sunless chilly day, the beauty rapidly fades, at least in the eye of the beholder.

shit-muckle-dun (*adjective*, Ramsey). A way of describing (usually with scorn) an unfamiliar or inappropriate or downright ugly color. "The neigh-bors have painted their house and barn. Looks like shit-muckle-dun to me."

old pelter (*noun*, Mendenhall). Some well-worn item, some "paltry" article of clothing or piece of machinery that the owner should probably discard, but is too fond of to do so. "I think that Fred would wear that old pelter of a coat to the President's Ball, if he was invited!" The word connects us with Elizabethan English (Shakespeare's characters speak of "poor pelt-ing villages" and "pelting farms") by way of southern Appalachia, where

Elizabethan English words and expressions (and pronunciations) have persisted.

pursy (*adjective*, usually pronounced "pussy," Mendenhall). Overweight, out-of-shape, to the point of sweating profusely. "Poor Millie, since Bob's death she's let herself get pursy-fat." Another word harking back to Shakespeare's English—Hamlet speaks of "the fatness of these pursy times."

orrey-eyed (*adjective*, Ramsey). Descriptive of someone so exasperated, so riled-up, that their eyes are, at least figuratively, fiery red. Some people are said to be "orrey-eyed" most of the time, by temperamental disposition. "Something set her off in church, and she was orrey-eyed all day." Oddly enough, in *The Dictionary of American Slang* the word is associated with "hoary-eyed," meaning "drunk."

cutthroat bread (*noun*, Mendenhall). Disparaging name for sliced bakery bread, used by someone (my grandfather Joe Mendenhall, for instance) who grew up accustomed to daily home-made biscuits.

blue-john (*noun or adjective*, Mendenhall). A local term for skim milk, etymology unknown, but obviously the "blue" describes the hue of skim milk, especially relative to the warm white of whole milk. The usage seems to indicate a strong prejudice for whole milk, as against skim: "Blue john— that's only fit for feeding hogs!"

grease gravy (*noun*, Mendenhall). Also known locally as "poverty sop," grease gravy was a staple of early homesteading cooking—made of bacon drippings, thickened with a little flour, a la the roux so crucial to Cajun cuisine. Usually served on biscuits. Presumably as homesteading families prospered and moved past subsistence-level poverty, their menus became more sophisticated—but there are still old-timers around who confess to a sentimental love of grease gravy.

pure quill (*adjective*, Mendenhall). Indicates the purest, most refined, most trustworthy form of something, whether a substance ("His brand of moonshine was always pure quill") or something intangible ("At the trial he told what happened that day, and his testimony was pure quill"). The expression apparently comes from the still-current practice of preparing both quinine and cinnamon bark for sale in rolled tubes, or "quills." The term is widely circulated, but oddly enough is not listed in *The Dictionary of American Slang*.

shuck (*transitive verb*, Mendenhall). Describes someone's abrupt and probably calculated severing of ties with another party, often a woman leaving her husband. "After Widow Jones cleaned out old Henry's bank account, she just shucked him and took off." Probably derives metaphorically from shucking husks off a corncob—done quickly and without fuss.

heavy keeper (*noun*, Ramsey). Someone, usually a woman but it could be a man, who is difficult, demanding, and expensive to maintain in a marriage or other relationship. "Everybody felt sorry for Hank because his wife was such a heavy keeper." Apparently derived from livestock terminology, in which a horse (or a cow) would be identified as costly to maintain in terms of both money and trouble.

skookum iktor (*noun*, Mendenhall). This, like the four following entries, is an instance of the assimilation into Central Oregon Anglo speech of words from Chinook Jargon, the lingua franca that was in extensive use here and throughout the Northwest as a "common language" between older Indians and their Anglo neighbors (and for that matter between Indians from different tribes), as late as the 1930s. My grandfather Joe Mendenhall, who grew up near the Grande Ronde Reservation in Yamhill County in the 1880s, spoke Jargon fluently and liked to sprinkle his stories with it for special effect. "Skookum" by itself means "mighty," "strong," "awesome"; "iktor" is an item or object. In my grandfather's usage, "skookum iktor" indicated some powerful, probably dangerous being or force.

tillikum (*noun*). In original Indian Jargon usage, "tillikum" generally meant "people" or "nation," but in Central Oregon Anglo usage at least it has come to mean "close friend."

kuitan (*noun*, pronounced "ku-i-tan"). Means "horse"; the Anglo usage probably reflects the fact that in earlier times in this region, Indians on the Warm Springs Reservation were great horse-traders to their white neighbors.

siwash (*noun*, *adjective*). From French *sauvage*, meaning "savage," "wild person." Presumably used by French speakers in the Northwest with racist overtones. But once in the Jargon vocabulary, Indians called each other "siwash" neutrally (they identified Anglos as "bostons"). Used by whites speaking English, however, the word carries a derogatory, racist edge, at least in my experience. "He always tried to horse-trade with some siwash on the reservation, and got taken every time."

muckymuck (*noun*). Chinook Jargon for food, typically (in Anglo use) a hearty meal—"Sunday dinners with them were always big muckymuck affairs." Oddly enough, the word in Anglo slang could also mean "important person," "potentate," "official," especially if the figure in question was self-important and pompous: "As an officer in the lodge, he thought of himself as a high muckymuck." Maybe the two usages are connected by associations between public figures (Indian chiefs?) and public feasts.

spizzrinktum (*noun*, Ramsey). Defined in *The Dictionary of American Slang* as "vigor," "pep," and dated to the 1940s. But my impression of family usage out here is that the word originated as teenage "flapper-era" lingo in the early 1920s, carrying on into the Depression, and serving as a kind of insider's code word, meaning "spirit," "enthusiasm," "vivacity," quite possibly in association with "hooch," "bathtub gin," and the like.

Before leaving the category of words per se, I want to register six words for which I know the origins to be strictly within my own immediate family (like the two I mentioned at the outset)—coinages, in fact, by specific individuals, but still in our familial usage after three generations, and possibly moving into wider circulation. I'm keeping an eye on them or, rather, an ear.

ti-ord (*adjective*, Ramsey). A special condition of being tired, emphasizing fatigue beyond ordinary levels. My mother, Wilma Mendenhall Ramsey, was a cheerful, energetic, and uncomplaining person, but on occasion she would let us know that she was especially "ti-ord," and needed sympathy.

punymae (*adjective*, Ramsey). In our family, someone who was "under the weather" was often described (not always very sympathetically) as being "puny," and for some reason my father (who had a Joycean appetite for torturing and combining words) took to describing himself when feeling unwell as being "punymae." His coinage was instantly popular in our household, and carries on to this day, although I'm not aware that it circulates beyond the family.

renovolate (*transitive verb*, McCoin). One day at lunch, my great-aunt Hazel, who used words exuberantly but not always precisely, reported to us how she was "renovolating" her kitchen. The force of this new word, as an indication of renovations beyond the ordinary, was immediately recognized by her listeners, and thus entered that very day into the family vocabulary, sometimes puzzling listeners who don't know our lingo.

doid (*noun*, Ramsey). The coining of words in families like mine is apparently ongoing, not just something the elders used to do. When she was very small, our eldest daughter Kate loved to play with Fisher-Price toys, many of which came with small rudimentary wooden dolls, nothing more than cylinders with heads, which fit as removable drivers or passengers into sockets in the toys. For lack of a designated word, either from Fisher-Price or us, Kate labeled these items "doids," and doids they have been ever since. I have considered offering the word to the company, to expedite inventories and customer reordering (doids are easily misplaced or lost).

crining (*participle*, Ramsey). My niece, Julie Talbot, coined this useful word as a child when she announced to her grandparents on a visit that she was not going to do any "crining" while staying with them. Small children do sometimes cry and whine simultaneously (perhaps when they are "ti-ord")—hence crining.

durrgh (*expletive*, Ramsey/Bland—spelling uncertain). One of my granddaughters, Madeleine Bland, at age eight invented an expletive for nearly every occasion (childish and adult) involving frustration, disgust, exasperation. The word is showing signs of "going viral"—through her immediate and extended family, through acquaintances as far away as England. Is it possible that durrgh has some linguistic connection with durgan (qv)?

The evolution of localisms is usually a leisurely process, like biological growth—but now and then, especially when "outside" forces are at work, familiar words can change their meanings and even their pronunciations with remarkable speed. Here are two examples of such accelerated adaptation.

yarrow—genus *Achillea*, sometimes called "whitetop," a vigorous, pungent white-flowered weed, said to have medicinal properties. Pronounced, according to all American dictionaries and in local speech until recently, to rhyme with "arrow," "sparrow," and so on. But when an upscale development was launched just east of Madras around 2000, and the developers chose "yarrow" as the brand name and emblem of their project, they insisted (against all the rules for pronouncing English vowels) on pronouncing the word with a broad *a*, as if it rhymed with "sorrow," "borrow," and the like. Whether this mispronunciation was inadvertent, the result of not knowing the word, or deliberate, as a way for PR purposes to give it a distinctive, vaguely British spin, is unknown. But whatever the reason for its sudden appearance here, "yarrow/sorrow" has pretty much prevailed hereabouts over the past decade, despite polite objections, being heard not just when natives mention the Yarrow Development, but even when farmers talk about the weeds in their fields! Maybe when linguists decide to recognize a North Central Oregon dialect, pronunciation of "yarrow" will become a defining marker, setting us off, like the Biblical test-word *shibboleth*, from speakers elsewhere in Oregon.

Muddy Ranch. This old "spread," since the early years of the last century a landmark and byword in Jefferson and Wasco counties, covered about seventy thousand acres of arid rangeland when it was owned and operated by the Prineville Land and Livestock Company. It was always to its neighbors and familiars just "the Muddy"—local folks would never have thought of calling it "the *Big* Muddy." Central and Eastern Oregon ranchers as a whole are laconic speakers, by habit given to understatement, and emphasizing the sheer size of the Muddy Ranch would have seemed like a ridiculous redundancy. Do Texans brag about their "[Big] King Ranch"?

But when the Rajneeshee cult bought the Muddy in the early 1980s, and it entered its bizarre years as the "Rajneeshpuram," visiting journalists who covered the story internationally began to identify its former self as the "Big Muddy Ranch," perhaps indulging in a little Hollywood-style verbal hype. The Rajneesh phase passed, happily, and the ranch is now a Christian youth camp, but "Big Muddy" has become, in just a couple of decades, the nearly universal original name for it. So, it seems, our words can rapidly change, bend, and twist under pressure of local usage, the objections of linguistic purists notwithstanding!

Now let's move on to phrases and sayings.

If a man . . . (Ramsey). This phrase, much used by my father and his kin-folks, and I think by local farmers generally, always introduced a theoretical proposal to be discussed as a possible solution to some farming or ranch-ing challenge. "If a man could somehow get rid of that rockpile, the corral could be built out another fifty feet at least."

I've worked so hard [in the sun], I've bleached my eyebrows! (Ramsey). This was actually declared (without irony) by a cousin who, although as strong as Li'l Abner, and the family's premier workaholic, did like to complain about his farming labors. It immediately entered the fam-ily dialect as a self-mocking exaggerated complaint.

If your nose itches, somebody's coming with a hole in his britches! (Ramsey, Mendenhall). This widespread expression probably had nearly 100 percent predictive power in early homesteading days, when britches would be worn and patched until—in another family saying—the britches were "more holes than otherwise."

cold as a blue flujeon; hot as the hubs of Hell (Ramsey). The men in my dad's family were in general given to exaggerating in their talk, espe-cially when holding forth together at family gatherings. I suspect both of these seasonal complaints were brought along to Central Oregon from Missouri. The second one has a nice fundamentalist biblical ring to it; the first is all the more evocative for being so mysterious. What is a "flujeon" (and I'm not sure about the spelling), and what color is it before extreme cold turns it blue? (I might add here that the tendency of our family's men to exaggerate became especially dramatic when they had something to swear about together. Then—or so it seemed to me as a child, eavesdropping—our generally flat laconic discourse expanded amazingly, became alarmingly inventive, and, as our saying had it, "the air turned blue," not for cold, but for heat!)

cuss, cry, and throw rocks (Ramsey). A popular epithet for someone recalling being terminally exasperated by some frustration on the job. At the moment of the screwup, there would be profanity, of course; then later this milder but alliteratively satisfying expression would come into play as a way of sharing the experience: "When the motor on the combine threw a rod just as we were about to finish harvesting, I tell you, I wanted to cuss, cry, and throw rocks!" There is a local story about a logger who went into the woods one morning to finish a job by himself, and everything went wrong. A tree fell sideways and pinched his chainsaw; his spare saw refused to start, and he'd forgotten to bring his tool kit; and then he noticed that his truck had a flat tire. He was ready to cuss (if not cry and throw rocks), but he lacked somebody or something to swear at. So he whittled a wooden peg about the size of a carrot, drove it into a nearby stump, and swore at *that* until he felt better and could get on with the job.

Now wouldn't that rasp ya? (Ramsey). Another favorite "clincher" in my family for some anecdote of irritation or exasperation. "When we broke down, the John Deere parts man ordered the wrong replacement parts, and they wouldn't fit—now wouldn't that rasp ya?!"

draggin' a hind foot (McCoin). Occasionally a cow or calf will suffer partial paralysis from injury or some malady, and thus drag a foot in walking. This expression was used to indicate reluctance about doing something, perhaps based on a sense of being incapable. "Tom said he would take Stan's sister to the Prom, but he's sure draggin' a hind foot about it!"

Looks like he smelled a wolf (Ramsey). Descriptive of someone whose hair is uncombed and standing on end, and also by metaphorical extension of someone who has been badly scared. Probably a very old expression: How long has it been since anybody in these parts actually observed a dog's reaction to catching the scent of a wolf?

I look like the Witch of Endor (Ramsey). My grandmother, Clara Yokum Ramsey, a great student of the Bible, liked to use this expression when an unexpected visitor found her with her hair uncombed and her old house-dress on. In Second Samuel, the Witch of Endor eerily prophesies to King Saul about his impending doom.

I see, says the blindman (Mendenhall). I've heard this expression used to suggest the experience of perceiving something not with the eyes but with the heart, much as Gloucester in *King Lear* exclaims that, although blinded, he now "sees feelingly." But in my family and roundabout it is more frequently used ironically to say just the opposite: that is, "I really don't understand what you're saying, any more than a blind person can see with his eyes."

I'm still kickin', but I'm not raisin' much dust (McCoin). Frequently used to good effect by Aunt Minnie McCoin Helfrich when she was well past ninety and casual well-wishers would ask her how she was doing. It's entirely possible, given her verbal gifts, that she made it up, but in any event it seems to be, forty years after her death, in wide circulation.

Eat the best food first (Mendenhall). A joking expression much used in the Mendenhall family. Even in jest it evokes the family's lighthearted, unprogrammatic approach to any outdoor adventure involving camping out and packing food—fishing, hunting, hiking. As a traditional dictum, it was always mentioned early on in the outing; I don't recall that we ever followed it, but it was a useful challenge, a sort of strategic reminder of alternatives. In the nature of packing (at least before the advent of freeze-dried food), most of the "best food" (fresh fruit and vegetables, meat) was the most perishable and probably wouldn't last over the whole trip, especially in hot weather. But eating "best first" would mean that what was left afterward would be mostly dry and canned stuff, dried beans and peas, macaroni and such, probably sustaining, but not very palatable. Once when my Uncle Max ritually proposed that we might go "best first" in our meals, I asked him what we would do after that? He answered, "Go home, I guess." The trick, as we both knew, was to maintain, meal by meal, a strategic balance between the fragile delicacies of the really good provender and the rest of our larder, extending the former as long as possible without letting it spoil.

Go back and run again (McCoin, Mendenhall). This cherished little saying is based on an anecdote dating back to the 1880s, and its persistence in our family illustrates the amazing durability of such things in oral tradition—always just one generation, after all, from oblivion. It embodies, as well as any of the words and sayings I've offered here, what I mean by "words marked by a place." Sometime in the late 1880s, at Gray Butte School on the northeast slopes of Gray Butte in Central Oregon, my grandmother Ella McCoin and her sister Minnie attended a "play-day" at the school (at which they were pupils), probably in the spring to be sure of good weather. These school play-days were eagerly anticipated community events that featured a potluck picnic, singing, games, athletic events like baseball and running races, and prizes. Aunt Minnie recalled that the boys' footrace was won by a boy whose family was the poorest, most hardscrabble family in the whole area. The prize was a big bag of "store-boughten" candy, and when the winner stepped up to claim the prize, his mother was heard to say to him, very seriously and with no trace of irony or amusement, "Go back and run again!"

So the saying was launched into the family memory, and although its modern usage has changed somewhat, meaning something like "Congratulations—and continue your good efforts!" it still, I think, retains something of the long-ago poignancy of the original story, wherein a little boy from an impoverished homesteading household once won a fine prize for himself and his family.

Other "localized" words and expressions come to mind spontaneously, almost never by my trying to summon them consciously, but just in the daily skirmish with language to say, or write, what needs to be said. I've learned that if I don't write them down when they appear, they just slip back into the mysterious pool where our occasional words lurk until their occasion arrives. But I hope that these few instances from my word-hoard will provoke my readers, especially those with Central Oregon roots, to consider their own special usages. Does anybody, I'm wondering, recognize any of these odd constructions from their own family or regional experience? And what vivid analogues and equivalents, I wonder, do you know for "blue flujeon" and "joober" and "go back and run again"—word artifacts marked, like them, by living where and how we have lived?

Ten
Farmers and Old Iron

On any old farmstead around here—ours, for example—if the fancy strikes you, you can tie a string on to a child's horseshoe magnet and idly drag it through the dry dirt in the yards and between buildings, and find it magically "whiskered" on both poles with tiny fragments of iron and steel.

After I tried this procedure a few times as a small boy, I was ready to conclude that our thin soil was hiding a fabulous undiscovered deposit of iron ore, like in northern Minnesota. My father told me he didn't think so, and offered an alternative explanation: that the "whiskers" on my magnet were mostly from iron and steel remnants, accumulated from odds and ends of equipment and scrap metal that had simply gone into the dirt over many decades of farming and householding. That seemed to me to be nearly as far-fetched as my iron ore hypothesis; but as usual, he was telling me the plain truth. When I experimentally dragged my magnet away from the farmstead, out in our fields and in the sagebrush, there was very little if any accumulation of iron filings.

But I had begun to wonder, what is it about farmers and iron? And I have come to think that there must be a very profound and ancient bond between the tillers of the soil and the ferrous metals that have made up their implements at least since the Industrial Revolution, and probably before. When John Deere invented the first moldboard plow, did he know that the rusty residue of his handiwork and that of his successors would literally become part of the soil they were meant to till? One wonders if archaeologists in the far distant, postapocalyptic future will sift through and analyze our Western agricultural sites and conclude that we were part of another Iron Age.

No doubt this affinity expresses itself in the passion of some farmers in the West and Midwest for collecting and restoring antique tractors and farm machinery, and proudly showing them off in annual threshing bees, plowing contests, and so on. But underneath all that devoted attention to ancient machines pulses, I think, a profound attachment to iron itself.

In the earliest, pre-railroad days of dry-farming in the interior of Oregon, of course, wood and leather were at least as important for the farmers' implements as cast iron. But with the arrival of the railroads in 1911, an age of "heavy metal" began, so to speak, with big plows, disks, cultivators, reapers, and grain separators arriving by the trainload and, after World War I, gasoline-powered tractors and combines. All were made of cast iron and steel, and generally on a monumental scale. My grandfather Mendenhall's first tractor, a Holt, as I recall, stood for years in rusty splendor in the yard behind his house after it wore out, an irresistible lodestone for every kid who came around. From the massive seat, there were pedals to stomp on and levers to yank, but it was so heavy on its massive wheels that none of us was strong enough to budge the big steering wheel. Eventually, it was hauled away by an antique tractor aficionado, who intended to restore it. I wish I could have taken it for a slow-motion spin around the south forty when he got it running!

The soil of much of Central Oregon, once cleared of brush and junipers, was found to be very hard on machinery, being abrasive and rocky, so plowshares, disks, weeder-rods, and so on wore out rapidly; by the late 1920s the bigger farms began to accumulate derelict machinery and parts thereof. Many of them designated remote corners of their properties and created what might be called "machinery boneyards," analogous to the legendary

Header in operation, with header box alongside, ca. 1912 (Luelling photo)

Derelict header at a machinery boneyard today

"elephant cemeteries" of Africa, where (supposedly) aging elephants go to die, leaving their bones in a kind of collective monument.

Our boneyard, over on the western rim of Agency Plains, drew from several branches of the family, and so by the time I had reached boyhood it had become impressive in both size and variety of junked machinery. There was a rusticated Model T truck, fondly remembered as "Old Gertie"; there were various iron-shod farm wagons, including (I was told) the "California rack" that carried the Advance Guard of the Ramsey clan in 1902 from the railhead at The Dalles south into Central Oregon. There were horse-drawn plows, disks, harrows, and weeders; and a strange-looking T-shaped "header" used during the first phase of harvesting grain, before the advent of combines.

This contraption consisted of a twelve-foot-wide sickle bar and reel, with an endless "draper" belt to convey the cut grain-heads sideways onto a low-sided "header wagon" running alongside. When this wagon was full it carried the load of grain-heads to the stationary separator to be thrashed into grain, and another wagon took its place, and so on. What was strange about the header itself was that it was mounted on the front end of a long metal beam or tube, on either side of which two or more pairs of horses were hitched, so that they *pushed* the header from behind, thereby facilitating careful steering through the field of grain, and of course allowing the horses to walk on stubble, rather than trampling down uncut grain.

One of the front wheels was a "bull-wheel" that drove the sickle-bar, reel, and draper-belt, by "ground power" as it moved forward. The rear end of the beam projecting back from the header framework rode on one or two smaller wheels, and the operator (who had to drive the horses, adjust the height of the sickle-bar, and steer everything around the field) perched insecurely up on a little elevated seat mounted over the rear wheels, high enough in the air that he could see over the horses and the machinery in front of him. The header was an ingenious if goofy-looking short-term transitional expedient between mowing and binding cut sheaves of grain and moving them in wagons to the separator, and the efficient all-in-one "combine" harvesters that became standard in the late 1920s and 1930s. It must have worked reasonably well on local farms during its brief heyday—but I remain curious about how it was steered, and how teams of work-horses, trained and harnessed to pull heavy loads behind them, adjusted instead to pushing the header around and around a field of grain.

The main iron specimen in our machinery boneyard (and in many others like it) was a stationary separator, another relic from the earliest pre-combine days. Ours, made by McCormick-Deering (soon to become International Harvester) was a huge, ungainly, dragonish thing, upwards of fifty feet long and ten feet high, its body made as much of wood as of metal, with sprockets, pulleys, ratchets, levers, and removable hatches protruding from one end to the other, and a twenty-foot length of jointed metal pipe mounted at the rear. This was the pipe for blowing chaff away from the separator when it was thrashing grain; for travel between fields, it was folded forward and stowed along the top, like the tail of a sleeping dragon, or so I fancied.

When in transit, the machine rolled on four iron wheels, with a wagon tongue fastened to the front axle, which pivoted for steering. Everything about separators converged on a clumsy functionality, geared to their single purpose of taking in pitchforks-full of wheat or barley stalks, violently whirling and sifting and blowing the dry kernels away from the heads, directing the separated grain to a side vent where sacks of grain were filled up, rapidly sewn shut by hand, and carried off to the warehouse, while the chaff pipe blew the chaff on to a growing pile off to one side and a dense cloud of dust filtered down on everything and everybody. What powered

Old grain separator on Agency Plains today

all the fans, beaters, and conveyors? A heavy and potentially very dangerous flat belt ran from the main power pulley to a steam or gasoline tractor
stationed thirty or forty feet behind the machine. You didn't want to be
close at hand if the belt slipped off under load and came flying, as it liked to
do if the separator and the tractor weren't exactly aligned.

Functional it was, although by report a working nightmare to maintain
and keep adjusted. But on our separator's undercarriage and wheels you
can still see, after a century of weathering, a whimsical, decidedly nonfunc-
tional touch: delicate hand-painted curlicues and spangles, in faded reds
and yellows, as if on a circus wagon. Somebody at the McCormick separator works in Chicago must have believed that art had to assert its claims
even in the vast wheat fields of the West. Whether my father's family, self-
described "dirt farmers" from Missouri appreciated this creative touch on
their separator, they never said.

Underfoot in the boneyard, or leaning against the implements, were
bits and pieces of old machinery: flanges, gears large and small, splined
drive shafts, cams, sprockets and chains, clevises, bearings, worn-down
cultivator disks, mysterious inspection plates, angle iron, bolts of every
size—all slowly rusting into the soil. To a mechanically inclined child it

was of course endlessly fascinating; often, in our missions to the site after possible spare parts and otherwise usable metal, my father and I would scrounge among these miscellaneous castoffs down in the weeds, and find more than we needed.

No doubt, at bottom, these family junkyards came into being out of convenience—simpler to pile up your worn-out equipment and scrap metal somewhere beyond the farmstead than to try to dispose of it. But the ingrained frugality of farmers, and a persistent intuition that if you save such stuff, down the line you might be able to cobble it up for some purpose requiring iron or steel, were also parts of the junkyard equation. One of the farming essentials that my grandfather brought out from Missouri to his Oregon homestead was a complete blacksmith's shop—forge and bellows, anvil, vise, hand operated drill press, and assorted iron-mongering tools. I don't know how skilled he and his older sons were at the forge (my father didn't follow their lead), but we still have, and regularly use, handy implements they remade from scrap, notably prybars and post-hole-digging tools reforged and hammered out of old drive shafts and hexagonal railroad construction hand drill-rods, the latter courtesy of Jim Hill's Oregon Trunk Railroad.

During harvest, when breakdowns were frequent and time was short, we made emergency visits in search of some piece or fitting that might serve as at least a temporary replacement or brace for something broken or bent on our combines. But our recycling of old metal wasn't always so driven by necessity. On the frivolous side of the ledger, for years our family Christmas trees were mounted on a heavy toothed drive gear from an old grain drill. When a schoolmate and I determined to build a revolutionary three-wheeled go-cart in our high school shop class, we appropriated Old Gertie's steering wheel for the project. (Eventually what was left of Gertie was given to a Model T enthusiast, and she was restored enough to appear—and often break down—in local parades.)

In the late 1930s, the Japanese government conducted extensive scrap-metal drives throughout the West. I don't know whether Japanese buyers were visible in these campaigns or they worked behind the scenes through American agents, but they offered undeniably good prices. Nonetheless, my dad and uncle and in fact most local farmers refused to deal, in part because, with the Japanese already in a warlike posture, they were suspicious of the buyers' purposes, but primarily, I think, because they were not willing to diminish their hoard of useful farm junk, even for cash. As it happened, in October 1940 an official US embargo on sale of scrap metal to Japan ended this campaign, but probably not before shiploads of cast-off American farm implements were sent across the Pacific for the making of Japanese ships, planes, and bombs.

After the war, another challenge to our boneyards appeared, with the arrival of a new generation of enterprising young farmers, many of them ex-GIs, who moved from elsewhere in the Northwest to take advantage of the opening of the North Unit Irrigation District. Like the first generation of dry-farmers a half century earlier, the newcomers had left their own farmstead scrap iron behind when they moved to Central Oregon. It didn't take some of them long to discover bountiful junk piles like ours, especially tempting when they were located out on the far edge of some remote field. It's hard at this distance to fairly sort out the ethics of what happened next. Perhaps the newcomers brought with them a different concept of derelict machinery and ownership thereof, a sort of "one man's junk/another man's treasure" attitude. But whatever their understanding, family machinery piles began to be visited without permission; items were removed, in identifiable pickups; unlicensed scavengers were caught more than once rusty-handed; and the county sheriff on at least one occasion was summoned to stop the raids. They stopped, short of arrests and lawsuits, and the community absorbed its scrap-iron crisis and moved on more or less harmoniously into the brave new world of irrigated farming together.

For the old-timers, however, one grievance persisted: in the course of their trespassing, a few of the borrowers had helped themselves to wagon wheels from old wagons on the sites, and these rustic trophies were promptly built into picturesque front-yard fences at several new farms in our neighborhood. Sure enough, our family's heirloom "California rack" was found to be sitting in the boneyard on its axles. But nothing could be proved, and in the interest of harmony, if not forgiveness, my mother instructed us to look the other way when we drove by those places.

At least, I thought, they didn't make off with our iron treasures. At the heart of my recollections of going with my dad on missions to the machinery pile is an impression that we went there on serious business, to a place where a certain solemnity was called for. Whatever our practical purposes for coming were (armed as we usually were with wrenches, prybars, and hacksaws), I understood that we were certainly not coming over here as

casual scavengers. My dad invariably pointed out relics like the giant separator and the California rack, and repeated their stories for my benefit.
Here was the first moldboard plow they'd used, better suited as it turned
out for the deep soils of the Midwest than out here, the sensuous curves
of its steel shares still dimly gleaming, polished by the mineral soil that
wore them out. Over there were the remains of a grain-drill that, he said,
had sowed the family's first big wheat crop, behind a team of horses whose
feeding, watering, and grooming was his job, age eleven.

Just old rusty metal, long since replaced by fancier machines with styl-
ish paint jobs, made of high-carbon steel, aluminum, even fiberglass and
plastic. But these angular shapes of old iron—he rested his hand on them
as he talked—"They were the first farm implements we had out here, all we
had to work the land with at first, and they did the job pretty well. Anyway,
they were made of good iron."

When we had found the piece we'd come for, and pried it loose, and
were ready to head for home, we usually left in silence.

Eleven
Rowboat Rescue on the Deschutes, 1940

The mountains, cliffs, canyons, and rivers of Central Oregon have drawn outdoor adventurers for well over a century, and inevitably there have been accidents, leading to major rescue efforts, both successful and unsuccessful. Of the former, for sheer do-or-die drama nothing equals the rescue of a badly injured young fisherman by rowboat, down the as-yet-wild Crooked and Deschutes Rivers, in 1940—and yet the story is all but forgotten now.

Sadaki "Doc" Akiyama grew up in Opal City and Culver and attended Culver High School in the 1930s with three brothers, Yasamasa, Utaka, and Minoru, and a sister, Tokiko. They were the children of Japanese immigrants from the Hiroshima area; Mr. Akiyama worked for the railroad.

July 28, 1940, was a Sunday, and Doc and some Culver High chums (including Ted Freeman and Rex Barber) decided they would go fishing below The Cove at the bottom of Crooked River Gorge, where the tidy fields and orchards developed by William Boegli (first judge of Jefferson County) had just become a state park. The boys, each probably carrying a wicker creel, bamboo fly rod, and a tobacco can of grasshoppers, parked by The Cove Bridge and started fishing down the rocky east bank. Somewhere near Kettle Rock on the way down to the junction with the Deschutes, Doc slipped while negotiating one of the numerous "shut-ins," riverside cliffs that made for hard going along the Crooked River, and fell thirty feet, to river level. When his fishing buddies reached him, he was in agony, with what seemed to be serious injuries to his back and one hand.

What to do? In those days, before the building of the Round Butte and Pelton Dams and the flooding of the Crooked, Deschutes, and Metolius Rivers, there was no easy prospect of rescue by water—and there were no service roads downriver from The Cove, or up the Deschutes. Several miles below on the Deschutes, near where Round Butte Dam is located, there was a famous fishing "glory hole" named Big Eddy, to which a well-made

Crooked River downstream from The Cove, before the dams. Courtesy Gifford Photograph Collection, OSU Libraries Special Collections and Archives Research Center

livestock trail had recently been built by US Resettlement Administration workers—but it was a long switchbacked trail out of the canyon from there, and Doc's injuries must have seemed too serious for rescue by horse and litter.

So one or two of his friends scrambled back up to The Cove, and from there drove into Culver and then Madras to alert the authorities—including Jefferson County sheriff Henry Dussault. The others, including Ted Freeman and Rex Barber, stayed on the river to do what they could for their

injured friend. As time wore on and night came, they built a warming fire
in a thicket of bushes nearby. It's not clear from contemporary reports, but
apparently some men from Culver, including Virgil Messinger and Merritt
Freeman (Ted's dad) hiked down to the accident site to offer support.

Meanwhile Sheriff Dussault had contacted his friend Thaddeus "Thad"
Dizney, Madras City watermaster and an experienced river-boatman.
Carrying Doc Akiyama out by boat—down into the Deschutes and so on
down fifteen miles of wild water to the Dizney place above Cowles Orchard
(today's popular raft-and-driftboat ramp, just off Highway 26)—seemed,
given what they knew about the boy's condition, the only alternative for
getting him out.

Had Dizney or anybody else ever attempted to run that stretch of swift
and rock-studded water, especially in summer's low water levels? Possibly
Thad had—certainly he knew the stretch from having bank-fished along it.
Another candidate would be my late uncle, Max Mendenhall, of Opal City,
who in 1937 had acquired an early model of the German-made Klepper
"Folbot" for the express purpose of running local rivers; and family tradition has it that sometime before World War II he set out from The Cove in
this collapsible, light, elegant rubber-hulled kayak, with a companion, possibly a friend from Max's recent stint with the CCC on the Oregon coast.

The nameless companion was soon so terrified by the unpredictable
power of the river that he demanded to be put ashore at the next stretch of
quiet water. So, somewhere near the confluence with the Deschutes, Max
landed on the east bank, and his distraught passenger was last seen scram-
bling up the steep slopes toward the rim, not looking back. With no place
to take out and retrieve the Folbot, it appears that Max continued his now-
solo run all the way down to Dizney's place or Cowles Orchard. He never
attempted it again, as far as anybody knows, and the Klepper was thereafter
relegated to occasional light-duty fishing use on lakes. Eventually he gave
it to me, and after eighty years, it's still a seaworthy work of art. Extremely
long, narrow, with canvas decking, it would not have been usable for a river
rescue even in its prime.

But now, in our story from 1940, it's the morning after Doc Akiyama's
accident, July 29, and at dawn Sheriff Dussault and Thad Dizney have
arrived with Thad's rowboat and a stretcher at The Cove Bridge. They make
an awkward launch into the river, and almost immediately Thad loses control and the boat crashes into a boulder, knocking several big holes in its

flat plywood bottom. Somehow getting it back to shore before it sinks, they hoist it up on rocks to dry and run back to their car. An hour or so later, they're in Madras, loading pieces of plywood, screws and nails, and some tools, and sometime around ten or eleven o'clock they're back at the boat, patching it as best they can.

For the second try, Dizney apparently decides that the rescue's chances will be improved this time if he goes alone. Both he and Dussault are big rangy men, and at least until he reaches Doc Akiyama, he'll navigate better without a passenger. This time he's able to oar his way through the initial rapids and swells and around the rocks, and reaches Doc and his friends under Kettle Rock about noon.

One of the friends, Ted Freeman, remembers that when the injured boy understood that the plan was to carry him out by rowboat, he adamantly refused—until Thad, a steady man with a calm manner, told him that under the circumstances he didn't have a choice, if he wanted to get out. So somehow he was eased into the stretcher, and placed as gently as possible in the stern of the boat, with his head against the transom, looking back over his feet at Thad amidships at the oars. (Almost certainly, Thad ran his rivers as modern driftboaters do, facing downstream with the blunt stern forward, to create some drag. And it was just as well that, if he was looking around at all, poor Doc could look only upstream, where they'd been, not downstream, the perilous way they were going.)

The others got them launched, irretrievably—down in rapid-y water past the mouth of the Deschutes, and another mile and a half or so past the influx of the Metolius, and by now the volume and force of the combined rivers were substantially increased. This would have been both advantageous (more water to maneuver in, around rocks) and disadvantageous (more sheer hydraulic force to cope with). What was Thad Dizney thinking about, in the occasional calm stretches when he wasn't flailing with his oars between boulders and whirlpools? Whatever he was thinking, underlying it all was the visceral certainty that if they capsized, or were caught broadside against a rock, he couldn't possibly save his injured passenger, or himself, for that matter, and there would be no witnesses. Did he, avid angler that he was, try to calm his nerves by prospecting for good holes and riffles as they flew past? Did he try to converse with Doc, to keep his spirits up?

It's about fifteen miles on the map from The Cove down to their destination of the Dizney place—probably a fair bit more than that, given the

Rescue Boat Wins Over Treacherous River

The bandaged and blanketed figure in the stern of the boat, above, is that of 20-year-old Sadaki Akiyama of Culver, who fell off a cliff near the Deschutes river while on a fishing expedition July 28 and who was rescued by Thad Dizney and Henry A. Dussault in a spectacular trip down the river to the landing at Dizney's ranch near the Warm Springs reservation. The oarsman is Mr. Dizney.

Thad Dizney and Doc Akiyama, their rowboat ordeal just ended (Madras *Pioneer* photo)

zigs and zags of the river's route in its canyon. It's possible that Thad briefly put ashore at Big Eddy, to stretch himself and attend to Doc. But if so, it was quickly back into the river, with some of the most dangerous stretches lurking ahead, where the river narrows and accelerates through the Pelton Dam site.

Probably it's in this long, harrowing passage that they encountered the near-catastrophes that the *Pioneer* mentioned in its August 1 front-page news coverage: "The trip nearly ended disastrously several times in turbulent rapids, and only Dizney's skill and knowledge of the river brought the craft safely to the landing 15 miles downstream."

But finally they were through the worst of it and into more civilized waters, past the mouths of Seekseekwa and Campbell Creeks, and at last in sight of the Dizney place, where Thad had grown up and first learned to manage rowboats on the river. A waving and cheering crowd welcomed them ashore. It was by now midafternoon.

The *Pioneer*'s page-1 photo in the August 8 issue is fuzzy, but shows the little boat apparently at the moment of arrival, with Thad still grasping the oars, and Doc Akiyama with his knees bent under a blanket, and his arms raised, shading his face, the poles of the stretcher under him sticking out over the transom. From here on, Sheriff Dussault must have taken over:

Doc was rushed to the hospital in Redmond, where his broken back and broken hand were diagnosed and treated. In a follow-up in the August 8 issue, the *Pioneer* reported that he was "recovering nicely."

Remember his Culver friends, Rex Barber and Ted Freeman, building a warming fire in some dry bushes the night after his accident? The bushes were actually poison oak, and after a night of inhaling poisonous smoke the boys soon had their own medical problem, as serious, albeit short-term, as their friend's injuries. Their air passages swelled up to the point that they had extreme difficulties breathing, and both needed medical attention after they got out. In an item from "Culver News" in the August 8 *Pioneer*, it's reported that "Rex Barber was released to his home here Saturday from Redmond Hospital, where he was a patient for several days with a severe case of poison ivy [*sic*]." For some reason, the circumstances of his affliction—his part in the rescue of his friend Doc—is not mentioned.

So the Great Rowboat Rescue of 1940 came to a happy end for everybody involved. But the details that make up what we think of as "local history" sometimes communicate mysteriously with the forces and patterns of history at large, and this story, seemingly complete in itself, soon took on larger meanings for some of its players. Before his rescue mission, Thad Dizney was locally well-known as a Deschutes riverman and guide, but in the 1940s and 1950s his renown grew, maybe in part because of his exploit in late July 1940, and he gained numerous celebrity clients, notably the famous stockbroker and investment guru Dean Witter, who regularly came up from San Francisco to fish the Deschutes and other Oregon rivers with him. In his memoir, *Meanderings of a Fisherman* (1974), Witter wrote gratefully about his fishing outings with Dizney—who died in 1961.

And Rex Barber: three years after helping to save his schoolfriend, he was flying P-38 Lightnings against the Japanese in the South Pacific. He became an ace and is credited with shooting down the mastermind of the attack on Pearl Harbor, Admiral Yamamoto. After an illustrious career in the air force, he moved back to Culver, where he served for a time as mayor, and died in 2001.

And Doc himself? A few months after Pearl Harbor, and less than two years after his adventure on the river, enactment of the War Relocation Act of 1942 meant that he and the entire Akiyama family were forced to leave their home in Culver and go into a Japanese internment camp in Tulelake, California, and then to another camp in Idaho, where they spent most of the war behind barbed wire. After the internment camps were closed in January 1945, the Akiyamas came back to Culver to reclaim the family car and other possessions, which they had left with the Freeman family, and moved to Spokane, where Mr. Akiyama and three of his sons worked for the Spokane, Portland & Seattle Railway. Doc, however, moved to Chicago, where he worked for the Japanese consulate there until he retired and moved back to Spokane to be with his family. He never married, and passed away in 2003.

The War Relocation Act was declared unconstitutional by the US Supreme Court (a few days after the internment camps were closed), but Doc Akiyama's story still, after three-quarters of a century, conveys a painful irony. His life was once saved, unconditionally, by his friends and neighbors, and by Thad Dizney, who probably didn't know him before the accident. And yet his government thereafter suspended his rights as an American citizen and incarcerated him and thousands of others without due process for being Japanese American. That's what happened to him, in 1940 and during the war, and it's left for us to try to make sense of the raw historical contradiction in his story.

Twelve
Airacobra

IN MEMORIAM 2ND LIEUTENANT
ROBERT L. CRANSTON, 1924–1944

I

Begin with the bare, unaccommodated memories, so far as I can find and focus them, after sixty-four years.

It is a raw, windy early-spring afternoon in 1944. I am six and a half years old and in the first grade. My father has picked me up at our little one-room school on the north end of Agency Plains; for some reason, my older brother Jim is not at the school to be picked up with me. On the way home, we stop to visit with our neighbor Floyd Evick at his place along the Market Road. As I remember it, Floyd and Dad are leaning against the pickup, talking, and I am standing alongside them, craning my neck to watch the aerobatics of an airplane nearly overhead, so high that all I can see are sun-flashes off the cockpit and propeller, and only then when there are gaps in the broken clouds. But I have already identified the plane as a Bell P-39 Airacobra, from a newly arrived squadron of them at the Madras Army Air Field at the south end of Agency Plains. I think it is a neat fighter, and I am already drawing pictures of it in my school books, with its bullet nose and unusual placement of the engine behind the pilot, and its small size, not as wide in the wings, even, as a Piper Cub.

Now, its maneuvers apparently completed, the plane pushes over into a power dive, and the noise of the engine revving up grows louder by the second. Dad and Floyd stop talking to watch it, and after a few seconds one of them says "I don't think he's going to pull out!" I remember a feeling of weakness, of helplessness, as if I am in the hurtling airplane, and then it

crashes, about half a mile east and a little north of where we stand. There
is a distant concussion, and a cloud of dust from the impact, but I see no
explosion and no smoke.

Dad and Floyd jump in the pickup, and I climb in the back, where I like
to ride when I'm allowed to, and we tear up the Market Road to the cross-
roads, and then east up Klann Road. As we near the crash site, on the north
side of the road in one of Fred Klann's wheat fields, near an old rock pile, I
can see wisps of steam and smoke coming out of the ground, but there is
nothing that looks like an airplane, just some twisted units of metal.

I jump out of the pickup bed and run across the borrow-pit and through
the barbed-wire fence before my dad and Floyd are even out of their seats. If
Dad yells at me to come back, I don't hear him.

The first piece of wreckage I come to, about a hundred yards into the
field, is the pilot's body. He is on his back, and still strapped in his seat, in
a shallow crater; and although his body is askew, his limbs flung out at odd
angles, he doesn't look broken up. He is wearing a flying suit or coveralls,
and a pilot's cloth helmet. As I draw near enough to see his face, there is
blood on it, and his eyes are open, staring at nothing, and there is dirt on
them. The fact that he's not brushing or blinking the dirt off his eyes is what
tells me that the pilot is dead.

By this time, Dad catches up, and pulls me back. As I recall it, he and
Floyd and I inspect from a safe distance the other pieces of the wreckage,
which are partly buried in their own craters, with steam and thin smoke rising over them, and the clicking sound of cooling metal. Then we get back in
the pickup and drive the five miles to the air base to report the crash.

I have to stay in the pickup while Dad and Floyd go past the MPs to talk
to the base commander. While they are gone, I think about what I've seen,
and what I will be able to tell my schoolmates the next day, but mainly I am
seeing the pilot's eyes. When Dad and Floyd finally come back, they are
talking about how, after they had given their statements, the commander
picked up his phone, dialed a number, and told someone on the other end
that there had been too many accidents with this plane, and he didn't want
any more of them on the base. After we take Floyd back to his place, we drive
back to ours, and Dad and I take unequal turns reporting to Mom and my
older brother.

At school the next day, Jim and I and the other boys hike up to the crash
site at lunch time, but there are soldiers all around, and they tell us to leave.

The next day, we come back, and find the site unattended. The pilot's body is gone, I can see as we cross the fence, but the wreckage is still there, so after inspecting it we each carry off a small piece of aluminum from the fuselage, painted military olive drab on the outside and bright yellow on the inside. They must have seemed precious to us then, those guilty souvenirs, but I'm unable to tell you what has become of mine.

II

Not surprisingly, I had nightmares about what I'd seen that afternoon, but I don't recall ever discussing the crash with my father again, maybe because it had gone in deep like a wound. In a few days the wreckage was carried away somewhere, by the air base I guess, and within a month the Klann's field was turning green with the year's new crop of wheat, which grew, ripened into yellow, and was harvested late that summer, as if nothing had fallen out of the sky along the road. But for several years pieces of metal would turn up when that stretch of the field was disked or plowed.

The next year, 1945, the war ended, just after wheat harvest, and the air base closed down abruptly, almost overnight it seemed. The sky over Agency Plains, once so busy and noisy with B-17 bombers and P-39 and P-38 fighters, was empty and silent again. Years ran on into years, and whenever I happened to tell the story of the crash to college friends and then to my own children, I would reflect, idly, on what I'd seen, and what I didn't know. Who was the poor pilot, where was he from? And what went wrong, so that he and his Airacobra lost their negotiated control of the air and plummeted two miles straight down into a farmer's planted wheat field? What if he'd pulled out, and landed, and finished his training, and been shipped out with his squadron in 1944 to Europe or the Pacific? Would he have gone on, using the skills he'd mastered flying over the fields and canyons of Central Oregon, to become an ace, like our family friend Rex Barber, who flew Airacobras over Guadalcanal before stepping up to the bigger, faster P-38 Lightning?

When I began to write poetry, and thus began ransacking my memory for things I'd been "given" to write about, inevitably I landed on the crash, and projected a long philosophical poem to be inspired by Charles Olson's "As the Dead Prey Upon Us," in which the poet tries by sheer force of imagination to levitate an abandoned car up and out of his dead mother's backyard. My efforts to do the same with the fragmented fighter plane in Klann's field didn't get very far. When I first read Kurt Vonnegut's *Slaughterhouse Five* and came upon the celebrated passage where he imagines reversing the events of a World War II bombing raid, as if in a film running backward, the bombers sucking up their bombs, or reassembling in the air after their crashes, flying backward to their bases in England and then back to their American factories and so on back into foundries and smelters and at last safely out of history and into the ore mines, I winced to think that I hadn't invented such a fantasy to deal with the fallen metal in *my* brain.

A few years ago, noodling on the Internet, I googled "Bell P-39 Airacobra Crashes," and to my astonishment conjured up accidentreports@comcast. net, an address that offered access to official US Army Air Force reports on military accidents. When I specified what I was looking for, information on a fatal crash involving a P-39 near Madras, Oregon, in early spring 1944, and added that the official file, if available, might include eyewitness testimony from my father, A. S. "Gus" Ramsey, the reply was breathtaking. Yes, a twenty-five-page report of the accident was on file, and it included accounts of the crash by Gus Ramsey and Floyd Evick!

So now, after seven decades, I've come to know some of the facts of the case. If it were a sack of wheat, it still wouldn't be full enough to stand on its own, but at least I now know something, whereas before I knew only what I'd witnessed as a child. The accident report, carelessly typed on military forms and ultimately filed with an "Accident Center" in the Army Air Force Office of Flight Safety in Winston-Salem, North Carolina, is in some ways quite detailed, regarding the pilot, especially, but in other respects, notably about the *cause* of the crash, it is pro forma and question-begging.

The pilot, I learned at last, was 2nd Lieutenant Robert L. Cranston, a native of Green Bay, Wisconsin. He was very young, a few months shy of his twentieth birthday; after graduating from West High School in Green Bay in 1942, he had started classes in engineering at the University of Wisconsin, but enlisted in the Army Air Corps in February 1943. After primary and basic flight training in Texas and California, he "earned his wings" at Williams Air Force Base in Arizona in February 1944, and after a brief stopover for reclassification at Santa Ana Army Air Base in California, he joined the 546th Fighter Squadron for training in P-39s in Madras, arriving only two weeks before his crash. According to his flight log, he had a total of only 225 hours of flight time, and since arriving at Madras Army Air Field he had logged three and a half hours in the P-39Q, the latest (and last) production model of the Airacobra. He was not yet rated for instrument or night flying—that training presumably lay ahead of him.

A page in the accident report headed "Civilian Experience" notes that, in high school, Cranston had participated in football, basketball, baseball, track, tennis, and skiing, belonged to the Boy Scouts (he was an Eagle Scout, in fact), YMCA, and "Hi Y," and built gas model planes—a new and relatively uncommon hobby in those days. At the time of his commission as a second lieutenant, he was 5 feet 11 inches tall, 151 pounds, with brown hair and brown eyes.

When Cranston arrived at Madras, the base was humming with flight training activity, being under the administration of the Fourth Air Force, which shared combat pilot–training duties with the Second Air Force. Madras Army Air Field had been established only in 1942, initially as a Second Air Force unit, and extensions of its two main runways (designed for heavy bombers—one was 7,400 feet long) were still under construction in spring 1944.

Two miles to the south, the town of Madras, county seat of Jefferson County, was in those days a raw dry-farming and ranching center of maybe six hundred people, somewhat overwhelmed commercially and socially by the near presence of the base; and although by the time Cranston came it had an active USO unit (organized by county Judge T. A. Power and the theatrically inclined wife of the founding base commander, Major Joseph P.

Old North Hangar at Madras Airport in 2017—a National Register of Historic Places building

Arnold), the base and its surroundings must have seemed over the edge of nowhere to newcomers.

In the "ready room" of the South Hangar (still in use today), young pilots like Cranston left their marks Kilroy-like in pencil along the walls. A few are patriotic and upbeat: "Take care of everything. Will be back when the Rising Sun sets!" But most are cryptic grumbles in the timeless GI style about the godforsaken place they were temporarily condemned to: "8-23-43—Came, looked, and left," and "3-1-44 to 3-29-44—And glad to go!" This last inscription was written, hauntingly, less than a week after Cranston's death. No doubt he, too, would have been "glad to go" if fate had permitted it, but in his few days at the Madras base I wonder if he had time enough to gain any impressions, negative or positive, of the territory he was in. Almost certainly he was billeted on the base, in the pilots' barracks—long frame-and-tarpaper buildings that, like most of the jerry-built facilities on the base, were dismantled soon after the war and reborn as chicken houses and sheds on local farms.

When I first discovered the availability of the official Accident Report, I was especially excited by the prospect of reading my father's eyewitness account of the crash, and that of our neighbor Floyd Evick, and comparing what they testified they saw that afternoon with what I remember seeing. How often do you get the opportunity to revisit something you saw as a child, through the written words of a parent who was also there?

When the report arrived, I was surprised to find that it included two additional testimonials. One was given by Floyd Evick's brother-in-law, George Rufener, who must have been visiting from his place at Grizzly when we stopped by. That my recollection has wholly excluded him is a reminder of how fallible the organ of memory is—did I edit George Rufener out because he was then relatively unfamiliar to me, whereas Floyd was one of my dad's chums? Whether he actually went to the crash site with us, I can't say; if he did not, or went separately, maybe that would explain how he has dropped out of the story in my mind.

The other "surprise witness" was clearly not on the scene at Floyd Evick's, and according to the record made his own deposition three days later, on March 26. C. S. "Chet" Luelling, my father's best friend since childhood, was plowing a stubbled field north of the crash, and the noise of the Airacobra power-diving was loud enough to make him notice it over the two-cylinder roar and racket of his old John Deere Model D tractor. My dad,

Floyd, and George were all in their late thirties, sharp-eyed and clear-headed observers, conditioned by farming, stock-raising, and hunting to pay attention to what they saw—but Chet Luelling, a little older, was as I remember him exceptionally observant, with an analytic turn of mind and habit with words. All four of them were a little too old for service in the war and were also deferred as farmers—a somewhat sensitive point with my dad, I think.

This much said by me, they should now speak for themselves, as they did in 1944:

GUS RAMSEY: I was in a Pick-up truck when George Rufener called my attention to the airplane. He said, "Look at that plane," and I did in the direction he was pointing. I could not locate the airplane until it just about struck the ground. It was burning and there were pieces of the airplane floating down after it. I am not sure whether it blew up just before or after it hit the ground.

GEORGE RUFENER: I was standing on the running board of a Pick-up truck when I heard an airplane. I looked up and saw the airplane coming down in a gradual curve. It appeared to make a V and then popped. When it got down a little lower it burst into flames, and seemed to explode just as it hit the ground.

FLOYD EVICK: I was sitting in a pick-up truck with Gus Ramsey when he called our attention to the airplane. When I saw the airplane it was in flames and falling. I could see only two points, and I believe the wing was off of the airplane then. I watched it fall with a sheet of flame trailing it. The flames seemed to get bigger as it fell and I could not tell whether it exploded before or after it struck the ground.

CHESTER LUELLING: I was plowing on the twenty-third day of March, when I heard the roar of a motor over the noise of the tractor I was using. Looking up in a southerly direction I saw a plane falling. An object in the sky, a little above and to the right of the falling plane, caught my eye. I could tell at this distance that it was a wing; another heavier object was falling vertically near the wing. Simultaneously I saw a group of smaller fragments in the air above the plane—I would say 200 or 300 feet above the plane. These fragments seemed to be almost motionless at first as if they had reached the apex of their flight and were mushrooming out in the air to start their descent.

About this time the plane landed. It had been descending at a steep angle and from my position looked as if it were bearing directly from west to east. The force of the impact threw up a sheet of dirt. Parts of the plane were hurled forward as the plane hit. Other fragments were hitting the ground at this time and kicking up a spurt of dirt.

There was no visible explosion when the plane hit the earth. I had not been conscious that the plane was in flames until reaching the ground a cloud of black smoke flared up but did not reach any great proportions.

One of my first reactions was to locate a parachute of the pilot. I kept looking at the sky which was filled with floating clouds. Directly above where I first saw the plane a cloud was being literally torn apart by some terrific force from below. The cloud was quickly swept away. I was almost due north of the scene of this crash, a distance of approximately three-quarters of a mile.

Reading through these terse statements, I am struck by their essential consistency, both with respect to the details of each, and with respect to my own memory of the event. Apparently, I alone had been watching Cranston's maneuvers, but we all took notice of the increasingly loud roar of the plane as it dove. Floyd Evick and Chet Luelling both saw a wing falling along with the rest of the plane; Chet and my father mention "fragments" or "pieces" falling, too—but I have no recollection that the plane had broken up. Nor do I remember it descending in flames, as Floyd did, or "exploding" just before or on impact, as Floyd and George Rufener recalled. Interestingly, Chet also indicated doubt that the plane came down in flames, and that it exploded either midair or on impact. On the other hand, his striking observation that "directly above where I first saw the plane a cloud was being literally torn apart by some terrific force from below" does strongly suggest a midair explosion of some sort, as does George Rufener's statement that it "popped."

Although the official accident dossier includes these firsthand accounts, it does not seem to make use of them in formally describing the accident and ascertaining its probable cause. The cover sheet merely declares: "authorized training mission . . . weather no factor . . . airplane crashed into the ground killing the pilot . . . cause of accident unknown." The engineering officer at the base, Lieutenant Edward Waters, and the crew chief of Cranston's plane, Sergeant Wesley Biesemeyer, attest that the plane had been properly serviced and "pre-flighted" before the flight. Biesemeyer adds that it was a "new ship," with only sixty-nine and a half hours on both the engine and the airframe.

The members of the base accident committee, Captain James R. Wilson and Captain Robert Santini, conclude from the evidence at the crash scene that "the plane came apart while in the air," and add that although an explosion in the air "was possible, the plane did not burn until after it had fallen apart."

According to the base flight surgeon's report, using what might be called medical euphemisms, Cranston's death was due to "evisceration of cranial contents"—a diagnosis confirmed in the State of Oregon's Certificate of Death, as filed by local physician Dr. W. H. Snook (who was our family doctor for many years). Dr. Snook adds that there were multiple skull fractures. Such a massive head injury could have been caused by a midair explosion blowing Cranston through the cockpit; or it could have happened on impact with the ground. That I do not recall seeing evidence of such a gruesome injury is probably because Cranston was wearing his pilot's headgear.

Much the fullest and most thoughtful commentary in the dossier was given by Cranston's own squadron commander, Major Andrew W. Salter, CO of the 546th Fighter Squadron. Salter visited the crash scene twice and prepared a rough map of the site, indicating where the pieces landed in relation to each other. He concluded, "It is definite that the plane disintegrated in the air, breaking the fuselage just at the rear of the engine. The right wing and fuselage did not burn and were found close to each other. The right wing bolts were found to have been pulled from the nuts, shearing threads of same."

From these details, unmentioned by the accident team in their report, he goes on to offer very tentatively an explanation of what caused Cranston's P-39 to dive out of control into the ground: "It is possible that the wing pulled off at leading edge, folding back over the fuselage, trailing edge whipping through fuselage, severing same, and at the same time, fuel cells (in the wing) being ruptured pouring raw gas over hot exhaust stacks causing explosion which catapulted pilot from the airplane. This is made clear due to the engine, cabin, nose section, and left wing burning on contact with the ground. The pilot, right wing, and fuselage showed no sign of burning."

Bell P-39Q Airacobra, in Russian-export colors, Erickson Air Collection, Madras

No doubt one of today's FAA's crash-investigation teams could have scrutinized the wreckage, perhaps reassembled its pieces, and reasonably solved the mystery of what led to Lieutenant Cranston's violent death. But such systematic forensic analysis of crashes was clearly not the order of the day in 1944, with a war in the balance and mounting quotas of trained pilots to be met. Still, as one of the witnesses of the crash, the only one in fact still living, I incline to think that Major Salter's scenario of right wing failure and fuel cell explosion very likely describes what happened, and it seems to be supported by George Rufener's observation that the diving plane "made a V and then popped."

But if Cranston's Airacobra did lose its wing, causing a fuel explosion, how could that have happened on a routine training mission? The P-39 did have, in all of its variants, a solid reputation for sturdiness, enhanced by a Bell pilot's 1941 power dive in it that reached a speed of 620 miles an hour! It was Cranston's fourth such flight, and its agenda, as outlined in the "Description of the Accident," called for the pilot to "take off, and climb to 10,000 feet, practice coordination exercises, climbing, gliding, and cruising for 10 minutes, establish normal glide, practice medium and steep turns for 10 minutes, practice precise chandelles [steep climbing turns] through 180 degrees both left and right." How, in the course of such a modest flight plan, was it possible to tear a wing off?

Major Salter, presumably an experienced P-39 pilot, concludes his statement with the hint of an answer; in doing so, he alludes to a sinister part of the Airacobra's reputation that began to circulate among aviators as soon as the plane entered service in 1941 and continues to be debated by aviation historians even now. "It is also possible," he says, "that the plane could have tumbled causing destruction of same, while in the air. From reports of planes that have tumbled, the terrific strain placed on the fuselage has caused same to twist and also wings to buckle. This possibly could have happened."

In a series of interviews with former P-39 pilots in his book, *Airacobra Advantage: The Flying Cannon* (1992) Rick Mitchell makes a point of asking his subjects about this dangerous trait (the result, so it has been claimed, of the plane's short-coupled configuration, with the Allison engine located at the center of gravity, and also of its small control surfaces). The thrust of Mitchell's book is to rehabilitate the P-39's somewhat mediocre historical standing alongside revered World War II fighters like the P-38 Lightning and the P-51 Mustang, and so the rumor of out-of-control tumbling is one of the Bell plane's "bad raps" that he is eager to correct.

One of his interviewees is Chuck Yeager, the celebrated hero of *The Right Stuff.* Yeager, who collected over five hundred hours in the P-39 before becoming an ace in the Mustang in Europe, gives the Airacobra high praise: "I would gladly have gone into combat with it" (Mitchell, p. 86). He emphatically denies that the P-39 would "tumble," adding that Bell Aircraft itself investigated the claims and found no credible evidence for it, concluding that what looked like tumbling was really a high-speed stall.

Another similar answer to Mitchell's question came from ace and Medal of Honor–winner William Shomo, who was intrigued by the stories while in advanced flight training and (always at a "safe" altitude of 6,000 feet) conducted his own investigation. His conclusion: what appeared at a distance to be tumbling was in reality a series of rapid whip-stalls, which could be initiated by flying inverted and then essentially pulling the stick back with full power. The ensuing gyrations could be recovered from (if you had enough altitude) by cutting power and releasing the controls until the plane settled down (!) into a flat spin. Films based on Shomo's findings and warnings were eventually added to the flight-school instruction of P-39 pilots; whether such materials were in use at Madras airfield in March 1944 is doubtful (pp. 64–65).

One other World War II P-39 pilot and ace interviewed by Rick Mitchell, Charles Falletta, reported that he had actually tumbled his Airacobra in combat, over New Guinea: "I was chasing a Zero straight up. The next thing

I knew I was in a position I couldn't get out of. I was falling, going over and over. I couldn't get control on my tail [surfaces]." After lowering his wing flaps (which tore off), he tried lowering his landing gear, and eventually slowed down, regained control, and landed. This harrowing (and never repeated) experience did not diminish Colonel Falletta's affection for the plane—"I have nothing but praise for the P-39." But he does add a final caveat: "You had to know what you were doing to handle it, or you would kill yourself" (pp. 84–85).

At this distance of time, with most of the Airacobra's pilots deceased and only one or two examples of the plane still flyable, we'll probably never get a definitive answer to the question of tumbling. But whether it *was* capable of being tumbled or, less sensationally, could be "just" put into a series of rapid whip-stalls that made it appear to be going end-over-end is maybe not so important for our purposes here. Clearly it *did* have, in certain extreme maneuvers, a dangerous tendency to get itself rapidly out of control and ahead of its pilots, and once *out*, it was clearly difficult for them to rein it in. I've read through the Bell P-39Q flight manual, and although it seems to be written with an eye toward creating pilot confidence in the plane ("Normal loops, slow rolls, and Immelmans are all done with ease"), and says nothing about tumbling per se, it does offer some pointed warnings ("deliberate spinning is not recommended . . . the spin is usually oscillatory in nature. . . . If [specified] procedures are not followed closely, the airplane may not recover"), and some unequivocal prohibitions, including outside loops and spins, snap rolls, and aerobatics in a tail-heavy plane.

Now it's probable that every first-line US military plane in World War II had an equivalent prohibited/not recommended list. Early models of the Lockheed P-38, for example, were initially "red-lined" for power dives, because its main control surfaces tended to freeze up under what came to be understood as the "compressability effect" of the airstream on the surfaces, rendering them impossible to actuate. But I have to wonder what COs like Cranston's Major Salter felt, as they saw their young trainees buckle up and take off on their first short solo flights in "hot ships" like the Airacobra.

The accident record for P-39s at Madras and nearby Redmond field between August 1943 and April 1944 lists thirteen reportable accidents of some sort. Of these, Cranston's crash is the only fatal crash I know of, but that many incidents in nine months at two low-volume training bases does seem to indicate a pattern of operational trouble, or, putting it in merely human terms, of high risk. This impression is underscored by the accident record at Oroville Army Airfield in California, another training base on about the same scale as Madras and Redmond. Between May 1943 and January 1944, seventeen accidents with P-39s were recorded, four of them killing the pilots. The phone call the Madras base commander made in my father's presence after Cranston's crash, asking for no more P-39s, now seems not unjustified. Whether his request was granted is unknown.

So where does all this sifting of old reports and details lead us, in our quest to determine what happened to 2nd Lieutenant Robert Cranston in the early-spring sky in 1944 above my dad and me, and Floyd Evick, George Rufener, and Chet Luelling ? Only to what might be termed a "documented speculation," along the lines of Major Salter's hypothesis already noted in the Accident Report: that in the course of finishing up his prescribed course of training maneuvers that afternoon, possibly because he felt like pushing the flight plan a little, kid-like, or maybe just in the course of trying to follow the plan out to the best of his limited capabilities, he let his plane get ahead of him and into trouble. Possibly one of the "chandelles" led into a full-power stall, and then a tumble or, if you will, a whip-stall and flat spin. And then, frightened and disoriented, quickly out of the depth of his meager flying experience, he over-controlled (possibly crossed the controls), quickly exceeding the plane's structural limits and tearing the right wing out of its roots, so that it folded back, according to Major Salter's theory, crashing into the right rear fuselage where the engine's hot exhaust stacks protruded, rupturing one of the rubber fuel cells in the wing and causing a brief but violent explosion that broke off the rear fuselage and blew the pilot and his seat out of the cabin and into free fall.

Remember the uncanny detail in Chet Luelling's report, about his looking up for an opening parachute above the falling pieces of the plane, but seeing instead a cloud being torn apart "by some terrific force from below"— that is, from where the plane may have just exploded. As Chet was watching this, Robert Cranston was already dead, or dying, and falling to earth with what was left of his plane.

III

After I learned Cranston's name and origins, and the exact date of his death, I was able to go looking for newspaper accounts of the accident. His home town daily, the Green Bay *Press-Gazette*, actually reported his death the day after it happened: "Lt. Cranston Dies in Crash," ran the headline. "Lt. Robert Cranston, son of Mr. and Mrs. Lee Cranston of 210 13th Avenue, was killed Thursday afternoon in the crash of a P-39 fighter plane he was piloting in maneuvers about six miles from Madras Army Air Field, Madras, Oregon, according to a message received Thursday night by his parents. No details were given."

From his obituary notices in subsequent issues of the *Press-Gazette*, I learned that he had actually been home on furlough in February after winning his wings and receiving his commission in Arizona. Other details emerged, adding to the impression that he was an outstanding young man, from a prominent family. He had been an Eagle Scout and a Sea Scout, and an Air Cadet at the University of Wisconsin before enlisting. His father, Lee Cranston, was a Green Bay attorney and civic leader (he would not die until 1982, at age eighty-three). The Cranstons also had a daughter, Gene, who later became a professor of nursing at the University of Florida, a nationally recognized expert in the care of newborn babies.

Her brother's funeral, originally scheduled for Tuesday, March 28, in Grace Lutheran Church, had to be postponed to March 31 because of delays in shipping the body from Oregon. Once in Green Bay, it was escorted by Lieutenant Henry Corbin (described in the obituary as a "buddy" from their flight-school days in Arizona) who stayed a few days with the family. Cranston's pallbearers were chosen from three institutions his family "felt had entered most into the life and development of their son, aside from his home and church—West High School, the YMCA, and the Boy Scouts." He was buried (as his father would be, nearly forty years later) in Fort Howard Cemetery.

In the files of our local weekly, the Madras *Pioneer*, I found, on the front page of the March 30, 1944, issue, a brief article headlined "Fatal Crash," not identifying Cranston by name (presumably because of military restrictions), but noting that the plane "had exploded in the air, and the pilot never had a chance to bail out." The article, after adding that the pilot had been "on a routine training trip," goes on to garble the details somewhat (again suggesting sparse military information): "When coming into the field, the plane suddenly went wrong, burst into flames, and plunged into the ground."

But what must have caught the brief attention of local readers (maybe especially my dad and his fellow witnesses) was this sentence in the lead paragraph: "It is thought that the young lieutenant's fiancée was on her way to Madras and an intended marriage but arrived one day too late."

What to make of this unutterably sad extension of our story? My own first reaction was skeptical—given Cranston's family background and his apparently straight-arrow boyhood, would he and his girlfriend have attempted such a bold step? And not at home in Green Bay, where it might have been arranged for his February furlough, but in Madras? However the *Pioneer* acquired the news of the crash, it had to omit the victim's name and hometown—so, lacking even this most basic documentation, is the story about the unnamed fiancée likely to be anything more than airbase scuttlebutt? What credibility lies behind the phrase "It is thought that . . ."?

Looking at the story another way, I found myself being tempted to recast the whole narrative of the crash in fictional terms. Given the poignancy of the material, and especially this final episode, wouldn't it make a compelling short story? Suddenly the possibilities of engaging all these technical details and factual gaps and uncertainties in a spirit of "what if" and making an imaginatively plausible story, a plot out of them, seemed liberating. What was there to lose in such a radical step?

But I soon recovered, reminding myself that I had taken up this project more than six decades ex post facto with the intention of proceeding as far as possible from my bare childhood memory of the crash into the real facts of the case, and thus to tell, the best I could, the story of the dead pilot in Klann's field. I now knew, unlike the readers of the Madras *Pioneer* in 1944, that his name was Robert Cranston, and what I would likely lose if I tried to reimagine the Cranston file as fiction would be my commitment to tell *his* story, for its own sake, "for the record."

So fiction-making, at least by me, would have to stay on the sidelines. But if not to inspire an affecting final scene, or be dismissed as implausible journalistic rumormongering, what should we do with the report of Cranston's fiancée arriving in Madras the day after his death? Considered in its historical and social context, such a step wouldn't have been all that implausible, or uncommon, in March 1944. The war was in its third and bloodiest year, with each month more soldiers being posted overseas, to places like Anzio and the Solomon Islands, from which reports of dreadful American casualties were circulating. Facing such grim prospects, trying to improvise a credible course for their lives beyond the war, a lot of GIs did get married hastily, perhaps imprudently, before shipping out. It must have been very much an "existential" act, not so much in the sense of trying in bad times to seize the moment, as in the sense of trying through the ritual of marriage to "invest" in a normal future. The Madras *Pioneer* noted several such GI weddings either on base or in town in 1943 and 1944.

Why didn't Cranston and his girlfriend arrange to marry in Green Bay, during his February furlough there? Perhaps his parents, or hers, wouldn't have approved. Or perhaps she was someone he had met in Arizona, Texas, or California, during his months of flight school. Or perhaps (assuming that she *was* a hometown girl), being together briefly during his furlough precipitated the decision to get married, when it was too late to do so at home.

Needless to say, the official Accident Report makes no mention of a fiancée, nor does it allude to Lieutenant Cranston's personal plans beyond completing his training at Madras Army Air Field. But it seems possible that Major Salter, his CO, knew about the marriage plan, and even more likely, his fellow pilots in the barracks and the ready room. Maybe it was through this informal connection that the *Pioneer* heard about the story, even though the official account was censored.

Or maybe the poor young woman's arrival in Madras (almost certainly by bus, after an arduous journey by train to The Dalles or Portland) was noted by sympathetic townspeople, who did what they could for her after she learned about her fiancé's death. From here, it seems best not to inquire too closely into a situation at once tragic beyond words and also beyond hope of substantiation. But the questions keep coming. What was her name? When she arrived in Madras, was she met by someone from the base (perhaps Major Salter), who had the duty of telling her the terrible news about yesterday's crash? Where did she stay? How was she consoled, and by whom, and when did she start her grief-stricken journey back home? Her story could well have entered local folklore—but I never heard it.

If she was real, I wish I knew at least her name. Knowing it would add something humanly tangible to the meager store of what we can ever share with Robert Cranston. But after so many years, the path of this tragic young woman out of her fiancé's brutally completed story seems to point nowhere and everywhere in postwar America. As so many other young widows and bereaved lovers did during the war, she would have had to somehow carry her broken hopes and dreams forward, into a world in which her beloved flyer would be only a memory and a set of records. I hope she found her way into a new life.

Robert Cranston would be in his late eighties now, about the age of some of my older cousins who survived the war. Visiting with them now, hearing their elderly voices, I find it hard to recollect the boisterous high spirits with which they enlisted and flung off to places far away from Central Oregon, to fight and win a war. But I know that the zeal and excitement were real in them then, beyond the palaver of recruiters. So I find myself thinking about Cranston, as he approached (unknowingly) his final moments in the sky over our heads. Was he, after more than a year of military indoctrination and intensive training, still energized by the aspirations and ideals that apparently attended his own enlistment as a college freshman?

In 1918, six years before Cranston's birth, the great Irish poet William Butler Yeats was struggling to make sense of the horrifying and seemingly senseless death in January of that year of his young friend and protégé Robert Gregory, accidentally shot down by his own Italian flying mates over northern Italy. Gregory, the son of Yeats's dear friend and collaborator Lady Augusta Gregory, was a painter, architect, and athlete, and was married with three small children. As an Irish citizen, he need not have enlisted in the British Army, but did so anyway, and volunteered to become a flyer. The plane he was killed in was a Sopwith Camel, as dangerous as any. In a remarkable series of poems, Yeats endeavored to come to honest terms with Gregory's death, straining to find affirmative meaning in it for himself and Gregory's family, beyond its seeming needlessness and waste.

Perhaps the greatest of these poems, one of the most perfectly wrought elegies in the English language, is "An Irish Airman Foresees His Death." In sixteen chiseled lines the poet audaciously makes Gregory himself declare a formal justification of his course of action, perhaps at the very moment of his death. The poem begins, "I know that I shall meet my fate / Somewhere among the clouds above;" and it concludes,

A lonely impulse of delight
Drove to this tumult in the clouds;
I balanced all, brought all to mind,
The years to come seemed waste of breath,
A waste of breath the years behind
In balance with this life, this death.
(*Yeats*, p. 135)

The poem's authority on its own terms seems absolute. Yeats's steely projection of Gregory's voice allows for no doubt that the aviator's balancing of the terms of his life in flight is utterly clear-headed, self-possessed, poised in the "lonely impulse of delight" in each moment of his flying—no matter the conventional military and patriotic motives for such heroics, no matter the anxieties of his friends and loved ones, no matter the future.

Perhaps Yeats felt that in writing "An Irish Airman" he had formulated an incontrovertible poetic rationale for Robert Gregory's death, and thus a measure of consolation for his grieving family. But he kept on writing other poems on the theme of his friend's death, and I am inclined to doubt that the poet believed, for himself, in the rationale he ascribes to Gregory. And I don't believe in it, either, as much as I'd like to, as a way of words to understand and reconcile myself to what I now know happened on March 23, 1944, to Robert Cranston. He must have been an exceptionally bright, talented, and ambitious young man, full of promise as we elders like to say, swept up in the great tumultuous weather of the war. It carried him high into the air and far away from home; but he died on the ground, in the mineral dirt of a field that would, not long after his funeral, turn green with sprouting wheat. I found him there, that afternoon after school, and I walked away.

Epilogue

A year or so after this essay was published in *Northwest Review*, in 2010, and found its way onto the Internet, I had a call from a man in California. He identified himself as Zack Harlwell; his mother, he said, had recently passed away, and in going through her keepsakes he had found a packet of letters, photos, and other items from a young Army Air Corps pilot named Robert Cranston, dated 1943 and early 1944. His mother's family name was Vivian Duganzich; she had grown up on her parents' fruit and nut farm near Mountain View, northwest of San Jose, and in 1943–1944 was a student at San Jose State. He said that his mother had never told him about Robert Cranston, but when he discovered and read the Airacobra article online, he resolved to help clear up the mystery in my narrative about Cranston's unknown girlfriend, and very generously offered to send me the packet of letters and photos. (They are now in the archives of the Jefferson County Historical Society in Madras.)

The letters were mainly from Cranston (his mother also sent several to Vivian after his death); the earliest is dated August 1, 1943, and the last was

Robert Cranston and Vivian
Duganzich, California, 1943

posted from Madras on March 22, 1944, the day before he died. Apparently they met in the summer of 1943, in San Francisco, possibly at a USO function; he probably had a weekend pass from his current training assignment at Salinas Army Air Base. From the start, his letters are passionate exclamations of love for his "Dear Dugy." As he shifted around from base to base in California and Arizona (Salinas, Sequoia/Visalia, Hamilton/Williams in Arizona, and back to Salinas), he seems to have found ways to visit her frequently, including several times in San Jose, and once at least at her parents' farm near Mountain View. "True love will find a way."

By early 1944 Cranston was already writing about their marriage, and at one point expressed his relief that Vivian's mother had given her consent—and also the anxious hope that his father, a prominent Green Bay attorney, would soon do likewise. Apparently the plan was for them to be married in California and live there together as long as they could before Cranston's next major transfer, possibly overseas. But at this point in the young couple's headlong planning, the iron realities of life in wartime began to catch up to them. First, Robert's letters to his parents, and specifically to his father about his plans to marry, were lost in the chaos of wartime mail, probably because of his frequent moves from base to base. They finally were delivered to Green Bay in a bundle the same day in mid-March that, in desperation, their son telephoned them with his plan! They were understandably astonished, and concerned, especially because during his brief furlough visit home in early February, he had only mentioned meeting Vivian and liking her—nothing as serious as marriage. As far as they knew, until his call, his only "serious" girlfriend was a young woman from Chicago he had met before enlisting.

The other military disruption of their marriage plans came in very early March in the form of an order for Robert's unit of pilot-trainees to report with the 546th Fighter Squadron to Redmond, Oregon, for training in P-39s. His next letter to Vivian is from Madras, and it conveys his extreme frustration over the turning of events:

> Ever since our marriage was thrown on the rock [he means his transfer to Oregon] we have been having trouble, and now you should see where I have ended up. I had to be eager and report to Redmond early Saturday [after a twenty-four-hour bus ride from Salinas], so what happens to me but that I have to be sent on up north to this hell of a place called Madras. You ought to see the town here. There are only about 430 people in town and is it ever a little jerkwater! Ouch! Remember what you and I agreed on, for you to come up here. Well, where the dickens you would live is beyond me. The base here has only 65 officer trainees so you can gather the size. Accommodations are very poor to say the least. There is only one consolation. No place to spend my money.

In an undated letter apparently written a few days later, their immediate prospects still looked bleak.

> The base here . . . is a hell hole, 38 miles from nowhere—Redmond—and 100 miles from anywhere—Portland, and longer than that from you—which is somewhere. . . . Captain Wilson . . . asked who was married and had their wives here. Two fellows raised their hands, and he said to them, "You had better go to town today and see them, for you won't see them for the remainder of your stay here." We fly 7 days a week and have to remain on the base.

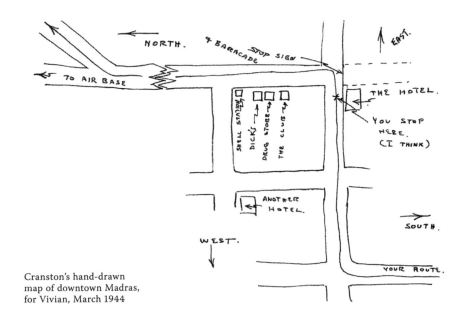

Cranston's hand-drawn
map of downtown Madras,
for Vivian, March 1944

Confirming this restriction, the "Guest Register" for the Madras USO for March 1944 records no visits from Cranston or any of his flying mates from the 546th Squadron.

But by March 21, his outlook was brighter: "Guess what I did today. I soloed the P-39. Gosh they are a sweet *little* ship. When I say little I mean very very tiny, or less. All motor, pilot, and guns." And in the same rush of excitement he hints (as much as he dares, given military restrictions on correspondence) about "some very good news"—evidently that by the end of March, his outfit will be transferred to Portland, meaning that she *can* come up (apparently Captain Wilson's no-off-base-pass order has been relaxed), they can get married in Madras, posthaste, and then she can move with him to Portland. He mentions that his best buddy in the 546th, Henry "Hank" Corbin, is planning to marry at Easter—so perhaps Henry's bride and Vivian can share an apartment in Portland while their husbands are stationed there.

Cranston's final letters to Vivian are feverish with plans and expectations, and crammed with logistical details about how she can make the long bus trip up to Madras, via Klamath Falls and Bend, and so on. He wants her to come either Friday (March 24) or Saturday (March 25), and, knowing that he may not be able to leave the base to meet her bus, he draws her a detailed map of downtown Madras as it was in 1944, highlighting the

Madras Hotel on Main Street, where he has reserved a room for her, and other local establishments she might need to know about, like Dick Doty's Café and the drugstore.

His last communication is a telegram, sent from Madras on Wednesday, March 22, at 1:12 pm:

> COME TO MADRAS LEAVE FRIDAY OR SATURDAY RESERVATIONS
> AT NEW MADRAS HOTEL ANSWER AND LET ME KNOW WHEN TO
> EXPECT YOU I LOVE YOU HAVE SOME VERY GOOD NEWS FOR YOU
> US WE WILL BE MARRIED VERY SOON AFTER YOU ARRIVE ALL MY
> LOVE BOB

Around 3:25 p.m. on the afternoon of Thursday, March 23, 2nd Lieutenant Robert L. Cranston was killed in the crash of his P-39Q Airacobra on Agency Plains, about five miles north of the airfield. Mercifully (if fate allows for any mercy), Vivian Duganzich had not begun her long bus trip from San Jose to Madras; someone, most likely Henry Corbin, must have telephoned her with the terrible news before she set out. Corbin—who went on with his unit to fly P-38s in combat in Europe—accompanied his friend's body back to Green Bay, Wisconsin, for burial. After the war, Vivian took flying lessons herself and earned her pilot's license; she eventually married, and it was her son from a second marriage, Zack Harwell, who contacted me and sent his late mother's packet of letters and photos.

After seventy years, we'll probably never know for sure what caused Robert Cranston to lose control of his Airacobra in the course of a short, routine training flight—again, the official USAAF accident report did not reach a conclusion as to cause. But reading Cranston's impassioned letters to his beloved "Dugy," and considering all that was competing for his attention during his hectic few weeks at Madras Army Air Field—distress at leaving California and giving up plans to marry her there, fretting about the silence from his parents on his request for permission to marry, then with the news of the impending transfer to Portland trying to cobble together arrangements for her to come to Madras, get married, and somehow set up housekeeping in Portland, and running through it all, seven days a week, coping with the grueling and nerve-racking work of trying to learn how to fly a dangerous fighter plane—considering all this, it's hard to avoid the speculation that his overloaded and distracted state of mind may have contributed to his crash. Quoting World War II Airacobra ace Colonel Charles Falletta again, "You had to know what you were doing to handle it, or you would kill yourself" (quoted in Mitchell, p. 85).

Seventy years, and the fields of Agency Plains and for that matter the little "jerkwater" town of Madras have changed greatly since Robert Cranston once flew over them. But the sad story of his romance with the beautiful girl from California still tells us some things worth knowing about the devotion and resilience of the people who have fought our wars, both in battle and at home. And it also testifies, as do so many other stories like it, to the terrible mind-numbing waste of human lives and dreams in time of war. That is why it is so important for Robert Cranston's last letters from Madras, and the USO guestbook he never signed, to be preserved in the local historical archives, and likewise for the old World War II hangars at what is now Madras Airport, where he and his mates once hung out, waiting for their chance to fly, to be faithfully preserved and visited. They are vivid pieces of our history, whose value is at once local and national.

Notes

Preface

Portions of this essay are based on a talk given to the staff and volunteers of the High Desert Museum, October 1, 2004. The only comprehensive history of Central Oregon is still Phil Brogan's *East of the Cascades* (1964), a well-informed and trustworthy guide—but after five decades of rapid changes in the area, it needs to be supplemented and updated. Arguably the most ambitious regional historical project since Brogan has been Steve Lent's excellent three-volume *Central Oregon Place Names:* Vol. I, *Crook County*; Vol. II, *Jefferson County*; Vol. III, *Deschutes County* (2001, 2008, 2015).

A pioneering study of Hispanic settlement in Central Oregon in the 1950s and 1960s is Jane Ahern's "The Origins of the Latino Community in Jefferson County," *The Agate* 6 (Fall 2016): 3–13.

The enterprises of local history and academic history (for lack of a better term) meet at least tangentially in the work of Carol Kammen, notably in the third edition of her *On Doing Local History* (2014). She recognizes, usefully, the need for historians of all types to cultivate the balanced interplay of local and wider perspectives in their work: "It is a task that calls for a microscope to see particular events and a telescope to see general patterns" (p. 136).

Chapter One

Thanks to Robert Sawyer's efforts, Henry Abbot's Oregon journal and field notes, and his personal map of the routes of the 1855 survey, are in the archives of the Oregon Historical Society. Loren Irving has made an excellent documentary video (DVD) of Fremont's 1843 march through Oregon, locating all thirty-one of his campsites and beautifully filming the Central Oregon country that he and Abbot both saw (*Finding Fremont in Oregon 1843*, 2010).

Chapter Two

For further references to the McCoins, see chapters 3 and 9.

Chapter Three

For further reading on heirloom fruits and the importance of homestead orchards, see *Pome News* (quarterly publication of the Home Orchard Society, Portland, Oregon); Roger Yepsen, *Apples* (1994); and Warren Manhart, *Apples for the Twenty-First Century* (1995).

Chapter Four

Another telling of the "race up the Deschutes" is Jane Ahern's excellent "The Last Railroad War," in *OnTrak Magazine* (Amtrak), Fall 2015, pp. 50–55. For the railroad and other Central Oregon photography of Ole Hedlund, see Jarold Ramsey and Beth Crow, "Ole Hedlund, Photographer of the Central Oregon Railroad Era 1909–1911," *Oregon Historical Quarterly* 111, no. 3 (Fall 2010): 343–371.

Chapters Five and Six

One item the Madras "raiders" did not carry off in their New Year's Day raid on the Culver courthouse was the big metal "Jefferson County Court House" sign on the building. It was somehow protected, and now hangs prominently in the Culver City Hall.

Chapter Seven

For a hilarious send-up of centennial celebrations and small-town theatricals run amok, see Christopher Guest's "mockumentary" film, *Waiting for Guffman*. For photos and additional commentary on the Jefferson County Centennial skits in 2014, see Jarold Ramsey, "How Do You Celebrate a County's Centennial?" in *Oregon Historical Quarterly*. For a discerning account of the historical value of one centennial celebration (Railroad Day 100, Madras, Oregon, February 19, 2011), see see Alexander Craghead, "Searching for Small Town Pride, " *Railfan* (Jan. 20, 2012): 4.

In *On Doing Local History,* Carol Kammen offers illuminating insights into her own work in adapting local upstate New York historical episodes for stage presentation—see "Going Back," pp. 122–129, and "Clio and Her Sisters," pp. 71–79. In *Enacting History* (2011), Scott Magelssen and Rhona

Justice-Mallory have gathered an interesting range of essays on staging (and filming) historical materials, some of them pursuing the theoretical implications of such adaptations. Oddly, neither these essays nor Kammen's take note of Michael Ondaatje's important work with Theatre Passe Muraille in rural Ontario communities.

Chapter Eight

Additional readings on western homesteading and homesteaders include: Barbara Allen, *Homesteading the High Desert* (1987); Ethel Klann Cornwell, *Rimrocks and Water Barrels* (1979); H. L. Davis, *Honey in the Horn* (1935); "Back to the Land—Oregon 1907," in *H. L. Davis: Collected Essays and Short Stories* (1986); Paul W. Gates, *History of Public Land Law Development* (1968); Molly Gloss, "Introduction" to Alice Day Pratt, *A Homesteader's Portfolio* (1993; Pratt's book came out originally in 1922); Gilma Endicott Greenhoot, *Rattlesnake Homestead* (privately printed, 1988); C. S. Luelling, *Saga of the Sagebrush Country* (unpublished MS in Jefferson County Library); "Many Hands," in *Jefferson County Reminiscences* (1998); Bess Stangland Raber, *Some Bright Morning* (1983); Jarold Ramsey, *New Era: Reflections on the Human and Natural History of Central Oregon* (2004); and Percy Wollaston, *Homesteading: A Montana Family Album* (1999).

Chapter Nine

In Oregon, spectacular antique tractor and farm machinery celebrations are held yearly at Dufur (The Dufur Threshing Bee, August) and Brooks (Antique Powerland—The Great Oregon Steam-Up, July).

Chapter Ten

In *The Stories We Tell: Oregon Folk Literature* (1994), editors Suzi Jones and Jarold Ramsey offer samplings of Oregon folk-speech and proverbial sayings, and examples of the specialized localized lingo of dry-farmers (pp. 141–144), cowboys (p. 146), loggers (pp. 166–170), and commercial fishermen (pp. 180–183).

There seems to be an international "topo-linguistics" movement under way to record and study local words and sayings, including place-names and words for topological and weather details, in terms of their etymologies and the ways they serve to name and reify important local features. Keith Basso's brilliant study of Apache Indian place-names and topological lore,

Wisdom Sits in Places (1996) is a landmark in this endeavor; other notable contributions are Barry Lopez and Debra Gwartney, eds., *Home Ground: Language for an American Landscape* (2006); and Robert McFarlane, *Landmarks* (2016), which concentrates on the British Isles. McFarlane mentions a project under way that aims at a global "topoglossary," listing topological terms from around the world, undertaken by a British scholar, Simon Fitzwilliam-Hall.

Chapter Twelve

The North Hangar at Madras Airport, built in 1942–1943 for B-17 bombers, has recently been listed on the National Registry of Historic Buildings. Elsewhere at the airport, the Erickson Aircraft Collection includes a Bell P-39Q, the same model that Robert Cranston was learning to fly from the airfield in 1944. For a short history of Madras Airport in its military and civilian phases, see Jarold Ramsey, "Madras Airport in War and Peace," *The Agate* (Jefferson County Historical Society) 2, nos. 1 and 2 (Spring/ Summer 2009): 1–6.

Bibliography

Unpublished and archival sources (the six sources below are all found in the Jefferson County Historical Society Archives)

Boegli, Willis. "Remembering the Cove and Culver." Unpublished ms.

"Robert Cranston File."

"Guest Register," Madras USO 1943-4.

"Larkin File."

McFarland, Janine, "Research Files for National Register of Historic Places Nomination for Cyrus and McCoin Homesteads and Orchards, Crooked River National Grasslands."

1913 Madras Land Office Records (Homestead Filings).

Newspapers and Newsletters

The Agate (Jefferson County Historical Society)

Bend *Bulletin*

Culver *Deschutes Valley Tribune*

Green Bay, Wisconsin *Press-Gazette*

Madras *Pioneer*

Pome News (Home Orchard Society, Portland, Oregon)

Portland *Oregonian*

Prineville *Central Oregonian*

Books and Articles

Abbot, Catherine C. *Family Letters of General Henry Larcom Abbot 1831–1927.* Gettysburg, PA: Thomas Publications, 2001.

Abbot, Henry Larcom. *Pacific Railroad Survey Reports.* Vol. 6. Washington, DC: Department of War, 1857. (Full title of series: Reports of Explorations and Surveys to Ascertain the Most Practicable and Economical Route for a Railroad from the Mississippi River to the Pacific Ocean. Vol. 6: *Report upon Explorations for a Railroad Route from the Sacramento Valley to the Columbia River*).

———. "Reminiscences of the Oregon War of 1855." *Journal of the Military Service Institute* 45 (July–December 1909): 436–442.

Ahern, Jane. "The Origins of the Latino Community in Jefferson County." *The Agate* 6 (Fall 2016): 3–13.

Allen, Barbara. *Homesteading on the High Desert.* Salt Lake City: University of Utah Press, 1987.

Amato, Joseph. *Re-thinking Home: A Case for Writing Local History.* Berkeley: University of California Press, 2002.

Basso, Keith. *Wisdom Sits in Places: Landscape and Language among the Western Apache.* Albuquerque: University of New Mexico Press, 1996.

Brogan, Phil. *East of the Cascades.* Portland: Binford and Mort, 1964.

Chinuk Wawa. Compiled by Henry Zenk and the Chinuk Wawa Dictionary Project. Grand Ronde, Oregon: Confederated Tribes of the Grand Ronde Community of Oregon, 2012.

Clark, Keith, and Donna Clark. "William McKay's Journals 1866–7." *Oregon Historical Quarterly* 74, no. 2 (Summer 1978), and no. 3 (Fall 1978).

Corning, Howard McKinley. *Dictionary of Oregon History.* Portland: Binford and Mort, 1956.

Cornwell, Ethel Klann. *Rimrocks and Water Barrels.* Winona, WI: Lakeside Press, 1979.

Craghead, Alexander. "Searching for Small Town Pride." *Railfan,* January 12, 2012.

Crook, George. *General George Crook: His Autobiography.* Edited by Martin Schmitt. Norman: University of Oklahoma Press, 1946.

Crow, Beth, and Jarold Ramsey. "Ole Hedlund, Photographer of the Central Oregon Railroad Era." *Oregon Historical Quarterly* 111, no. 3 (Fall 2010).

Curtis, Edward S. *The North American Indian.* Vol. 8 (1911). New York: Johnson Reprint Co., 1970.

Davis, H. L. "Back to the Land—Oregon, 1907." In *H. L Davis: Collected Essays and Short Stories,* pp. 282–300. Moscow: University of Idaho Press, 1986.

———. "The Homestead Orchard." In *H. L. Davis: Collected Essays and Short Stories,* pp. 227–248. Moscow: University of Idaho Press, 1986.

———. "Oregon." In *Collected Essays and Short Stories.* Moscow: University of Idaho Press, 1986.

———. *Honey in the Horn.* New York: William Morrow, 1935.

———. *Team Bells Woke Me and Other Stories.* New York: William Morrow, 1953.

Dolan, Susan. *Fruitful Legacy: A Historic Context of Orchards in the United States.* Washington, DC: National Park Service, 2009.

Downing, Andrew Jackson. *The Fruits and Fruit Trees of America.* New York: John Wiley, 1871.

Fremont, John Charles. *Memoirs of My Life.* New York: Cooper Square Press, 2001 (1887).

Gates, Paul W. *History of Public Land Law Development.* Washington, DC: US Government Printing Office, 1968.

Gloss, Molly. "Introduction." In *A Homesteader's Portfolio*, by Alice Day Pratt. Corvallis: Oregon State University Press, 1993 (1922).

Grande, Walter. *The Northwest's Own Railway.* Portland: Grande Press, 1992.

Guide to Willow Creek Canyon Trail. Salem: Oregon State Parks and Recreation, 1993.

Hoeg, Larry. *Harriman vs. Hill: Wall Street's Great Railroad War.* Minneapolis: University of Minnesota Press, 2013.

Irving, Loren. *Finding Fremont in Oregon, 1843.* Video. Bend: TVStoryteller, 2010.

Jones, Suzi, and Jarold Ramsey, eds. *The Stories We Tell: Oregon Folk Literature.* Corvallis: Oregon State University Press, 1994.

Kammen, Carol. *On Doing Local History.* 3rd ed. New York: Rowman and Littlefield, 2014.

Kipfer, Barbara Ann, and Robert L. Chapman. *Dictionary of American Slang.* New York: Collins, 2007.

Klinkenborg, Verlyn. "Apples, Apples, Apples." *New York Times*, November 5, 2009. http://www.nytimes.com/2009/11/06/opinion/06fri4.html.

Lent, Steve. *Central Oregon Place Names.* Vol. 1, *Crook County*; Vol. 2, *Jefferson County*; Vol. 3, *Deschutes County.* Bend, OR: Maverick Publishing, 2001, 2008, 2015.

Lopez, Barry, and Debra Gwartney, eds. *Home Ground: Language for an American Landscape.* San Antonio, TX: Trinity University Press, 2006.

Magelssen, Scott, and Rhona Justice-Mallory, eds. *Enacting History.* Tuscaloosa: University of Alabama Press, 2011.

Manhart, Warren. *Apples for the Twenty-First Century.* Portland: North American Tree Co., 1995.

"Many Hands." In *Jefferson County Reminiscences.* Portland: Binford and Mort, 1998.

McFarlane, Robert. *Landmarks.* London: Penguin Books, 2016.

Mitchell, Rick. *Airacobra Advantage.* Missoula: Pictorial Histories Publishing, 1992.

Nabhan, Gary Paul, compiler and editor. *Forgotten Fruits: Manual and Manifesto: Apples.* RAFT Alliance (online), 2010. https://www.google.com/url?sa=t&rct=j&q=&esrc=s&source=web&cd=1&ved=0ahUKEwiX0caRvZvYAhWphlQKHXqoArEQFggpMAA&url=https%3A%2F%2Fwww.albc-usa.org%2FRAFT%2Fimages%2FResources%2Fapplebklet_web-3-11.pdf&usg=AOvVaw3QFLssCwmGgxY9LQ_oyYss.

Olson, Charles. *The Collected Poems.* Berkeley: University of California Press, 1979.

Ondaatje, Michael. *The Clinton Special: The Farm Show.* Toronto: Canadian Filmmakers Distribution Center, 1974.

Peck, Gunther. *Reinventing Free Labor.* New York: Cambridge University Press, 2000.

Power, Evada. "Hay Creek." In *Jefferson County Reminiscences,* pp. 9–53. Portland: Binford and Mort, 1998.

Raber, Bess Stangland. *Some Bright Morning.* Bend, OR: Maverick Publishing, 1983.

Ramsey, Jarold. *Coyote Was Going There.* Seattle: University of Washington Press, 1977.

———. "How Do You Celebrate a County's Centennial?" *Oregon Historical Quarterly* 116, no. 1 (Spring 2015): 130–135.

———. *Love in an Earthquake.* Seattle: University of Washington Press, 1973.

———. "Madras Airport in War and Peace, *The Agate,* 2 (Spring-Summer 2009): 1–6.

———. *New Era: Reflections on the Human and Natural History of Central Oregon.* Corvallis: Oregon State University Press, 2003.

———. *The Stories We Tell: An Anthology of Oregon Folk Literature.* Edited by Suzi Jones and Jarold Ramsey. Corvallis: Oregon State University Press, 1994.

Sawyer, Robert. "Abbot Railroad Surveys, 1855." *Oregon Historical Quarterly* 33, nos. 1 and 2 (March 1932 and June 1932).

Schubert, Frank N. *Vanguard of Expansion: Army Engineers in the Trans-Mississippi West, 1819–1879.* Washington, DC: Department of the Army, Office of the Chief of Engineers, 1980.

Schwantes, Carlos. "Problems of Empire Building: Oregon Trunk Railway Survey, 1911." *Oregon Historical Quarterly* 83, no. 4 (Winter 1982): 371–400.

Speroff, Leon. *The Deschutes Railroad War.* Portland: Arnica Publishing, 2006.

Stevens, John. *An Engineer's Recollections.* New York: McGraw-Hill, 1936.

Stewart, George R. *Names on the Land: A Historical Account of Place-Naming in the United States.* New York: Houghton Mifflin, 1945.

Taft, Robert. *Artists and Illustrators of the Old West 1850–1900.* Princeton, NJ: Princeton University Press, 1993.

Thoreau, Henry David. "Wild Apples." In *Henry David Thoreau: The Natural History Essays.* Salt Lake City, UT: Peregrine Smith, 1980.

Turner, Howard. "Madras." In *Jefferson County Reminiscences,* pp. 114–173. Portland: Binford and Mort, 1998.

Vonnegut, Kurt. *Slaughterhouse Five.* New York: Delacorte Press, 1969.

Williams, William Carlos. "Kenneth Burke." In *Selected Essays of William Carlos Williams.* New York: New Directions, 1969.

Witter, Dean. *Meanderings of a Fisherman.* San Francisco: James Barry, 1974.

Wollaston, Percy. *Homesteading: A Montana Family Album.* Foreword by Jonathan Raban. New York: Penguin Books, 1999.

Yeats, William Butler. *William Butler Yeats: The Collected Poems.* Edited by R. J. Finneran. New York: Macmillan, 2003.

Yepsen, Roger. *Apples.* New York: Norton, 1994.

Index

A

Abbot, Lt. Henry Larcom Abbot,
1–23, 70
  work on Pacific RR Survey
    Reports Vol. VI, 20–23, 38, 39,
    191
  career after 1855, 23
Accident-reports.net, 170
Agency Plains, 62, 134,167, 169
Ahern, Jane, 192
Akiyama, Minoru, 159
Akiyama, Sadaka ("Doc"), 159–168
Akiyama, Tokiko, 159
Akiyama, Yasamasa, 159
Albee Township, Saginaw County,
  Michigan, 117, 118, 122
Allen , Barbara, 193
Amato, Joseph, x
An-ax-shat, Sam, 1,2, 14, 17, 18, 21,
  25–42
Anderson, A. D. ("Dick"), 94
Army Air Force Office of Flight
  Safety, 170
Army Air Force 546th Fighter
  Squadron, 170
Arnold, Major Joseph D., 171, 172
Ashley, A. W., 83
Ashwood, 71, 76, 127

B

Barber, Rex, 159, 160, 164, 169
Barber, William ("Bill"), 81, 88, 94
Barlow Road, 11, 21, 22
Basso, Keith, 193
Bear Springs, 15

Bell P-39Q "Airacobra," 162–170,
  172, 180
  liability as a trainer, 178
  tendency to "tumble," 177, 178
  training crashes of, 178
Bend, 64
Biesenmeyer, Sgt. Wesley, 175
Black, Sheriff Ira, 92
Blizzard Ridge, 118, 122, 134
Blanchard, A. E., 78
Boegli, William, 21, 46, 77, 79, 159
Boeing B-17 "Flying Fortress," 169,
  171
"boneyards" of farm machinery,
  152–158
Brewer Reservoir, 126
Brogan, Phil, 191
Brown, George (Oregon Attorney
  General), 82
Budd, Ralph, 62
Burlington and Northern (BNSF), 69

C

Camas Prairie, 15
Campbell Creek, 163
Central Oregon localisms, 137–150
  words, 137–146
  phrases, 146–150
Central Oregon railroads, 59–70
  economic advantages of, 65
Chenowith, H. V., 78
Chinook, Billy, 11
Chinook Jargon, 1, 2, 11, 14, 36–39,
  142, 143
Clark, A. P., 86

Clark, Jim, 47, 48
"close-up" and "zoom" lenses on
    history, xi, xiii
Cockerham, J. C., 79
Cook, Riley, 125
Cooper, Joanie, 45
Corbin, Lt. Henry ("Hank"), 180,
    187, 188
Corvallis, 20
Country schools, 33, 34
County seat conflicts in Oregon, 84,
    85
Cove Orchard, The, 46, 47, 77, 159,
    160
Craghead, Alexander, 192
Cranston, Gene, 180
Cranston, Mr. and Mrs. Lee, 180,
    182, 185, 186
Cranston, 2nd Lt. Robert L., 170–
    189
    certificate of death, 174
    final flight plan, 176
    marriage plans, 185, 186, 187
    personal history, 171, 180
Crook, Lt. George (later, General), 7,
    19, 20, 38
Crook County, 71, 75, 76, 131
Crooked River, 159–162
Crooked River RR Bridge, 63, 70
Crooked River National Grasslands,
    48
Cross Keys, 78
Crow, Beth, 192
Culver, 59, 63, 71, 76, 81–94, 159,
    161, 164, 192
    Crawdad Festival, 95
Curry, Governor George, 19
Cyrus, Enoch, 49, 50
Cyrus orchards, 49–51

D

Dams on Deschutes River (Pelton
    and Round Butte), 159
Davis, H. L., 23, 52, 132, 133
Deschutes County, 76

Deschutes River, 4, 8, 12, 14, 59, 64,
    159, 162
    "Big Eddy" on, 159, 160, 163
    "Cowles Orchard" on, 161
    "fishermen's specials" railroad
        service on, 68
Des Chutes Railroad, 59, 61, 63, 65,
    131
"Deschutes Railroad War," xii, 4, 61,
    62
    cost of, 64
Dictionary of American Slang, 139,
    141, 142, 143
Dizney, Thad, 160, 161–165
Dolan, Susan, 53, 55
"Domenich," 11, 14
Donahoe, Rick, 117, 118
Downing, Andrew Jackson, 55
"dragoons" (U.S. Army), 7, 8, 18
drought in Central Oregon, 53, 130
Duganzich, Vivian, 180, 181, 185–
    188
Dussault, Sheriff Henry, 160, 162,
    164

E

Ecker, Duane, 48, 53
Eliot, T. S., 136
Elkins, Sheriff Frank, 76
"Elkins Place" (4th of July
    celebrations at), 128
Erickson Air Collection/Museum
    (Madras), 194
Estacada, 16
Eugene, 20
Everett, Susie (Abbot), 11, 23
Evick, Floyd, 167, 170, 172, 173, 179

F

Fairview School, 127
Faletta, Col. Charles, 177, 189
Federal Resettlement
    Administration, 48, 50
Fort Dalles, 8, 11

Fort Lane, 20
Fort Reading (CA), 11, 20
Fourth Air Force, 171
Freeman, Ted, 159, 160, 164
Freeman, Merritt, 161
freighting in Central Oregon, 25, 48
Fremont, Capt. John, 5, 6, 11, 191
fruit varieties, heirloom, 44, 48,
     49,50, 54
Fryingpan Lake, 16

G

Gates, Paul W., 193
Gateway, 62
Gard, Roscoe, 77, 79, 81, 94
Gloss, Molly, 193
Grande, Walter, 59
Grandview, 71, 79
Grant County, 131
Gray Butte, 25, 48, 50
Green Bay, Wisconsin, 170, 185, 188
Greenhoot, Gilma Endicott, 193
Gregory, Major Robert, 183
Grizzly (community), 71, 125, 127
Grizzly Mountain, 13, 74
Guest, Christopher, 192

H

Haner, J. H., 73
Hanley, Bill, 64
Harriman, Edward, xii, 59, 60, 70
Harwell, Zack, 184, 188
Hay Creek Ranch, 118, 120, 126, 128,
     130
"headers" (farm machines), 153. 154
Hedlund, Ole (photographer), xii, 61,
     62, 63, 192
Helfrich, Minnie McCoin, 25, 148
Henderson, Perry, 83
High Rock, 16
Hill, James J., xii, 59, 60, 70, 96–99,
     139
Hoeg, Larry, xii
Home Orchard Society, 45, 50, 57

homesteading, xi, xii, 25–38,
     117–134
   "proving up" for title,130
   local newspapers and, 130
Howsley, L. B., 79
huckleberries, 15, 16
Hughes, Charles Evans, 83

I

Indian wars in Oregon, 7, 18, 38
"initiative and referendum" ("Oregon
     System"),72, 82, 83
internment camps for Japanese-
     Americans, 165
   revocation by Supreme Court,
     165
irrigation, 71
Irving, Lewis H. ("Turk"), 79, 94
Irving, Loren, 191

J

Japan, pre-war scrap-metal
     collection by, 156, 157
Jefferson County, 71–94
   county separation (from Crook),
     72–76, 83
   creation of boundaries of, 73–75
   temporary county seat marathon
     vote, 78, 80
   conflict over permanent county
     seat, 83–86
   "court-house raid," 91–94,
     99–104
Jefferson County Historical Society,
     x, 45, 117, 119, 184, 189
John Day River, 74
Jones, Suzi, 193
Justice-Mallory, Rhona, 193

K

Kammen, Carol, 191, 192
Kentner, Jim, 122
Kentner, Mildred, 123
Ketrenos, Harry, 48, 53

Kibbee Creek, 43
King, John M., 77, 79, 81, 94
King, S. K., 77
Klamath Country, 8, 64
Klann, Fred, 167
Klepper "Folbot," 161
Klinkenborg, Verlyn, 45
Kuckup (Warm Springs/Tygh
    leader), 14

L

Lamonta, 71, 76
Larkin, Alma, 192
Larkin, Almon Wakefield, 124
Larkin, Ben, 118, 122, 124
Larkin, Cora Goff, 129
Larkin, Ethel, 118–134
Larkin, Gaylord ("Gay"), 118–134
Larkin, Gladys, 123
Larkin, John, 122
Larkin, Lewis, 130
Larkin, Lilia, 122
Larkin, Mildred, 118, 122, 127, 128
Larkin, Minerva, 130
Larkin, Selma, 130
Larkin, William, 123
Lent, Steve, 191
local history as an endeavor, x–xiv
    and academic historians, x
    alternative ways of "doing," xiv,
        25–42, 95–116
Lockheed P-38 "Lightning," 169
Longfellow, Henry, 15
Lopez, Barry, 193
Luelling, C. S. ("Chet"), 173, 179, 193
Luelling, Henderson, 44

M

Madras, 59, 62, 63, 65, 71, 76, 84, 94,
    160
    Centennial in 2011, 95
    "women's revolt" in 1922, 105–112
    Eleanor Roosevelt's 1934 visit,
        113–115

"Railroad Day" 1911, 59, 62, 96
    World War Two and, 171, 186
Madras Airport, 189, 194
Madras Army Air Field, 69, 168, 170,
    171, 189
Megelson, Scott, 192
Manhart, Warren, 192
Martin, Major, 20
Mason, M. C., 83
McCallister, T. F. ("Ferd"), 46
McCoin, Julius and Sarah, 25, 48, 49,
    55
McFarlane, Robert, 193
McGraw, Larry, 57
McKay Creek, 131
McKay, Dr. William, 18
McKenzie Pass, 9
McKenzie River, 11
Mecca, 62, 67
Mendenhall, Ella McCoin, 25
Mendenhall, Joseph R
    1911 family trip to Portland, 66,
        142
Mendenhall, Max, 56, 57, 148, 161
Messinger, Virgil, 161
Metolius, 59, 63, 76
Metolius River, 12, 13, 159
Meyers, W. P., 82, 94
Meyers, Mrs. W. P., 92
Michigan and Oregon farming
    terminology, 127
Mitchell, Rick, 176, 177
moldboard plows, 158
Moore, Cecil, 57
Mt. Hood, 11, 16, 21
Mt. Jefferson, 12
Muddy Ranch, 145

N

Nabhan, Gary Paul, 45
Newberry, Dr. J. S., 7, 8, 12
Newman, Charles, 129
North and South hangars (Madras
    AAF), 171, 172, 189

North and South Junctions, 61, 62
North Unit Irrigation District, 157

O

odometers, 2
Olson, Charles, 169
Ondaatje, Michael, 95
Opal City, ix, 63, 71
Oregon City, 11, 18, 20, 83
"Oregon Mounted Volunteers" in 1855, 20
Oregon Trunk Railroad, 59, 65, 96–99, 131
    route-sharing with Des Chutes Railroad, 64
    abandonment of North Junction-Metolius section, 66
    recycling of trackage by farmers, 68
Oroville (CA) Army Air Field, 179

P

Pacific Railroad Survey, 1, 4, 5
    Reports, 21
Paiute Wars, 18
Peck, Gunther, xii
Pelton Park, 68
People's Railroad, the, 60
poison oak, 164
Pound, Ezra, 136
Powell Butte "Lord's Acre," 95
Power, Evada, 47
Power, (Judge) Tom, 127, 171
Preuss, Charles, 5
Priday, H.L., 78
Prineville, 25, 71, 72
Prohibition, 92, 104–108

R

Raber, Bess Stangland, 193
railroad "speeders," 69
Rains, Major G. J.
Ramsey, A. S. ("Gus"), 151, 167, 170, 173, 179

Ramsey, Clara Yocum, 148
Ramsey, James, 135, 167
Ramsey, W. H., 134
    family wagon trip to Coast, 66
Redmond, 63, 117, 164
Redmond Army Air Field, 179, 186
Resettlement Administration, 38, 53, 134, 160
Rogue River Indian uprisings, 18
Roosevelt, Eleanor, 113–115
Rufener, George, 172, 173, 174, 176, 179

S

Saginaw County, Michigan, 117, 129
Salem, 20, 83
Salter, Major Andrew W., 175, 176, 179, 182
Santa Ana Army Air Base (CA), 170
Santini, Capt. Robert, 175
Sawyer, Robert, 2, 3, 19, 191
Second Air Force, 171
Seekseekwa Creek, 13, 163
Shomo, Col. William, 177
separators, stationary, 154, 155
Shawe, Bruce, 127
Shawe, Victor, 127
Shepherd, Shaun, 45
Sheridan, Lt. (later Gen.) Phil, 7, 17, 18
Shiawassee River (MI), 121
Shipp, Jack, 72
Sophocles, 136
Sopwith "Camel," 183
Speroff, Dr. Leon, 59
Spokane, Portland, and Seattle Railway (SP&S), 69
Springer, Judge Guyon, 73
Stevens, John F., 60, 62, 70
Strong National Museum of Play, ix, xi
Suffrage, 71

T

Theater Passe Muraille, 95
The Dalles, 25, 130
Thomas, Lorenzo, 77
Thoreau, Henry David, 54, 55
Three Sisters, 8
"topo-linguistics," 193
Turner, Frederic Jackson, xi
Turner, Howard, 73, 79, 92, 94
Tygh Valley, 11, 14

U

U'Ren, Charlie
U'Ren, William S., 73, 83, 94
U.S.O. (United Service
    Organization), Madras, 187

V

Verboort Sausage and Sauerkraut
    Festival, 95
Vonnegut, Kurt, 170

W

Wapinitia, 15
War Relocation Act, 164, 165
Warm Springs Reservation, 12, 13,
    17, 18, 37, 143
Warner, Capt. William, 6, 7

Wasco County, 71, 74
Wasco Indian oral traditions, 26,
    39–42
Waters, Lt. Edward, 175
Watts, Lillian Ramsey, 92
West, Gov. Oswald, 72, 77, 79
Wheeler County, 74
Wilder, Laura Ingalls, 25
Williams Army Air Base (AZ), 170
Williams, William Carlos, 136
Williamson, Lt. Robert S., 1, 4, 6, 8,
    18, 19, 20, 27
    illnesses of, 19, 20
Willow Creek Canyon, 62, 63, 70
Wilson, Capt. James R. 175, 186
Wilson, Pres. Woodrow, 84, 130
Withycombe, Gov. George, 92
Witter, Dean, 164
Wollaston, Percy, 193
World War One, 126

Y

Yamamoto, Admiral Isoruko, 164
Yarrow (Madras subdivision), 145
Yeager, Gen. Charles ("Chuck"), 177
Yeats, William Butler, 183, 184
Yepsen, Roger, 192
Young, John, 7, 8, 13, 14